Tourism in Mountain Region

About the Authors

Dr. Udai Prakash Sinha, (b. 1956), former Vice Chancellor, Central University of Haryana, currently Professor of Economics, T.M. Bhagalpur University, Bhagalpur. He is national level Professor of Economics, SME for Commission for Scientific and Technical Terminology, Ministry of Human Resource, Government of India, New Delhi and Consultant—State Planning and Development Department, Bihar State Planning Council, Government of Bihar, Patna. He has been editing of "*Journal of Economic Issues*" since year 2000 published by Planning Forum, and Anga Economic Society, University Department of Economics, T.M. Bhagalpur University, Bhagalpur. He has been a life member of Indian Economic Association and has been Chairperson of conferences of Indian Economic Association and other international conferences and seminars. He has completed three UGC major research projects as principal investigator and presently working on UGC sponsored major research project entitled "*Ecological Imbalances and Plan Perspective for Rural Bihar*". He has been Resource person of academic staff college of many universities and has delivered lectures at various universities nationwide. He has 100 research papers to his credit published in reputed National and International journals. He has authored 14 books, 37 Research scholars have already been awarded Ph.D. degree under his able guidance. Micro-level planning and regional economics are his areas of research and expertise.

Dr. Santosh Sharma, is presently Assistant Professor of Economics, Government College, Rhenock (Sikkim). He has contributed more than 15 research papers to the reputed National and International journal of economics and other behavioural sciences. He has also participated and presented papers in the National/ International symposium. He is a creative and passionate teacher dedicated to fostering a student oriented classroom environment.

Tourism in Mountain Region

Retrospect and Prospect

Udai Prakash Sinha
Professor, Department of Economics
T.M. Bhagalpur University, Bhagalpur (Bihar) and
Former Vice-Chancellor (Actg.)
Central University of Haryana
Mahendragarh, Haryana

Santosh Sharma
Assistant Professor
Department of Economics
Government College, Rhenock
East Sikkim, Gangtok, Sikkim

CONCEPT PUBLISHING COMPANY PVT. LTD.
NEW DELHI-110059

ISBN-13: 978-93-86682-33-8

First Published 2018

Published and Printed by

Concept Since 1974

Concept Publishing Company Pvt. Ltd.
A/15-16, Commercial Block, Mohan Garden
New Delhi-110059 (India)
T: 25351460, 25351794, *F*: 091-11-25357109
E: publishing@conceptpub.com, W: www.conceptpub.com

Cataloging in Publication Data—Courtesy: D.K. Agencies (P) Ltd. <docinfo@dkagencies.com>

Sinha, Udai Prakash, 1956- author.
Tourism in mountain region : retrospect and prospect / Udai Prakash Sinha, Santosh Sharma.
pages cm
Includes bibliographical references and index.
ISBN 9789386682338

1. Tourism—India—Sikkim. I. Sharma, Santosh (Assistant professor of economics), author. II. Title.

LCC G155.I4S56 2018 DDC 338.479154167 23

Preface

With the abundant natural resources, cultural, religious, archaeological heritage, etc. of the various important economic resources in the developing nations, tourism holds very prominent place, which can be easily established, promoted and developed by minimum investment. So, it is the major sector for the development of the developing nation's economy in general and India in particular. Tourism is an activity that generates the number of social and economic benefits. Natural beauty and rich tradition and culture are the significant sector of India's tourism industry, which embrace and develop the various activities of traditional, cultural and religious together. It support rural economy and have a pivotal impact upon the entire tourism industry of the State.

Among the many facts of tourism, rural tourism is becoming widely popular both theoretically and practically. India has already started Community Based Rural Tourism in few states with comparative success. The subject continues to trigger numerous discussions and debate among scholars, entrepreneurs, students, researcher about the models, benefits and challenges of promoting rural tourism and thereby helping economic development at local level. Despite of all it is surprising to note that there is little availability of text-books on rural tourism to help and aid the ever growing number of scholars and students in their research and study. For lack of any useful publication, students are at a great loss from the opportunities to home their wit and intelligence in the subject. This has directly affected the quality of education. Studies are limited to theoretical concepts with almost no real life practical experiences. The growing importance of tourism in the study area, its traditional development, and institutional development, socio-economic upliftment of the rural locals who were deprived from economic and social status has been viewed in this context. The study have been made using some relevant research designing procedure like observation, group discussion, some feedbacks from tourism expert as well as using some relevant research questions like: How can we highlight the prospects of village tourism? What are the appropriate strategies for making village tourism attractive and fruitful for the locals as well as tourists? And what is the significant contribution of tourism to uplift the standard (socio-economy) of locals?

It was observed that tourism has received the attention of the Government from the very beginning. Many programmes were launched from time to time. Many Government and Non-Government as well as public sectors were also involved in promoting tourism in various places. But all their efforts have not been so effective, if we talk regarding tourism industry of Sikkim. Due to the lack of significant resource allocation for tourism development and the lack of publicity in the regional fields, tourism sector in various areas have not been flourished as it should have been. The study focused not only the natural potentiality of tourism available in the study area, but also the traditional and cultural tourism. The study highlights the different innovative ideas to make one more destination for tourists who can enjoy various expects of tourism and stay for a few days.

This book intends to take the stress and anxiety of the eco-tourism in Sikkim and is the pioneer tourism activity which would introduce Sikkim as its unique natural product to tourists in the international markets. Due to the presence of immense snow-capped Himalayas of different awesome height and dimensions, Sikkim has immense potentials for the development of tourism and can accrue large economical benefit to the people of Sikkim. Despite possessing high socio-economic advantages, Sikkim still could not have fully mobilized and exploited these immense natural gifts appropriately. Insufficient physical infrastructure and unskilled/inexperience tourism entrepreneurs along with deficiency of other supportive things tourism has not yet progressed in a desirable manner in the State. Until now, the contribution of tourism in the State of Sikkim economy is felt in the field of foreign exchange earning mainly in the area of employment opportunities and royalty. However, its contribution is nominal. The government starts more attention and starts functioning for overall development from where tourism may be able to generate significant socio-economic advantage in the State.

This study continues with its tradition of touching on many of the most important questions about the purity and potential of eco-tourism in the face of so many competing demands—demands that will not go away because they appear to a function of who we are at the very core; a function of human nature. This book is a useful aid to students, giving an authoritative and comprehensive review of key issues that continue to both plague eco-tourism and make it one of the most dynamic sectors in the tourism industry. This accessible book covers a breadth of themes and geographical regions. It also focuses on various issues of tourism, it got have linkage with other sector of the economy as well as all aspects of our society. Apart from its importance to economic changes, human socio-cultural activities and environmental development, tourism is related to other academic subjects such as geography, economics, history, languages, psychology, marketing, business and law, etc. Therefore, it is necessary to integrate a number of subjects to study tourism. For example, subjects such as history and geography help us understand more abou the development of the historical and geographical resources of a tourist destination. Besides, subjects like marketing and business help us understand the promotion and marketing of tourism products.

Book highlights tourism as a complex field of study because it includes a variety of disciplines which are either directly or indirectly related to the understanding of tourism. The study of information technology enhances our understanding of the importance of the global distribution system and its effect on tourism business. The study of religion and culture provides information on the cultural resources of a destination and opportunities to develop it as a cultural destination. Tourism is so vast, so complex, and so multifaceted that there is a wide range of subjects related to tourism. The vast majority of business organizations such as travel agents, meeting planners, and other service providers including accommodation, transportation, attractions and entertainment are classified as travel and tourism related business. In practice, these organizations are closely linked in the provision of services to the travellers. Tourism is so vast, so complex, and so multifaceted that the practitioners need to obtain a wide range of knowledge related to tourism.

Tourism industry is the core economic sector in Sikkim. People start shifting their profession towards tourism. In the view of natural, cultural resources or heritage, there is high potentiality of tourism development to generate multi-economic and social advantages in the study area. In the field of foreign exchange earnings, employment generation, regional development and advancement or modernization of rural life, tourism can significantly contribute to the nation in general and Sikkim in particular. Tourism industry in Sikkim has marked significantly multiplier effect. Eco-tourism is the second tourism activity in the State.

This book also discusses on various economic issues like economic impact on employment opportunities, local business opportunity, development of infrastructure, improved standard of living, foreign exchange tax in income and other respectively. Major economic impacts pointed out are from tax, foreign exchange, souvenirs, improved standard of living, business opportunities, better infrastructure and the gap between poor and rich increase respectively as mentioned by tourism entrepreneurs. Also discuss on various hospitality sectors which would benefit to the local people in an around tourist destination, like location, quality of food, behaviour of staff regarding hotels, hospitality, language communication, agencies, guide and tourism vendor and behaviour of local people and solid waste management. Similarly, with the some aspect of tourism like international airlines, domestic airlines, immigration, shopping facilities, currency exchange and naturally satisfied with tourism information centre, customs banking services.

Some recommendations are also highlighted in this text; To sustain multiplier effect and to prevent the leakage of income, inputs of tourism activities should be made available locally. Cable car and ropeways services should be expended. Wildlife tourism should be developed in mountain areas in national parks. The entry formalities must be strict in parks and conservation areas for sustainable tourism. Organic tourism must be given more importance as Sikkim is only organic state in the country.

To sum-up tourism in Sikkim is marked by different weaknesses and shortcomings as mentioned in this book. Until and unless we show keen interest to avoid such weaknesses associated with tourism development, Sikkim's tourism cannot play significant role in our economy. That is why, it is necessary for the government to consider seriously to get rid of such shortcomings as early as possible whereby, sustainable and more productive tourism activities will emerge in the state in the days to come.

We hope this book has been appropriately timed to serve the growing interests in rural tourism of all residents of the society and would be considerably helpful and motivate concerned stakeholders, researchers, policy-makers to build upon the knowledge of rural tourism and further help in expanding and exploring its horizon. This book is intended to be used primarily as text-book for college and university courses in tourism and hospitality management. However, the book also provides valuable information and guidance for nationals, states, provincial and local tourism, offices, chambers of commerce, tourism promoters and development, transformation, attractions and others business, transportation carrier, oil and automotive companies and many other organizations interested or involved in the movement of people from their homes or business destinations.

Udai Prakash Sinha
Santosh Sharma

Acknowledgements

To conduct the field research investigation is a joint endeavour and in such cases the success depends upon the whole hearted cooperation of everyone involved in the preparation of the present book. It is the devotion of the work as well as proper suggestion, guidance, moral and financial help that determines the outcome of such work.

Firstly, we would like to share our gratitude to all the tourists, entrepreneurs and tourism related persons willingly participating in our research survey and gave valuable information without which the study would not have been completed. We would like to thank the Department of Tourism, Government of Sikkim, State Central Library, CEDA, TAAS, ECOS and DSME Government of Sikkim and Central Library, T.M. Bhagalpur University, Bhagalpur, Bihar for providing us information and kind support in the course of our study.

Our especial thanks go to Shri Bikram Pradhan, Member of Legislative Assembly, Chujachen Constituency and Shri Bimal Chandra Rai, PRO, Chief Minister, Government of Sikkim for encouragement and support in the course of our study.

Our gratitude goes towards our families who have supported us in every difficulty while preparing this study. We are also thankful to Raj Madhavan for neat and clean computer typing and editing. Finally, we would also like to thank all helpful friends including, Md. Sami-Praveen Gautam, Yon Tsiring Lepcha, Dhiren Gurung, N.B. Chetti and Fojen Lepcha for necessary help and advice.

Udai Prakash Sinha
Santosh Sharma

Contents

List of Tables

List of Figures

Abbreviations

AD	After Death
BC	Before Christ
BoP	Balance-of-Payment
CTC	Canadian Tourism Commission
ECOS	Environmental Council of States
EGCF	Economic Gain Conversion Method
EGT	Employment Generation through Tourism
EM	Economic Multiplier
EUSH	Experience Unique Sikkim Himalayas
GDP	Gross Domestic Product
GSDP	Gross State Domestic Product
IASET	International Association of Scientific Expert in Tourism
ICAO	International Civil Aviation Organization
IHCAE	Indian Himalayan Centre for Adventure and Eco-Tourism
INGOs	International Non-Governmental Organizations
LDCs	Lower Developing Countries
LTC	Leave Travel Concession
MICE	Meeting, Incentives, Convention and Exhibition
MOTCA	Ministry of Tourism and Civil Aviation
MPC	Marginal Propensity to Consume
MPS	Marginal Propensity to Save
NGOs	Non-Governmental Organizations
NTAs	National Tourism Administrations
OECD	Organization for Economic Cooperation and Development
PATA	The Pacific Area Travel Association
PPT	Pro-Poor Tourism

PSU	Public Sector Undertaking
RTDC	Rajasthan Tourism Development Corporation
SAARC	South Asian Association for Regional Co-operation
SIC	Standard Industry Classification
ST-EP	Sustainable Tourism-Elementary Poverty
TAAS	Travel Agent and Association of Sikkim
TALC	Tourist Area Life Cycle
TEFT	Total Earning From Tourism
TIES	Trade Infrastructure for Export Scheme
TSA	Tourism Satellite Account
TTA	Total Tourist Arrival
UK	United Kingdom
UNWTO	United Nations World Tourism Organization
USA	United States of America
USPs	Unique Selling Propositions
WTO	World Tourism Organization
WTTC	World Travel and Tourism Council

1
Introduction

Extent of the Study

In the world, travel is as old as mankind and by nature human beings are fond of travelling. Human travel has started since nomadic times when they travelled and migrated for food and shelter due to natural compulsion. The true consciousness and the anxieties of human nature encouraged travelling for finding new things. Thus, "the origin of tourist industry can be traced back to the earliest period of human habitation in the globe. Of course, there exists difference between modern travelling and travelling during the early period. Travelling in those far off days was a must for the survival and existence of early men. But with the advent of civilization and change in the human outlook, the meaning of travelling has been shifted from the necessity to the desire of taking marvelous adventures".

During the Neolithic Age, several innovations in the field of transport changed the very nature of travel. In Egypt, sailing vessels were built around 4000 BC. This resulted in conscious travel in order to explore and see the world. The invention of wheel and money by the Sumerians (Babylonia) around 3500 BC marks the beginnings of the modern era of travel. The money invented by the Sumerians was used by them in their various business and travel dealings. Many traders could pay for transportation as well as accommodation either with money or by exchange of goods. Shulgi, the ruler of ancient Babylonia, claimed to have protected roads and built rest houses at various places for respectable wayfarers. The forerunners of modern day accommodation, these rest houses were the ideal places of rest for the travellers of those days.

The Sumerians deserve to be accredited as the father of the travel business as they not only coined the idea of money, but also invented cuneiform (of or using writing composed of wedge-shaped marks) writing and the wheels. Apart from this, almost as early as five thousand years ago, cruises were arranged and conducted from Egypt. In all probability, the maiden journey ever made with the objective of peace and tourism was the one by queen Hatshepsat to the land of Punt (believed to be the present Somalia) in 1400 BC and one can find the description of this tour recorded on the walls of the temple of Deity Bahan at Luxor.

Travel in the distant past was not a thing of pleasure, as is the case now. The traveller of the past was a merchant, a pilgrim, a scholar in search of ancient text, or even a curious wayfarer looking forward to new and exciting experiences. Trade and commerce were the strongest force in the ancient time; it made travel to distant lands possible in order to seek fortunes, because with the opening of the trade routes travel became easier and more regulated.

Early travel in the orient, particularly in India and China, was also largely based on trade and commerce. Travel to the orient, especially to India, was undertaken by travellers from all-over the world. This was done for a variety of reasons the most important among them being trade and commerce. India and China enjoyed the reputation of being countries of fabulous wealth.

The concept of pleasure travel as it existed in the West can be associated with the Roman Empire. Romans probably were the first pleasure travellers in the world. Travel received a great stimulus from the great communication system and security of the Roman Empire. There existed a fine network of roads and new roads were built increasingly wherever the Roman went. Travel literature was published extensively giving routes, the name of the major roads, distances between places and the time required in travelling them. The Romans were able to travel over a hundred or more miles in a day using relays of horses. They journeyed primarily to see famous temples on the Mediterranean areas, particularly the monuments and the famous pyramids of Egypt.

The Romans also travelled during holiday occasions, particularly during the famous Olympic Games. Spa and seaside resorts which developed during this period may be associated with pleasure travel. Medicinal baths and seaside resorts which later were named as spas were very popular with the Romans. The inland spa had its origin in the belief in the efficacy of its mineral water for medicinal purpose, either by drinking the water or by immersing in it. However, the fall of the Roman Empire in the fifth century was a great setback for pleasure travel in Europe.

The first medieval traveller to reach the orient was probably Benjamin of Tudela, a Jewish scholar, who left Saragossa in the year AD 1160. He wrote a detailed account of his thirteen year long journey through Europe, Persia and India, giving information on the Jewish communities and the geography of various places he had visited. Yet another famous traveller who recorded interesting accounts of his travel experiences was Ibn Batutah. Ibn Batutah wrote a detailed diary of his travel experiences. He was born at Tangier in AD 1304. In the year 1325, he left his home and passing through various countries in Africa and West Asia, crossed the Sindhu in AD 1333. His travel took him to places as far as Indonesia and China. Out of a total of more than 17,000 miles, he covered more than 14,000 miles in the course of his travels through India, the Maldives and Ceylon (Now Sri Lanka). Marco Polo, the fearless traveller, spent almost twenty-five years in Asia during the latter part of the thirteenth century. His wanderlust could have well been inherited from his father. Young Marco Polo left Venice in the year 1271 with his father and uncle. The three together travelled through Persia and Afghanistan to the "Roof of the World" the then unknown Pamir Plateau. After crossing the windswept Gobi desert, they reached Kublai Khan's Palace and remained in China for over twenty years. On his way back home, he stopped in Sumatra, Java and Ceylon.

The Era of Pilgrimage

The emerge of a large number of temples and shrines associated with the martyrs and saints of different religions and extensive missionary activities during medieval age led to massive pilgrimage tours. The Royal patronage of Buddhism in India and the visits of Buddhist missionaries to different countries, establishments of *Dhams* in the four corners of India by Adi Sankaracharya, the travels of Christian marks all-over the world to spread Christianity and the visits of Muslim religious leaders to different countries contributed to pilgrimage tourism. Visits to distant shrines and holy places associated with the religious beliefs of people became social phenomenon amongst various societies. Pilgrimage was regarded as a release from poverty, sickness or any other misery. Pilgrims always travelled in groups and used the facilities created for traders in the past. In due course, the rulers and societies also created facilities for the exclusive use of pilgrims.

The Age of Exploration

Technological advances and extensive explorations since the beginning of modern age opened up new horizon for tourism. The expedition of Christopher Columbus in 1492, John Cobot in 1497, Vasco da Gama in 1498, and Ferdinand Magellan in 1520-21 resulted in the discovery of several nations and establishing sea routes between them. The explorations were later replaced by exploration of continental interior to study the flora, fauna, topography and resources during nineteenth and twentieth century.

The Grand Tours

The tours undertaken by the rich aristocrats through the major cities of Europe for culture, education and pleasure during the eighteenth century are popularly known as "Grand Tours". It was the first extensive movement of tourists for which primary source of information like letters, journals and diaries of tourists were available. The Grand Tourists respected learning, antiquities and social refinement of the world. The thirty years period from 1763 to 1793 is considered to be the golden age of grand tours.

Paid Holidays

There were, however, no general public holidays until the time of the industrial revolution. The introduction of paid holidays was the product of industrial revolution. The introduction of paid holidays in Europe was yet another important landmark which enabled many people to undertake travel in large number during the eighteenth century. The annual holiday was the forerunner to the paid holiday which later on was responsible for an extraordinary growth of tourism during the twentieth century. The term holiday derived from holy days associated with religious observances.

Paid holidays are now established all-over the world and in most countries, a minimum duration of one to three week is specified either by law or by collective agreements between the employers and the workers. The employers have realized that the paid holidays have not adversely affected industrial production. There are more than 500 million wage earners worldwide roughly half are in Europe, little less than 30 per cent in the Americas and the rest in Asia and the Pacific. Presently, the main potential for tourism market is made up of wage earners and their family.

Technological Revolutions

Technological revolutions in the field of automobiles, railways, sails and ships, aircrafts, computer and communication helped in the promotion of tourism. The first automobile was a large, clumsy and three wheeled vehicle with a speed of about 3 km/hour and was built by Nicholan Joseph Cughot, a Captain of French Army in 1769. Gasoline-powered automobiles came into existence by 1864 and the first commercially successful gasoline three wheeler cars were built in 1886. By 1895, Benz built four wheeled vehicles, which were light, strong and simple to operate. By the beginning of twentieth century, car offering luxury and power came into existence.

The technological innovations in railways have been more astounding than the case of automobiles. George Stephenson built the first successful steam locomotive engine in the locomotive 'Rocket' built by him in 1829 could attain a speed of 47 km/hour and it was run between Liverpool and Manchester. By twentieth century, diesel engine and gas-turbine engine locomotive were built and regular rail-traffic came into existence in different parts of the world.

In the early 1870s first class railway travel was introduced by an American, named G.M. Pullman, who developed the Pullman Coaches with their luxury furnishing and having dining facilities. The longer distance in America necessitated ensuring greater passenger comfort. Long distance travel can now be undertaken in comfort and with pleasure. The Pullman Coaches manufactures in America were being imported by some railway companies in England and other countries in Europe. In India, it was on April 16, 1853 that the first train (in the east) took off from Bori Bundar in Bombay to Thane, covering a distance of 33 kilometer. Four hundred guests were selected from various segments and were invited to travel by the first train in India. From a small beginnings on April 16, 1853, when the first train steamed off from Victoria Terminal for Thane, 33 kilometer away, the railway system in India has grown into the world's second largest system under one management, second only to the former USSR. The shipping, like the railways, made a significant contribution to travel during the nineteenth century.

The concept of mass tourism emerged along with the introduction of paid-holiday with pay. It was in the last quarter of the nineteenth century that increasing attention was paid on the desirability of holiday with pay and at least of cheap holidays for working class people.

The introduction of annual paid holidays is very largely of English origin and this had important repercussions on the development of mass tourism. By the year 1939, in UK, some eleven million people were covered by the Holidays with Pay Act (1938).

Soon after the First World War tourists began to appear in countries where tourism had been practically unknown a few years earlier. The major tourist countries enjoyed an unprecedented boom in the twenties. In the year 1929, there were nearly one and a half million visitors to Switzerland, over one million to Italy and about two million to Austria, France, Spain and Great Britain received a considerable number of visitors. The unprec dented boom in tourist movements in the twenties especially in Europe and America can be directly linked to the introduction of the private motor car. The motorized private and public road transport and the improved road condition led to tremendous growth of travel. The motor car revolutionised holiday habits of the Europeans and Americans. It became increasingly important in the pursuit of leisure and tourism. The provision or good motor roads and the road service were important factor in the development of both domestic and international tourism.

The post-Second World War period brought in a rapid development of tourism. As the world began to settle down after the years of readjustment, immediately after the war ended in year 1945, there has been a remarkable rapid increase in domestic as well as international tourism. The United Nations reported that in the ten years period between 1955 and 1965, the number of tourist arrivals in some sixty-five countries increased three-fold around 51 million to over 157 million.

Although commercial travel was introduced even before the Second World War, air transport for the masses has essentially been a post-Second World War phenomena. With the tremendous increase in speed, safety and comfort provided by the new civil aircraft like Douglas DC-65, and DC-7, and Super Constellations, there was a noticeable increase in the long distance international as well as intra-regional tourism. In the year 1952, the two-class travel was introduced and this was made possible by the larger capacity of new aircrafts. The increase in the aircraft capacity was also responsible for lower airfares. The steady fall in the cost of flying also resulted in the increased traffic across the Atlantic. This period also saw the first attempt to introduce a package holiday around air transport, which subsequently became the model approach for most of the present day's global tourism. The most dramatic event, which introduced an entirely new dimension of speed, comfort and efficiency to air transport and brought mass travel to its present level was the advent of the jet travel in the year 1958.

Introduction of 'inclusive tours' is yet another decisive development during this period responsible for mass tourism. In all inclusive tours' travellers are carried on charter flights at rates substantially below those of normal scheduled service.

Patterns and Growth of International Tourism

The tourism traffic specifically started growing after Second World War. In 1950, there were only 25 million international tourist arrivals and most recent figure reached to 991.6 million in 2013 (Fig. 1.1). During 63 years of time span (1950-2015), the international tourist arrivals grew more than thirty-seven times and international tourism receipts by about 330 times, i.e. in 1950, US$ 2.1 billion and in 2013, US$ 886.4 billion (Table 1.1). WTO/OMT's 'Tourism 2020 Vision' forecasts that international arrivals are expected to reach 1.56 billion by the year 2020, which is further broken down into 1.2 billion intra-regional travellers and 0.4 billion long haul travellers.

Apart from the remarkable growth in international arrivals there was also a diversification of destinations during the past decades. While in 1950, 15 countries, all of them from Europe plus USA and Canada, accounted for about 88 per cent of total international arrivals, in 2009, their share of market had fallen to around 37 per cent. On the other hand many developing countries saw their tourist arrivals increase significantly.

The same Table 1.2 show that, in 1950, among ten destinations, eight were from Europe and two from North America. But, in 2014, the scenario of the number of top ten destinations changed and two nations were added from Asia (i.e. China and Malaysia). Similarly,

Table 1.1: Tourist Arrivals and Receipts in the World (1950-2013)

Year	*International Tourist Arrivals (Million)*	*Year*	*Receipts Billion US$*
1950	25.3	1950	02.1
1960	69.3	1960	06.9
1970	159.7	1970	17.9
1980	284.9	1980	102.4
1990	455.9	1990	264.1
2000	687.3	2000	473.4
2010	940.0	2010	693.0
2011	956.9	2011	711.6
2012	974.3	2012	753.8
2013	991.6	2013	886.4

Source: World Tourism Organization.

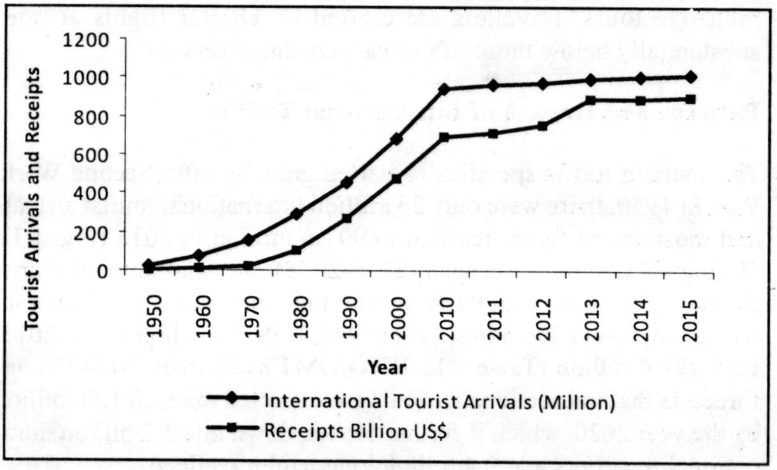

Fig. 1.1: Tourist Arrivals and Receipts in the World (1950-2015).

more than 75 countries receive more than one million international tourist arrivals.

(a) Most Visited Countries' growth Patterns of Tourism in terms of International Tourist Arrivals, Receipts and Expenditure

The growth and development of tourism in any country depends on many factors. These may include tourism policy and planning of the country, status of infrastructure development, economy of the country,

Table 1.2: World's Top Tourism Destinations by International Tourist Arrivals

Rank	*1950*	*World Share*	*1980*	*World Share*	*2004*	*World Share*	*2014*	*World Share*
1.	USA	71%	France	38%	France	34%	France	31%
2.	Canada		USA		Spain		USA	
3.	Italy		Spain		USA		Spain	
4.	France		Italy		China		China	
5.	Switzerland		Hungary		Italy		Italy	
6.	Ireland		Austria		UK		UK	
7.	Austria		UK		Hong Kong, China			
8.	Spain	17%	Mexico	19%	Mexico	15%	Germany	19%
9.	Germany		Germany		Germany		Malaysia	
10.	UK		Canada		Austria		Mexico	
Total	**Others 25 million**	**88%**	**Others 465 million**	**57%**	**Others 760 million**	**49%**	**Others 880 million**	**50%**

Source: World Tourism Organization, 2014.

political stability, governance, safety and security of tourists, behaviour of host population towards tourists etc. In this section, top ten destinations of international tourist arrival, receipts and expenditure patterns are described.

Table 1.3 reveals that in terms of maximum number of international tourist arrivals in any specific country, the market leader is France where the highest number of international tourist pay their visit. Since long time France has achieved first rank. United States was holding second position in 2000. In 2006 and 2011, Spain forced USA to 3rd position. However, it became successful to achieve second position in 2012 and 2013 by forcing Spain to 3rd position. Tourism is rapidly growing in the People's Republic of China. This country was at the 12th rank in 1990. It achieved 5th rank in 2000 and 4th rank from 2006 to 2013. United Kingdom has been able to maintain its 6th rank since 2000. Although, the international tourist arrival is not much encouraging. The number of arrivals was 25 million in 2000 and which reached only 28 million in 2013. Turkey and Malaysia are two countries where the growth pattern of international arrivals were much encouraging. Both these countries were much lower in rank up to 2000 (i.e. lower than 15th rank). Recently, Turkey gained 7th rank in 2012 and 2013. Similarly, Malaysia achieved 10th rank from 2006 to 2012 and 9th rank in 2013. The number of international

Table 1.3: Top Ten World's Tourism Destination (Arrivals)

Rank							*Country*	*International Tourist Arrivals (million)*						
2000	*2010*	*2011*	*2012*	*2013*	*2014*	*2015*		*2000*	*2006*	*2011*	*2012*	*2013*	*2014*	*2015*
1st	1st	1st	1st	1st	1st	1st	France	75.6	77.9	80.9	79.2	74.2	70.2	67.6
2nd	3rd	3rd	2nd	2nd	2nd	2nd	United States	50.9	51.0	56.0	57.9	54.9	51.4	48.9
3rd	2nd	2nd	3rd	3rd	3rd	3rd	Spain	47.9	58.0	58.7	57.2	52.2	48.2	45.1
5th	4th	4th	4th	4th	4th	4th	China	31.2	49.9	54.7	53.0	50.9	48.9	47.2
4th	5th	5th	5th	5th	5th	5th	Italy	41.2	41.1	43.7	42.7	43.2	44.7	46.4
6th	6th	6th	6th	6th	8th	9th	United Kingdom	25.2	30.7	30.9	30.1	28.0	25.0	22.0
—	9th	8th	7th	7th	6th	6th	Turkey	—	18.9	22.2	25.0	25.5	26.2	28.2
10th	7th	7th	8th	8th	9th	8th	Germany	19.0	23.6	24.4	24.9	24.2	23.2	22.4
—	10th	9th	9th	9th	7th	7th	Malaysia	—	17.5	21.0	22.1	23.6	25.6	28.1
8th	8th	10th	10th	10th	10th	10th	Mexico	20.6	21.4	21.4	22.6	21.5	20.8	19.0

Source: World Tourism Organization (WTO).

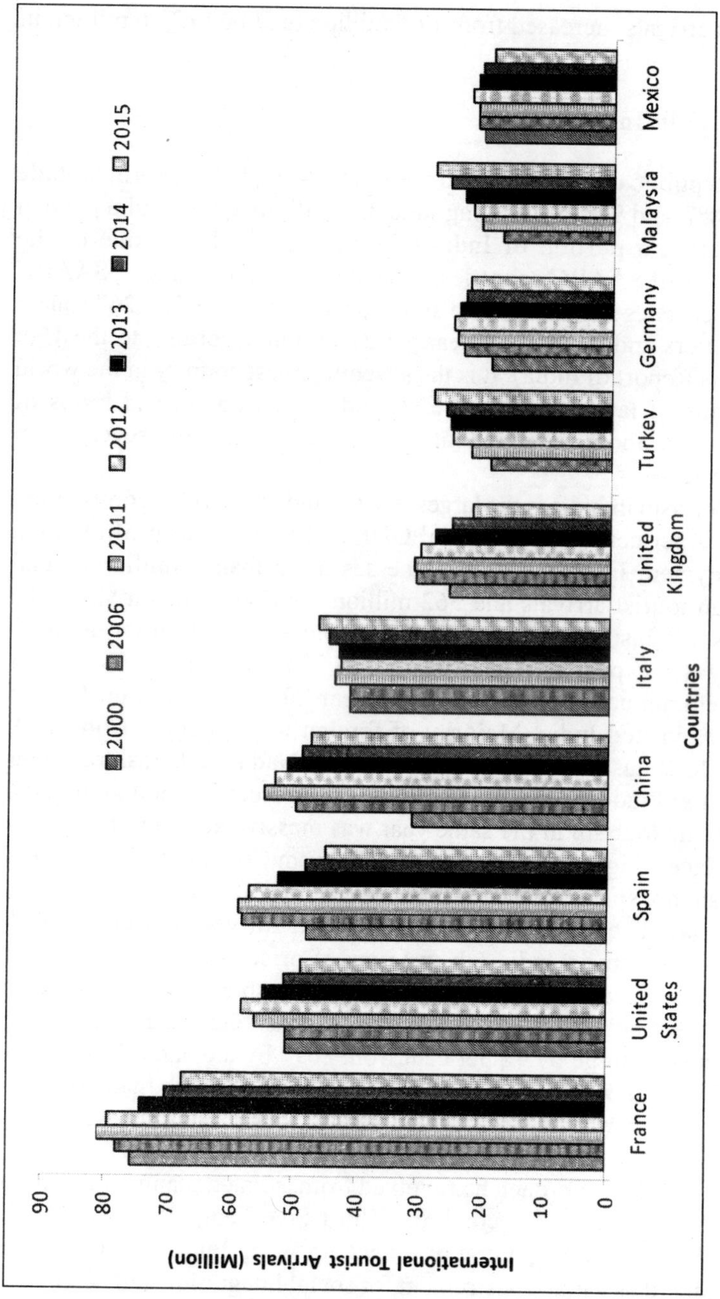

Fig. 1.2: Top Ten World's Tourism Destination (Arrivals).

tourist arrivals increased from 17.5 million in 2006 to 23.6 million in 2013.

Tourism in India

The Republic of India, located between 8°4' and 37°6' north latitude and 68°7' and 97°25' east longitude, lies entirely on the India plate in the northern portion of Indo-Australian plate. India, one of the members of SAARC countries, is the largest country among SAARC member states in terms of area and population (Area 3,287,263 square kilometers and population nearly 1.21 billion according to the 15th Census Report of India). It is the seventh largest country in the world in terms of land area and the second largest country in terms of population. India is divided into twenty-eight states and seven union territories.

Tourism in India is the largest service industry, with a contribution of 6.23 per cent to the national GDP and 8.78 per cent of the total employment in India. India witnesses more than 5 million annual foreign tourist arrivals and 562 million domestic tourism visit. The tourism industry in India generated about US$ 100 billion in 2012 and that is expected to increase to US$ 275 billion by 2018 at a 9.4 per cent annual growth rate. In the year 2013, 5.11 million foreign tourists visited India. Majority of foreign tourists come from USA and UK. Rajasthan (Land of Kings), Tamil Nadu, Maharashtra, Delhi and Uttar Pradesh were the top five states to receive inbound tourists. Domestic tourism in the same year was massive at 650 million.

According to World Travel and Tourism Council, India will be a tourism hot spot from 2009-2018, having the highest 10-year growth potential. The Travel and Tourism Competitiveness Report 2011 ranked tourism in India 6th in terms of price competitiveness and 39th in terms of safety and security. Despite short and medium term setbacks, such as shortage of hotel rooms, tourism revenues are expected to surge by 42 per cent from 2011 by the end of 2017.

Tourism development in India has passed through many phases. At government level, the development of tourist facilities was taken up in a planned manner in 1956, coinciding with the Second Five Year Plan. The approach has evolved from isolated planning of single unit facilities in the Second and Third Five Year Plans. The Sixth Plan marked the beginning of a new era when tourism began to be considered as a major instrument for social integration and economic development. However, it was only after the 1980s that tourism activity gained momentum. The government took several significant steps. A national policy on tourism was announced in 1982. Later in 1988, the National Committee on Tourism formulated a comprehensive plan for achieving a sustainable growth in tourism. In July 1991, tourism was also declared as a priority sector for foreign investment. In 1992, a National Action Plan was prepared and in 1996 the national strategy for promotion of tourism was drafted. The other major developments that took place were the setting up of the India Tourism Development Corporation in 1966 to promote India as a tourist destination, and the Tourism Finance Corporation in 1989 to finance tourism projects. Altogether, 21 government run Hotel Management and Catering Technology Institutes and 14 Food Crafts Institute were also established for imparting specified training in hotel and catering.

Though inbound tourism statistics of India manifest a substantial increase in terms of numbers and growth rates, that is from 17,000 in 1950 to 5.11 million in 2013 (Fig. 1.3), it is very insignificant compared to global tourism (0.58% of the world). A decade-by-decade analysis reveals that up to 1990, while the growth rate was declining, it was comparatively less volatile. However, the growth in the liberalized economic environment (since 1990) has not been very encouraging because of slower growth rate and fluctuating inflow patterns (Table 1.4). Indeed, in the post-liberalized Indian economic context, tourism should have grown faster and steadily due to favourable growth environment, like opening up of the economy, currency devaluation, industry automation, use of information communication technology in marketing and promotion, growth in international trade and the like. But, the reasons for the country's inbound tourist traffic not growing up to the visualized potential could be attributed to the internal contradiction, supplemented with a volatile global tourism business environment.

The earnings from inbound tourism are also reflective of India's insignificant position at the global level, though tourism continues to be a major source of foreign exchange. India's share in the world receipts ranging from 0.57 per cent in 1990 to 0.84 per cent in 2005, that is, US$ 1.5 billion and US$ 5.7 billion respectively in real term (Table 1.5). Further, comparison of foreign tourist arrivals and corresponding receipts in India shows that on account of the country's

Table 1.4: International Tourist Arrivals: World and India (*Figures are in millions*)

Year	*Global Tourist Arrivals*	*Annual Growth Rate (%)*	*Foreign Tourist Arrival India*	*Annual Growth Rate (%)*	*India's Share to World (%)*
1960	69.3	—	0.12	—	0.18
1970	165.89	13.9	0.28	12.8	0.17
1980	286.24	7.3	0.80	18.5	0.28
1990	455.90	5.9	1.70	11.3	0.37
2000	696.70	5.3	2.65	6.7	0.38
2010	808.00	3.2	3.91	4.6	0.49
2013	880.00	—	5.11	—	0.58

Source: Tourist Statistics, Department of Tourism, Government of India.

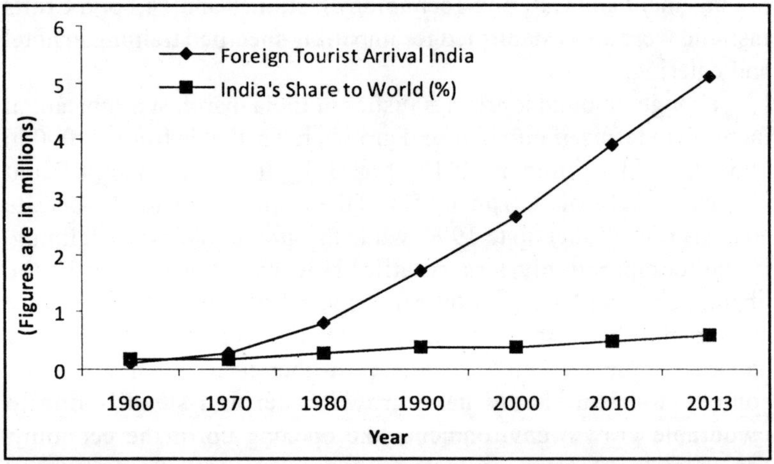

Fig. 1.3: International Tourist Arrivals: World and India (*Figures are in millions*).

growth rate and share of the world total, the receipt have been exceeding the arrivals possibly due to longer duration of stay being estimated at about a month, and an increase in average daily spending.

A study by National Council of Applied Economic Research (NCAER, 2004) using the Tourism Satellite Account (TSA) methodology estimated the value added by tourism at 2.78 per cent of Gross Domestic Product (GDP) in terms of direct impact, and 5.8 per cent of GDP in indirect effects. Further, though tourism generated employment estimations are often refuted, it would be pertinent to consider some recent studies to gauge the potential of tourism. For instance, the National Action Plan for Tourism (NAPT) Report by the Department of Tourism stated tourism to have generated 13-14 million employments directly and indirectly. The National Council of Applied Economic Research (NCAER) study stated above estimates tourism's share in the total number of direct jobs as 4.59 per cent, which rises to 8.27 per cent when indirect effects are also included.

Table 1.5: International Receipts: World and India

Year	*World Tourist Receipts (billion US$)*	*Annual Growth Rate (%)*	*Tourist Receipts Indian (billion US$)*	*Annual Growth Rate (%)*	*India's Share to World Receipts*
1990	266.2	—	1.51	—	0.57
1995	406.2	10.5	2.69	18.5	0.64
2000	474.4	3.4	3.18	6.0	0.67
2005	682.0	8.8	5.70	15.8	0.84
2013	944.88	—	—	—	—

Source: Tourism Statistics, Department of Tourism, Government of India.

Tourism in Sikkim

Tourism is one of the mainstays of the mountain and hill economy and Sikkim is second to none in this regard. The mighty Kanchenjunga offer brilliant mountain scenery, healthier and invigorating climate. The snowy winter and cooler summer serve to invite many tourists to this tiny hilly state. Sikkim is a place where fusion of culture is distinctly visible. Sikkim has great beauty ranging from the mountains and multitude of rivers and lakes, which are considered as the *sine-qua-non* of Eco-tourism. Sandwiched in the hills and mountain, Sikkim has now started gaining importance as a major eco-tourism destination. It has everything which a tourist can dream of as a land of fairs and festivals, snow-clad mountains, holy lakes and peaks, religious centres, hot springs, trekking, water-rafting, pleasant valleys, flora and fauna and so on.

Sikkim, one of the smallest states in the north-east India and the second smallest state in the country lies between 27.50 and 28.10 north and 88.40 and 88.580 east longitude. Spread across an area of just 7,096 sq. km, this state has a varied terrain climate and altitude resulting in a wide range of bio-diversity. Three foreign countries surround it—Nepal in the West, Bhutan in the East and Tibet and China in the North and West Bengal in the South. Till the middle of 1970s Sikkim was under the monarchy government when the 35th Amendment Act made it an associate State of Indian Union and finally on 16th of May, 1975 (38th Amendment Act), it was made a full-fledged state of India. Since, then there has been a constant flow of tourist in Sikkim, which has played, great roles in boosting up the economy of the state.

Sikkim is a hilly state traversed by rivers and mountains that define its boundaries. Two principle mountain ranges—Singalila on the western border that marks its boundaries with Nepal and the Chola on the eastern border with Tibet. A low altitude range Panglakha marks the boundary between Sikkim and Bhutan. Most of the peaks above (20,000 ft) are on the western border of Sikkim (Kanchenjunga -28,168 ft; Kabru-20,000 ft; Sinolchu, Pandim, Simvo). Paunhri peak (22,000 ft) is the highest point on the eastern border of the State. Another mountain ridge separate Teesta and Rangit valley, which include the peaks like Tendong (8660 ft), and Maenam (10,612 ft).

There are many glaciers too in Sikkim, some of the important glaciers of Sikkim are the Zemu glaciers (largest in state), Rathong and Lonak glaciers. Mountain ranges are incomplete without passes, so numerous passes are found in the huge mountain range of Sikkim, the most important of which are—Nathu La (La meaning Pass) (14,140 ft), Jelep La (14,350 ft), Chiwabhanjang (10,300 ft).

Sikkim is gifted with a number of lakes, which are not expected on such a rugged terrain. The serene lake Tsomgo Lake (12,320 ft), Bidan Tso, Memencho, Kheceopalri Lake are the few to name. Gurudogmar Lake is the largest lake in the state located in the northern part of the state. Teesta and Rangit are two important rivers of Sikkim, which gives off numerous tributaries along its course. Starting from a height of 18,000 ft, Teesta travels down in 100 km to a height of just 3000 ft. These rivers never dry out, even during the winter as they are fed both by snowmelt as well as rains. There are numerous hot springs in Sikkim, which have medicinal as well as therapeutic value. Phurchachu, Yumthang, Yumey Samdong, Ralang are the important hot springs of Sikkim which are rich in Sulphur content and have an average temperature of 500° C.

The climate of Sikkim ranges from the tropical to alpine. Places with an altitude of 19,900 ft and above are snowbound and places as low as 9,850 ft come within the snowline in the winter. The temperature in the lower altitudes fluctuates between 40–35° C and places with moderate height like Gangtok experiences temperature between 10–25° C. In the high altitude area (above 13,100 ft), the mercury never rise above 15° C and slides down below the freezing point in winter. Because of its close proximity to Bay of Bengal and the obstruction of the path of monsoon clouds by mountains, most of the part of the state receives heavy rainfall throughout the year. It is only during the month of October—March that the state remains dry.

Tourism in the state is growing at a rapid pace in a very well thought of and planned manner. Sikkim now has become one of the best hill destinations at the global level. The leadership is very much committed and the Government has been extremely effective and successful in educating and guiding the people regarding tourism on the basic principle of Sustainable Development. Sikkim is now the only organic state in the country. There are certain strong steps which have been taken up to preserve culture, tradition, heritage and environment/ecology of the state. A number of well planned programmes are being introduced to educate the people by organizing capacity building programmes for the youth and other stakeholders engaged in tourism sectors. In order to procure license for registration of travel agents, hotels and lodges and other sectors relevant to it, single window clearance system is being adopted.

The people of Sikkim are persistently encouraged to preserve the old monuments and heritage sites. The Green Mission programme has been launched under which every individual, agency and the Department contributes towards the planting of trees all-over the state. Village tourism is encouraged to preserve culture, heritage and handicrafts and to create better economic and employment opportunity in the rural area. Floriculture is being promoted and all the hotels and restaurants have been requested to use natural flowers instead of artificial flowers. Plastic is banned in the state and the tourists are educated to respect local culture and tradition.

Sikkim is one of the hottest tourist destinations in India. What oil is to Arab, tourism is for Sikkim. Eco-tourism as we know from the definition given by TIES is responsible for travel to natural areas that conserve the environment and sustain the well being of local people.

Sikkim has an excellent setting for Eco-tourism. This state is purely rural in nature with about 40 per cent of the total land comprises of fixed land and another 30 per cent land is under snowcapped mountain, glaciers and rivers. Here one can travel from a level of 300 m to 8598 m in a span of just 110 km. This variation in altitude has given rise to a rich biodiversity in Sikkim. Therefore, this region is one of the most sought eco-tourist destinations. The demand of tourist to see the culture of local people helped in the revival of the interest within local people regarding their culture. The people of Sikkim make it a natural tourist destination because of their friendly and hospitable nature, peace and tranquility. Most of the areas are unventured and unspoiled thus creating an area of mystery around it.

A good amount of the tourism resources in the area can be utilized to develop and promote Eco-tourism. There are numerous Eco-tourism products available in this region. "Wildlife in natural setting" is the most important product while the nature based recreational activities like camping, rafting, hiking and trekking are also found to contribute towards promotion of Eco-tourism.

(A) Adventure Tourism

Adventure tourism is one of the most neglected forms of tourism, which has an enormous potential of growth and development in Sikkim. Today's generations love fun of adventure and Sikkim has everything to contribute to the adventure tourism of the state. Adventure tourism in Sikkim includes mountaineering, trekking, mountain biking and water rafting.

(B) Trekking

Trekking in Sikkim can be a wonderful experience—an antidote to the stress of daily life and a memory to cherish rest of life. While trekking, an individual can relish the pure air and the silence of wilderness and feels the awakening of senses dolled by urban living. Though each and every nook and corner of the state is worth trekking, following trek routes are worth while to be discussed here:

- Gangtok—Penlong—Tinjure—Rumtek.
- Lachung—Yumthang—Yumey Samdong.
- Damthang—Tendong—Ravangla—Maenam—Sirwani.
- Ravangla—Maenam—Borong—Tashiding.
- Yuksom—Dzongri.
- Hilley—*via* Sombarey—Varsey—Soreng.

- Hilley—Varsey—Dentam—Singalila—Chiwabhangang.
- Mangan—Lingzin—Sakyong—Royot Patam—Dzongri—Yoksum.

(C) Mountaineering

The first European to explore Khangchendzonga area was Douglas W. Freshfield in 1899. Famous Sikkimese Everester Sonam Gyatso climbed the summit of Siniolchu. Though mountaineering activities now a days is not frequent yet the activities are usually taken by Sonam Gyatso Mountaineering Institute.

(D) Rafting

Under the category of water sports, White River rafting is the latest adventure sport in Sikkim. Teesta and Rangit are the ideal rivers for rafting. The following two routes are the most desired by the rafters:

- On River Teesta : Chungthang—Dikchu—Singtam—Melli
- On River Rangit : Legship—Jorethang—Melli

(E) Mountain Biking

This class of adventure tourism is recently introduced in this hilly state of Sikkim. Since most of the roads of Sikkim are accessible by motorbikes, this sport can gain momentum in the near future. Following routes are advisable:

- Gangtok—Rumtek—Sang—Sirwani—Temi.
- Damthang—Rabongla—Kewzing—Tashiding—Yuksam—Khecheopalri.
- Jorethang—Sikip—Reshi—Rinchenpong—Bermiok—Dentam.
- Jorethang—Melli—Rangpo—Singtam—Gangtok.
- Gangtok—Phodong—Rangrang—Dikchu—Makha—Sirwani—Temi-Singtam—Gangtok.

(F) Wildlife Tourism

Due to the variation of altitude from sea level to the mountain tops, Sikkim possess a wide and varied spectrum of flora and fauna. It has one of the richest assemblages of habitat in the world. The zoological and botanical richness and diversity is excellent, boasting of more than 4,000 species of plants, 300 species of fern and its allies, 11 species of Oaks, 8 species of tree fern, 30-40 species of primula, 20 species of bamboos, 144 species of mammals, 500-600 species of birds (30% of all birds found in Indian sub-continent), over 400 species of butterflies and moths, together with many reptiles, medicinal herbs and shrubs. The state can be broadly classified into three zones:

(a) Tropical (Sea Level –1500 m)
(b) Temperate (from 1500 m to 3500 m)
(c) Alpine (above 3500 m)

The jungle of lower altitude harbor Jungle cuts, Mongoose, sparrow and has abundance of bamboos, trees firm, walnut and oak. More than 600 species of orchids are found in Sikkim, which are indeed the jewels in the crown. The most important of them are—Cymbidiums, Vanda Cuttaleya, Haberina, and Paphiopedilum. Nobile orchid (*Dendrobium nobile*) is declared as the State flower. The fauna of Temperate Zone comprises of common Langur, Leopard cats, Red Panda, Musk deer, Himalayan black bear and the flying squirrel. The arid cold alpine region of Sikkim harbors snow leopard and wild ass roaming amongst rhododendron, the state hosts around 30 species of Rhododendron. The Rhododendron Nevium is the state tree of Sikkim. Parks and Sanctuaries played an important role in promoting eco-tourism in Sikkim.

References

Bhatia, A.K. (2010): *Tourism Development: Principles and Practice,* New Delhi: Sterling Publishers Private Limited.

Goswami, B.K. and Ravindran, G. (2001): *A Textbook of Tourism*, New Delhi: Har Anand DSB Management Service.

Ranjit, Sanuraja (1978): Tourism Industry with Special Reference to Foreign Exchange Earnings and Resort Development, Unpublished Masters Dissertation, T.U., Kathmandu.

Ratti, Hanish (2007): *History and Geography of Tourism*, New Delhi: Rajat Publication.

Singh, A.K. and Rana, P.S. (2006): *Tourism Geography*, Lucknow: New Royal Book Co.

Sinha, U.P. and Kumar, Swargesh (2011): Bihar Tourism: Retrospect and Prospect, New Delhi: Concept Publishing Company (P.) Ltd.

Sutheeslina, B.S., *et al.* (2008): *Tourism Development Revisited*, New Delhi: Response.

Tewari, S.P. (1994): *Tourism Dimensions*, New Delhi: Atma Ram & Sons.

WTO (1994): *Recommendation on Tourism Statistics*, Madrid: World Tourism Organization.

2
Tourism Research and Methodology

The purpose of this chapter is to present the different approaches to estimating the economic impacts of tourism. We have summarized economic impact concepts and methods as they apply to tourism. In this chapter we apply the methods to illustrate cases in order to demonstrate some practical approaches. Three specific examples have been presented. These represent a range of alternatives for estimating the economic impacts of visitor spending. The techniques covered range from methods based largely on judgement, to methods that utilize secondary spending data and published multipliers, to the use of visitor surveys and input-output models. This study discusses survey methods for measuring visitor spending and includes sample spending instruments. While the construction and operation of tourist facilities also has economic impacts, we will restrict our attention here to the impacts of visitor spending and future potentiality of Sikkim tourism industry.

Need of the Study

Tourism holds a place of prominence in economic development. Today, every economy has elaborate economic development programmes and many list tourism as one of their most important economic sectors. Along with business, service and technology, tourism is considered to be significant contributor to a country's prosperity and image. The degree of reliance of local economy on tourism does have a statistically significant impact on the level of the capital outlays, transportation, police protection, protection from natural disasters, parks and recreation, financial administration and public expenditure. The economic activities associated with tourism improve the quality of life as such. Much of the analysis of this industry has focused on the positive impact on employment, income, tax revenue and economic growth and development in general. Tourism is not an isolated industry, but is a bundle of complementary services.

In broader terms a tourist is any visitor in a community who comes to spend money and enjoys local services. So, the travel and tourism industry represents the major segments of national economy and is a significant economic sector in many states and local economies. It is thus considered as an important indicator of the process of economic development without hampering ecology and environment of the potential places.

Several studies have been conducted in this field by different researchers, institutions and scholars. However, most of these are concerned with specific areas only. This study mainly focuses on tourist inflow in Sikkim. This study tries to highlight trends, causes of tourism, and portrays the socio-economic condition of the study area. Hitherto, no such study has been conducted regarding these issues in Sikkim.

Statement of Problem

The present endeavour is attempted to study at the micro-level with the main objectives to address the following questions:

1. To what extent do the people living in and around the tourist spot economically depend on tourism?
2. What is the opportunity cost of the tourist spot in terms of other economic activities?
3. Tourist inflow in the study area?
4. To find out Social-Cost Benefit Ratio of tourism industry of Sikkim?

Research Hypothesis

Sikkim has three resources to build-up Indian economy; they are agriculture, hydropower and tourism. Among them, tourism is the key industry which can be easily promoted and developed by minimum investment. So, it is the major sector for the development in economy. Tourism is an activity which generates number of economic and social benefits which are given below:

1. The economic exploitation of natural and cultural wealth are closely associated with the development of tourism in Sikkim (the study area).
2. It provides a vast spectrum of employment ranging from high skilled persons to unskilled.
3. It opens up new horizons of employment, career building capacity, empowerment and self-independence among the peoples which directly or indirectly depend on tourism.
4. Linkage of tourism sector with other sectors of economy can be viewed in terms of multiplier effects of tourism expenditure.

Objectives of the Study

The objectives of the study are focused on the estimation of local and national economic effects of tourism industry which were as classified below:

1. To examine the tourist inflow in Sikkim and analysis the tourist trend of last ten years.
2. To study the various kinds of tourism in the study area.
3. To estimate the opportunity cost of tourism industry in the study area.
4. Income analysis of tourism industry.
5. Future potential of tourism industry in Sikkim.

Limitation of the Study Area

The limitation of this study is that it is confined to the State of Sikkim only. It is not possible to generalize or to represent the entire tourism industry of the country as a whole. The study has following limitations:

Firstly, the micro-level study is limited only on the economic impact of tourism industry of the Sikkim. The study has only focused on the people those who were related with tourism for their livelihood, and it also measure social-cost benefit ratio of tourism industry to make the study more realistic.

Secondly, the study has only focused on the inflow of foreign and domestic tourist, the effect of tourism in economy, opportunity cost in terms of other economic activities based on field surveys through interviews, using questionnaires for individual tourist and the local people who were directly or indirectly dependant on tourism for their livelihood, through empirical observation and focus group discussion. The survey will be completed spread over a period of six months.

Research Methodology

The following research methods has been used for the research:

Research Design

The study will be designed as exploratory and conclusive in nature. As an exploratory research, search of secondary data, survey of knowledgeable persons and case study will be made. As conclusive research case study and statistical tools like trend analysis will be done in order to draw conclusion.

Sources of Information

The present study is based mainly on primary cross-section data and secondary data. The main sources of primary data are households and visitors and surveys conducted through the formal method of interview in a designed questionnaire. Two stage random sampling has been followed for household survey. The area selection at the first stage and the household selection at the second stage will be conducted. For the visitor survey, foreign visitors and domestic visitors from different countries and the states of India will be selected purposively at random.

The concept of "Comity Village" has been introduced to indicate the environment friendly region. The term 'Comity' is meant for harmonious friendliness. This research work strives for the environmental friendly co-existence in and around the tourist spot.

Tourism Models

System Approach

System approach is useful in many types of research and in many fields of study, for it provides distinctive ways of understanding (Emery, 1981). While its best known application has been in the development of computer technologies, it has profoundly shaped

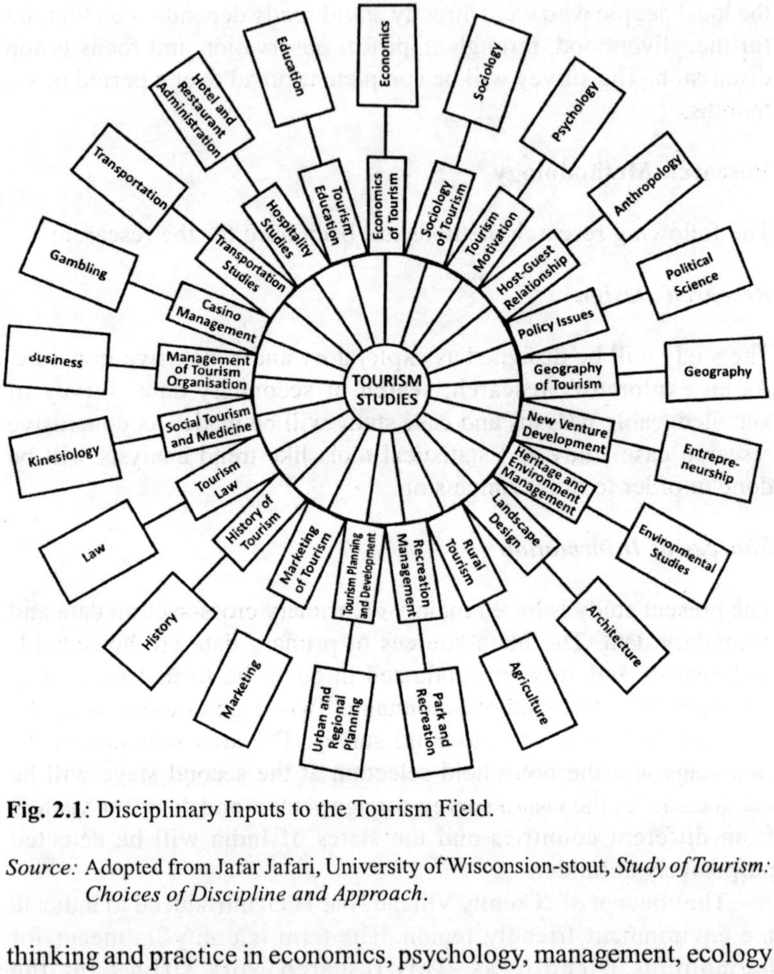

Fig. 2.1: Disciplinary Inputs to the Tourism Field.

Source: Adopted from Jafar Jafari, University of Wisconsion-stout, *Study of Tourism: Choices of Discipline and Approach*.

thinking and practice in economics, psychology, management, ecology and many other areas. System approach is especially valuable in multidisciplinary education on applied fields. For all these reasons, its relevance to tourism studies and tourism industries is pervasive and diverse.

System thinking can be distinguished from system approach. The former is a way of looking at things (concrete systems) or ideas (abstract systems) which attempts to be holistic and cohesive. The search for holistic vision means attempting to view a whole entity rather than focusing on some parts, ignoring others. The search for cohesion means attempting to understand how the parts are arranged and how they function in combination as a system. System thinking has been evident for two thousand years in the work of isolated scholars including Aristotle, Ptolemy, Copernicus, Galileo, Ibn Khaldun and Vico.

System approach is newer. It was created in the 1930s and continues to develop. It formalizes system thinkings, as a quasi-discipline, an organized body of knowledge, for the study of systems. Several applied sciences have grown from it, including cybernetics, information theory, game theory, decision theory, topology, factor analysis, systems engineering operations research. Central to all this is general systems theory, devised by Bertalanffy and others (1972).

The distinctive purpose of general systems theory is to deal with any thing or any idea that seems complex. The aim is to reduce the complexity. The value is that after complexity has been reduced, things and ideas become easier to understand, analyse and manage. The strategy for achieving this is, broadly, breaking down a whole (thing or idea) into its elements, and then identifying the crucial attributes of elements to see how they are connected. Element, attribute and systems hierarchy are basic concepts in systems theory, where these terms have particularly meanings. An element is a component which must exist for the system in question to exist. For example, useful models of whole tourism systems have (tourists) as an element, since without tourists there can be no tourism. They also have destination region and origin (or generating) region as two more elements, by the same logic.

Attributes are features or characteristics of an element that makes it part of a system, linking it to the other elements. For example, urban congestion and pollution are attributes of many of the world's traveller-generating regions. Those features influence many residents to seek temporary escape *via* tourism, a behavioural process which involves those residents becoming tourists, visiting places beyond their home city, places which are destinations.

Elements forming a system do not do this because of their imminent qualities, but by their arrangement in that system, where they are not significantly connected except with reference to the whole. That axiom indicates a distinction between relationship thinkers and system thinkers. If the former sees beautiful scenery, they imagine that the region is (or should be) a destination because of its beauty, the two facts seem related. System thinkers understand that beautiful scenery is an immanent quality which, on its own, does not and cannot make a region a destination, nor can advertising or business investment (Leiper, 1995). For a place to become a successful destination, a number of connected elements are necessary.

Certain systems can be seen in hierarchies. In principle, every system has superior and subsystems. The latter are derived by analysing elements and attributes in their fundamental components 'Whole system' is a heading for the superior system in a field. Common concepts of systems approach include whole systems and subsystems, framework and clockwork system, inputs and outputs, environments, feedback, entropy, negative entropy, proliferating variety, dynamic systems and homeostatic systems, interdisciplinary and multidisciplinary. While all those concepts are mentioned in the tourism literature, to date few have been explored in depth.

Tourism generally involves notable open system, so environmental interactions are a major interest. In some places, environmental impacts are reduced, or altered, by closing off parts of the system, reducing its open qualities. One strategy for this is integrated resorts. A number of researches have devised simple framework and clockwork models of systems. Theoretical research on feedback and proliferating variety in relation to tourism has been conducted by Leiper (1995). This has helped analysis of part industrialisation, which has implications for all elements of tourisms and their environments.

Systems thinking's pervasion of traditional discipline has been a counterbalance to the main approach in modern academia. That approach has allowed a rapid expansion of knowledge in specific physical and social sciences. But it involves concentration on analytical fact finding and narrow theory building. Countering this fragmentation, system theories are serving as a unifying bridge, a means of co-ordinating multidisciplinary education and research.

Butler's Tourist Area Life Cycle (TALC) Model

Tourist Area Life Cycle (TALC) model, developed in 1980 by Richard Butler is based on the product cycle concept. In his seminal article presenting his model, Butler acknowledges the contribution of others who have perceived a similar cycle in the real world.

Butler has suggested a tourist area life cycle, where resorts evolve from discovery through development to eventual decline. Although, the life cycle approach has its own critics—who feel it is difficult to operationalize the main utility of the approach as a way of thinking about resorts, an explanatory framework for their development and as a means of integrating supply-side developments with the evolving market of a resort. After all, the type of tourist who visits at introduction will be very different from that visiting in consolidation or decline (Fig. 2.2). The tourist area life cycle is as follows:

1. *Exploration*—Small number of adventurous tourists, main attraction is unspoilt nature or cultural features.
2. *Involvement*—Local initiatives provide facilities and some advertising ensues. Larger number of visitors during tourist season and public sector involvement follow.
3. *Development*—Outside investment is attracted to the destination as a well-defined tourism market emerges. Accessibility is enhanced, advertising becomes more intensive and extensive, and local facilities are displaced by more elaborate and up-to-date ones. This results in a decline in local participation and control. Artificial attractions supplant original ones. Imported labour and auxiliary facilities and services become necessary to support the rapidly growing tourist industry.
4. *Consolidation*—The destination is now a full-fledged part of the tourist industry; the rate of increase of visitors is reduced. Marketing and advertising efforts are further

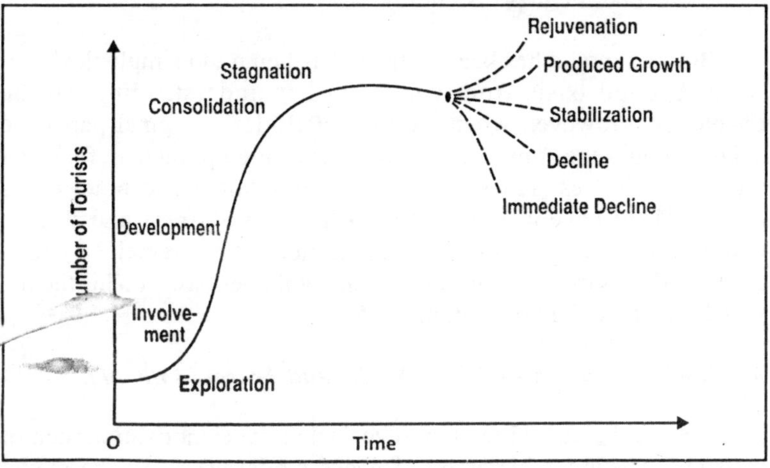

Fig. 2.2: The Tourist Area Life Cycle.

widened to extend the tourism season and attract more distant visitors.

5. *Stagnation*—Peak visitor numbers have been reduced as the destination is unfashionable with environmental, social and economic problems. Major promotional efforts are needed to maintain visitor numbers.
6. *Decline*—Tourists are drawn away towards newer destinations. Those remaining are mostly weekend or day visitors. Tourism facilities become replaced by non-tourism establishments as the area disengages from the industry. The destination either becomes a tourism slum or finds itself devoid of tourism activity altogether.
7. *Rejuvenation*—A dramatic change in the resource base is established. Either a new set of artificial attractions is created or a previously unexplored natural resource is utilized.
8. *Reduced Growth*—The effects of competition mean that even with the new development plans, the destination is never able to return to the levels of previous growth and development.
9. *Stabilization*—The destination is able to maintain its market share, but there is little, if any, continued growth and development.
10. *Immediate Decline*—Visitor numbers fall quite rapidly and the tourism base severely contracts, resulting in a local economic depression.

Butler's model has been criticized as being too simplistic, but it forms a good basis from which further understanding can be developed. However, when we look at Butler's original paper, he acknowledges the complexity of what he is attempting to define, and recognises that testing will be needed to ascertain the accuracy of his model. There have been hundreds of academic papers and student dissertations either using or refuting the model, yet it remains a strong theory today as can be seen by two recent volumes based on his theory, which he had edited by Butler, 2005.

Maslow's Hierarchy of Needs Model and Travel Motivation

A review of the travel literature reveals that travel motivations can fit well into Maslow's hierarchy of needs model in 1943. The model suggests that lower needs in the order of hierarchy warrant priority

Table 2.1: Maslow's Needs and Motivations Listed in Travel Literature

Need	*Motive*	*Tourism Literature Reference*
Physiological	Relaxation	Escape, Relaxation, Relief of Tension, Sunlust, Physical, Mental relaxation of tension.
Safety	Security	Health, Recreation, Keep oneself active and healthy for the future.
Belonging	Love	Family togetherness, Enhancement of kinship relationships, Companionship Facilitation of Social interaction, Maintenance of personal ties, Interpersonal relation, Roots, Ethnic, Show one's affection for family members, Maintain social contacts.
Esteem	Achievement status	Convince oneself of one's achievements, Show one's importance to others' Prestige, Social recognition, Ego-enhancement, Profession/business, Personal development Status and prestige.
Self-Actualization	Be true to one's Own nature	Exploration and evaluation of Self-discovery Satisfaction of inner desires
To know and understand	Knowledge	Cultural, Education, Wanderlust, Interest in foreign areas.
Aesthetics	Appreciation of beauty	Environmental Scenery.

attention and satisfaction—Maslow's idea of prepotency. The hierarchy of needs proposed by Maslow can be represented as follows:

(a) *Physiological*—Hunger, thirst, rest, and activity.
(b) *Safety*—Security, release from fear and anxiety.
(c) *Belonging and love*—Affection, giving and receiving love.
(d) *Esteem*—Self-esteem (the need to exhibit strength, achievement, mastery, competence, and independence and esteem from others, described by notions such as reputation, prestige, status, and recognition).
(e) *Self-actualization*—Personal self-realization from the above list, it is clear that the needs are mainly psychological in nature except that of the first one, which is physical in nature. To this list of needs, two specific needs were added later which are intellectual in essence.
(f) *Acquisition of knowledge* –To learn and understand.
(g) *Aesthetics*—Appreciation of beauty. Although, the relationship between the above said three types of needs—physical, psychological and intellectual is ill-defined, it is

> considered that the intellectual needs stand on their own. Nevertheless, the correlation between the needs, motives, and references from the tourism literature is presented in Table 2.1.

The people for whom the prime motivation behind travel is "to escape" or "to relieve tension" can, indeed, be seen as aspiring to satisfy the basic physiological need. For such travellers, the motivation may be to get physical or mental relaxation. Holidayers generally return home from a tour mentally revitalized and refreshed, but physically exhausted. And here arise the need to differentiate between people opting to undertake an active holiday or a passive one, though both are motivated by a need for relieving stress and strains. The active holidayers achieve the objective of reduction in tension through physical activity. This activity can also be considered as being related to self-esteem and/or of achievement and mastery of environment. On the contrary, a passive holidayer tries to achieve the objective of tension relief by giving in or surrendering to environment. From such surrender comes the very let-up from tension that will bring on the return of the holidayers/vacationers as refreshed and rejuvenated. This proposition also well explains the fact that, at any one time, one may be motivated to satisfy multiple needs. Moreover, drawing on the idea of prepotency, that is, before the satisfaction of higher level needs are considered, the lower level needs in hierarchy framework should be satisfied to a level, implies that products and services including holidays targeted towards the satisfaction of lower-level needs would be deemed as more of a necessity than a luxury and would, as such, be more resilient to external pressure of time and money.

Projection Method

Another projection method is to build a computer model that will simulate tourist demand. Typically, the demand for tourism to a particular area is a function of factors such as levels of income of tourists, the cost of travel from the tourists' homes to the destination, price-levels, competition, currency exchange rates, and distance or journey time. These relationships are usually identified using multiple regression, as discussed above.

Simulation models include a complex set of equations that will usually combine both the trend-line extrapolation methods and the regression-technique models into a more comprehensive systems simulation. Relationships between many variables are specified through interrelated equations. Simulation models rely on historical data for input and model calibration. Once a model gives reasonably accurate distributions for past years, it can be used to predict probable future distributions.

Simulation models require specially trained personnel with a high degree of technical expertise to set-up original model and data processing programmes.

Knowledge of time-series, cross-sectional and causal relationships and change processes is required. Also, powerful computing resources and high data precision are necessary. These are serious problems that have to be faced by any tourism organization that might consider using this approach. Simulation forecasting is best suited for a problem that is complex with known and quantifiable relationship and some feedback effects. It is also suitable for long forecast horizons.

Several statistical methods or econometric analyses can he used to project demand. All require a degree of statistical or mathematical sophistication, familiarity with computers, and a clear understanding of the purpose (and limitations) of such projections. Listed are several such methods with brief explanations.

(i) Trend Analysis Method

The trend analysis method involves the interpretation of historical demand data. For instance, if a record of the number of tourist arrivals in an area on an annual basis is available, then demand for future years can be projected using this information. The first step is to plot the available data on a graph: time (in years) against the tourist arrivals. Once this has been done, a linear trend can be established which best captures the changes in demand levels in the past. Demand projections for future years can now be made by extending the trend line up to the relevant year and reading the demand estimate off the graph. Fig. 2.3 illustrates this procedure. The points represent the levels of demand for the six-year period for which data are available.

A linear trend in demand levels can then be determined (say, line AB). If a demand projection for year 10 were needed, the trend line AB can be extended to a point such as C. Finally, the projected demand level in year 10 can be determined to be approximately 1,80,000 arrivals, as shown in Fig. 2.3.

The advantage of using trend analysis is that the data needed are rather basic and easy to obtain. Only one data series is required: visitor arrivals or some other measure of demand on a quarterly or on an

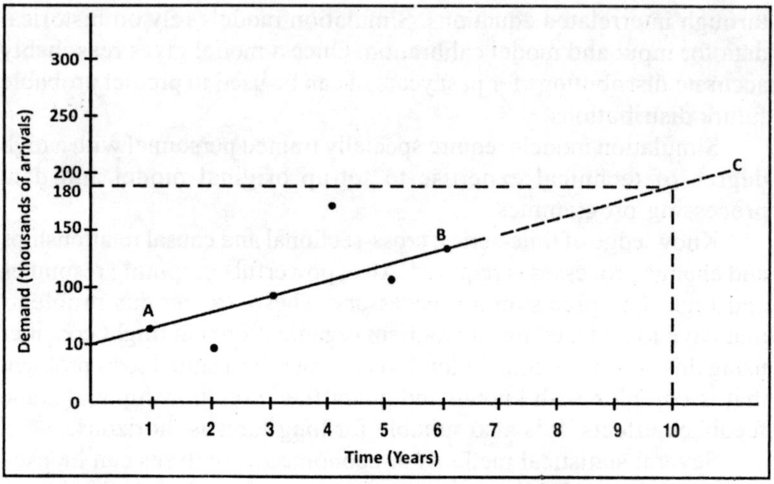

Fig. 2.3: Trend Analysis.

annual basis for the past few years. In addition, the method is simple and does not require a great deal of mathematical sophistication. Characteristically, however, the simplicity of the model is to a large extent a trade-off for the usefulness of the results. For instance, the future demand estimates obtained in this manner should be interpreted with a great deal of caution. There are several reasons for this. First, trend analysis does not "explain" demand in any way. In other words, if demand changes from year to year, we would expect this to be because of changes in the components of demand. Trend analysis does not add knowledge the influence that these variables have on demand levels and, therefore, cannot explain why it changed. Second, to extrapolate from a linear trend (extending the trend line AB to point C) is to assume that past growth trends will continue without change. Such an assumption is tentative at best. Estimates based on a constant growth rate tend to become very unrealistic in rather short period of time, due to the nature of compounding.

(ii) Simple Regression: Linear Least Squares Method

In simple regression, information on demand levels for past years is plotted against one important determinant of demand, say, income or prices. Then, through the application of a statistical technique called least squares regression, a straight line is used to "explain" the relationship between demand and the particular variable being considered (such as income levels of tourists). Consider, for example, the hypothetical data in Table 2.2 for demand levels for ten years and the income levels of tourists for these same years.

Table 2.2: Relationship between Income and Travel Demand

Years	*Number of Tourist Arrivals (in '000)*	*Per Capita Income of Tourists (in ₹)*
1.	75	6300
2.	90	7200
3.	100	7000
4.	105	7400
5.	95	6800
6.	110	7500
7.	105	7500
8.	100	7200
9.	110	7600
10.	120	7900

By plotting the pain of arrivals and income data on a graph, we obtain a relationship between income and travel demand, illustrated in Fig. 2.4. The points represent the annual observations, and the line AB represents the line of "best fit". It is obtained by the least squares method. We can now obtain demand projections from this method based on what we expect income levels to be in the future. Suppose we wish to estimate demand for year 15. In this year, income is projected to be $8,300 per capita. As shown in the Fig. 2.4, the estimate of demand for this income level is 1,28,000. Because income is a major determinant of demand, simple regression 'explain' demand to some extent. It is superior to trend analysis for this reason. Besides, the methodology is still relatively simple and can be presented visually. Data needed for this method are relatively easy to collect, when compared to the data needs of the two following projections methods.

(iii) Multiple Regression: Linear Least Squares Method

The major drawback of simple regression is that only one variable can be considered at a time. In reality, demand is affected by all the factors that influence propensity and resistance, as discussed earlier. It may not be feasible to include all these variables at one time, but it is certainly practical to isolate a few that are particularly relevant to

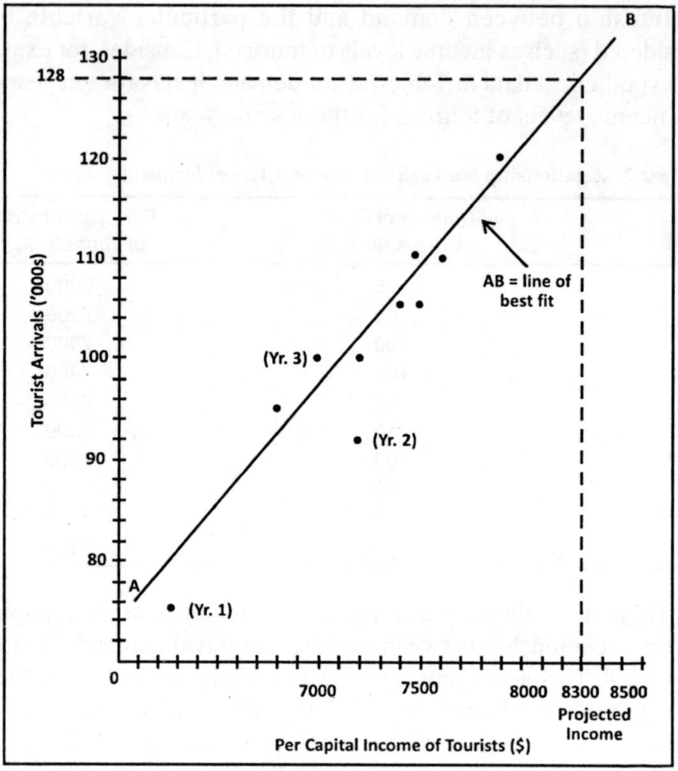

Fig. 2.4: Relationship between Income and Travel Demand.

determining demand and deal with these in one model. Multiple regression is one way to do this. It is essentially the same as simple regression, except that now more than one variable can be used to explain demand. Through a mathematical formula, a relationship is established between demand and the variables that we have chosen to consider in the model. For example, suppose that we had data on the prices of tourist services at a destination in addition to the incomes of the tourists. We could then regress demand on these two variables (income and prices) and obtain a mathematical relationship between them. To estimate future demand, projected income and price-levels for the relevant year can simply be substituted into the mathematical formula. The resulting estimate of demand will be more reliable than will one obtained by the simple regression method, because the former incorporates the combined effect of income and price on demand.

Indeed, the analysis is not restricted to these two variables alone. Conceptually, any number of variables can be used to explain and predict demand-levels. But there are some practical limitations. As the number of "explanatory" variables increases, the calculations become increasingly complex. In addition, the costs involved in collecting the additional data and solving the mathematics of the technique are considerable. In some instances, the incremental reliability of the estimates may not justify these expenses, because estimates are after all only estimates, and not certain to materialize—no matter how comprehensively they may be calculated.

In addition to the expense involved, another drawback of multiple regression is that the relationships cannot be depicted graphically, as the results of the two earlier methods can be. The reason is, of course, that we get into multi-dimensional planes. Up to dimensions can be depicted visually, but beyond that it becomes impossible.

(iv) Schematics of Tourism Process

The course that a tourist destination takes has been represented in various models of tourism process 12—15. These models assume that the tourist destinations have a lifespan and their journey from evolution to decline follows a life cycle. They have a boom phase, which is followed by a bust phase 12, 13. The life-span of tourist destinations depends upon the destination characteristics, tourist type, and the host community. The models by Butler and Murphy, which most aptly describe the life cycle of tourist destinations, are reproduced in Fig. 2.5. The Tourist Area Life Cycle (TALC) model developed by Butler is an amalgam of the product life cycle model and the model of population growth. This correlates the different stages and the course of evolution of destination areas or tourism development with the stages of product life cycle and population cycle by linking tourism experience, which is consumed, with product and carrying capacity. Murphy explains the rise and fall of tourist destinations in terms of tourist-host interactions/transactions and social carrying capacity.

The concept of these models is based on the premise that like the trends of animal population or the sales performance of a product in the market, the number of tourists visiting an area initially grows at a gradual pace. Later, because of the hospitality and with the growth and development of infrastructure, the tourist population enters a phase of continuously increasing growth, reaches a point of maximum growth. Thereafter, it follows a declining rate, reaches a stagnation

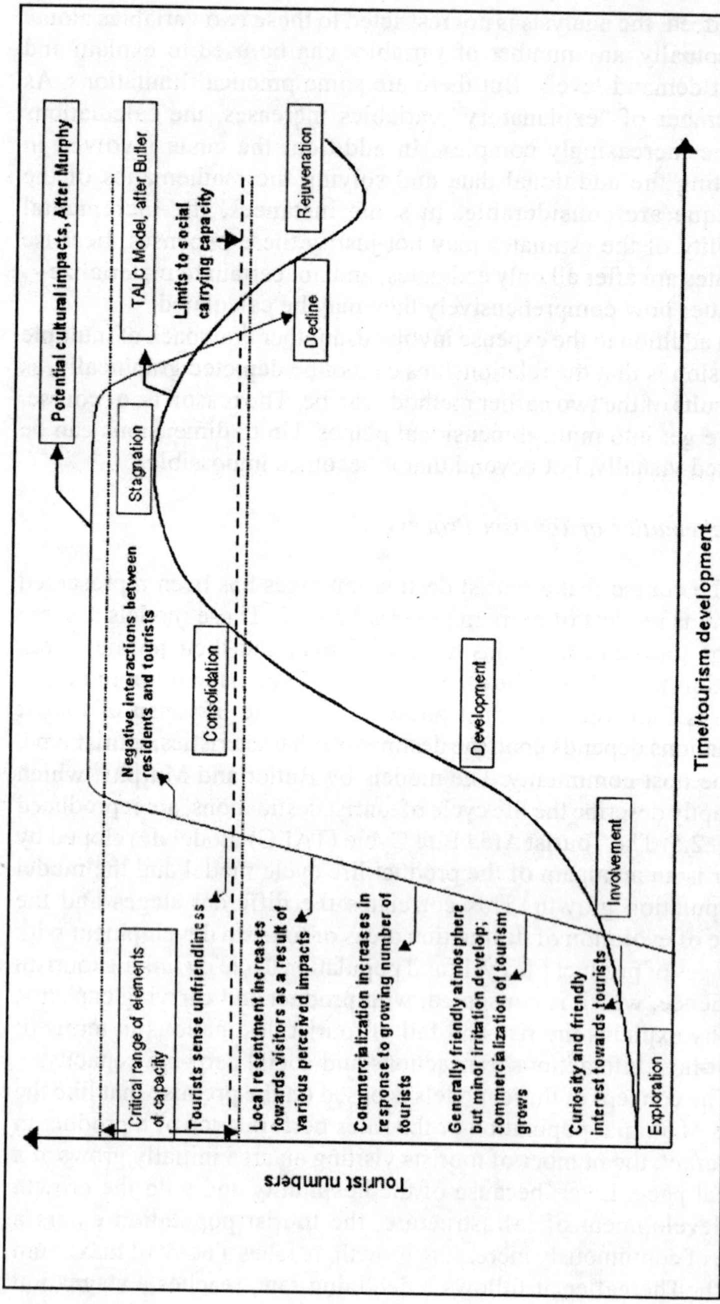

Fig. 2.5: Schematics of Tourism Development.

stage as the social, biological and environmental carrying capacities are exceeded, and after a peak the tourist population starts declining due to degradation of resources, over crowding, negative tourist-host interactions, and decline of overall tourism experience. The best course becomes a norm unless efforts for restoration are made. The cyclic pattern of tourist trends, the inevitability of carrying capacity violations and the decline after the peak are the three basic elements of these models. The models also acknowledge the scope and importance of management for resurrection of tourism from its bust phase, or the expansion of the boom phase before the breach of carrying capacity cut-offs. The sustenance of tourism through revival from bust course or by regulation of tourist numbers within carrying capacity limits, therefore, requires special efforts towards tourism management, and conservation and sustenance of the host environments. The patterns of tourist influx trends therefore can be useful in identification of the state of progress of tourism, its future course, impacts and likely implications for the sustainability of the environment and tourism.

Delphi Method

An important purpose in market research is to estimate future demand or to forecast the future prospect. There are a number of forecasting methods which are being used in diverse fields including business forecasting, demand forecasting, economic growth forecasting. These methods can be broadly categorized as:

(a) Qualitative methods,
(b) Time series projection methods, and
(c) Causal methods.

The time series and causal methods belong to the class of quantitative methods of forecasting. Qualitative methods include Jury of Executive opinion method and Delphi Methods.

In this method, views/opinions of experts on the specific subject are galvanised into a forecast through a mail survey. The steps involved are the following:

- A group of experts are identified as panelists and a questionnaire is sent to them by mail to express their views.
- The responses received from the experts are analysed and a

summary of the results are sent back to the experts with another questionnaire to assess the reasons for extreme views without disclosing the identity of the experts.

- The process is repeated one or more rounds till a reasonable agreement emerges in the views of experts.

Delphi method is more accurate and less expensive than the traditional face-to-face group meetings. The method permits a spread of opinion so as to reflect the uncertainties. The method, however, requires the co-operation and support of a group of experts.

Carrying Capacity

The concept of carrying capacity has a long pedigree. It was originally developed by resources in agriculture and forestry to determine the cropping levels that pieces of land could sustain without nutrients and other food sources being depleted. Of course, in tourism, the concept has a similar meaning. Quite simply, carrying capacity refers to the ability of a destination to take tourism use without deteriorating in same ways. In other words, "it defines the relationship between the resource base and the market and is influenced by the characteristics of each. One of the best definitions as that of Mathieson and Wall (1982)." The maximum number of people who can use a site without unacceptable alteration in the physical environment and without an unacceptable decline in the quality of experiences gained by visitors.

Carrying capacity can be managed and there is no absolute number for any destination. For example, open heath land can appear crowded with very few visitors' present, while wooded area can absorb many more visitors before appearing crowded.

There are different types of carrying capacity:

From the Point of View of the Resources

Physical carrying capacity refers to the number of facilities available—aircraft seats or car parking spaces for example. It is easy to measure and can be calculated on a simple percentage basis.

Environmental or biological carrying capacity is more difficult to measure and refers to limits of use in the ecosystem. There is increasing interest in the capacity, not only of the flora to take tourism use, but also in terms of fauna such as tourism based on whale or dolphin watching, or in the African game reserves.

From the Point of View of the Visitor

Physiological or behavioural carrying capacity refers to the point at which the visitor feels that additional tourists would spoil their experience. This is less straightforward than may appear at first sight. For example, completely empty spaces are just as problematic as crowed ones, and the type of tourist also has an effect on perception of crowding.

From the Point of View of the Host Community

Such carrying capacity is a measure of the ability of the host community to tolerate tourism. It is a more recent addition to typologies of capacity, but is becoming an important issue. Indeed, one of the most important tests of a sustainable tourism destination is the level of involvement of the local community in plans and decisions relating to tourism development. Whilst there is a concern that local residents have a lack of knowledge about tourism, new techniques such as "destination visioning", where the locals determine the future of tourism and "limits to acceptable change" where they determine levels of future development, are increasingly being adopted as a form of capacity management.

Various Economic Methods

That the study quantifies the objectives of study areas are as follows:

Economic Gain Conversion Factor (EGCF)

The EGCF will be derived on the basis of opportunity cost of the tourist spot. The existing practice of the agriculture and other related economic activities in and around the tourist spot is considered as the basis for the estimation. The lump-sum annual net income from one unit of economic activity is taken as the conversion factor to obtain the total benefit foregone from the tourism.

Logit Binary Choice Model

This model is used to estimate the future potential of tourism industry. The present study selects the YES-NO type dependent variable. It is in the form of binary choice of the visitor, either to visit or not to visit the tourist spot. Logit Binary Choice Model is useful in the case of dichotomous dummy dependent variable. The SPSS computer package is used for the desired model estimation with reiterative process.

Flow of Income Study Method

This method is based on the distribution of income from tourism into various sections of people. The present study concentrates on the economic value of time used by the people with tourist spot in the study area.

Relevant secondary sources will also be used to complete the study. Such secondary sources will be collected from different offices and organizations such as Department of Tourism Sikkim, Travel Agent and Association of Sikkim, Central Library Namchi, Newspapers and Journals published by Governments, several published and unpublished documents.

Sampling Procedures

Sampling is the process by which inference is made to the whole by examining only a part. In this research work different sampling procedures would be used to collect data such as simple random, stratified, multistage, etc. as per the need of the study.

Statistical Methods

Statistical method is the statistical tools and techniques used to facilitate the analysis and interpretation of numerical data secured from a single individual during the research work. Different statistical tools as per needs such as Percentage, Mean, Frequencies, Standard Deviation, Correlation and Regression etc. may be used.

Processing of Data

After the collection of research and analysis of data, interpretation of the result will be conducted. Analysis of data comes prior to interpretation. The fact and figures collected are to be processed with a view to reducing them to manageable proportion. So, for management and interpretation of the research conclusion, the research should use different process such as editing, coding, categorization and tabulation, etc.

Structure of the Study

The present study has been designed to draw a conclusion to fulfil all the objectives. To fulfil all the objectives, the chapter has been distributed as, in Chapter I—Introduction of the study has been made. Simultaneously in Chapter II—Research and Methodology, Chapter III —Review of Past Literature, Chapter IV—The Various Kinds of Tourism in the Study Area, Chapter V— Tourist Inflow and Analysis of the Tourist Trends of the Last Ten Years in the Study Area has been made. For The Opportunity Cost and Income Analysis of Tourism Industry the Study Area, Future Potential of the Tourism Industry in Sikkim, and Summary, Conclusions and Suggestions for Further Research in Chapter VI, VII and VIII respectively. Lastly, Standard Questionnaire, Interview Schedule, Group Discussion has been applied to fulfil the objectives.

References

Bertalanffy, L. Von. (1972): General System Theory: A Critical Review, In J. Beilshan and G Peters (Eds.), *System Behaviour*, London: Open University Press, 29-49.

Butler, R.W. (1980): The Concept of Tourist Area Cycle of Evolution, Implications for Management of Resources, Can. Geogr., 24, 5-12, as displayed in p. 203, in *Tourism, Environment and Sustainable Development, Environmental Conservation* (Ed. Butler, R.W.), 1991, Vol. 18, pp. 201-209.

Cooper, C.J., Fletcher, D. Gilbert, R. Shepherd, and S. Wanhill (Eds.) (1998) : *Tourism: Principles and Practice*, Essex, UK: Longman.

Goeldner, C.R., Brent, J.R. and Robert, M. (2000), *Tourism Principles, Practices, Philosophies*, New York: John Wiley & Sons Inc..

Goswami, B.K. and Ravindran, G. (2001): *A Textbook of Tourism*, New Delhi: Har Anand DSB Management Service.

Mathieson, A. and Wall, G. (1982): *Tourism: Economic, Physical, and Social Impacts*, New York: Longman, p. 208.

Pasricha, A. (2009): *International Tourism*, New Delhi: Regal Publications.

Sharma, A.S. (2009) : *Tourism Management*, New Delhi: Essential Books.

Sirgy, M.J. and Su Chanting (2004), Destination Image, Self-congruity, and Travel Behaviour: Towards and Integrative Models, *Journal of Travel Research,* 38(2): 340-352.

Wagner, J.E. (1997) : Estimating the Economic Impacts of Tourism, *Annals of Tourism Research*, 24, 592-608.

3
Tourism: A Precedent Study

Despite the short history in Sikkim as compared to other states of India and other Asian countries, there is various kind of wealthy literature available on Tourism, tourism activities and tourism product related to Sikkim. In this chapter, an attempt has to be made to provide the theoretical foundation of tourism and eco-tourism, opportunities cost of tourism, etc. which has to be found rare. In dealing with this tourism concept some selected Books, magazines, Policies, Regulation and Dissertations that are directly and indirectly relevant to proposed study were reviewed. Tourism is an ancient phenomenon of inherent nomadic urge in man. From the very earliest historical period, travel has remained a fascination for man. In ancient time pilgrims, traders and few scholars and adventurous souls had to undertake journey in order to satisfy their respective urges.

Cohen (1979) has identified some characteristics of tourism as commercialized hospitality, democratized travel, a modern leisure activity, a modern variety of the traditional pilgrimage, an expression of basic cultural themes, an acculturative process, type of the ethnic relationship, a form of neocolonialism. He mentioned travelling as a human instinct. The industrial revolution led to development of trade and commerce. The industrial development led to urbanization, changed the working environment, increased their income and living standard. Moreover, they realized the need for the leisure and pleasure.

Leiper (1979) gave a technical definition of tourist must clearly define the category of the travel and visits, the time element and the particular situation. The categories of travel and visitors may or may not be included for particular purpose. The minimum and maximum period in terms of length of stay away from home or in terms of stay at particular situation, this may obtain for particular purpose and determine whether they are regarded under the purview of tourism. As tourists are temporary visitors staying at least twenty-four hours in the country visited and the purpose of whose journey can be classified within leisure and business. Excursionists are temporary visitors staying less than twenty-four hours in the country visited.

Mathiesen and Wall (1982) defined social perspective of tourism that "Tourism is the temporary movement of people to destination outside their normal places of works and residence, the activities undertaken during their stay in these destination, the facilities created to later to their needs. The study of tourism is the study of people away from their usual habitat, of the establishments which responds to the requirements of the travellers, and of the impacts on the economic, physical and social well-being of their hosts. It involves the motivations and experiences of the tourists, the expectation of and adjustments made by residents of reception areas, and roles played by the numerous agencies and institutions which intercede between them".

Jafari (1983) defines tourist as "the study of man away from his usual habit of the industry, which responds to his needs, and of the impacts that both he and the industry have on the host's social-cultural, economic and physical environment".

Satyal (1988) said that, in general, tourism denotes the journey of human beings from one place to another, whether it may be in own country or second countries for various purposes. The word 'Tourism' is derived from the French word 'tourisme' which was originated in the nineteenth century, later, this word was popularized in 1930s, but its significance was not fully realized until today when 'tourism' has a wider meaning and significance.

Negi (1990) mentioned that today marketing has become one of the major as well as challenging jobs of any business organization. For the success of any business activities, proper marketing system is essential. Marketing denotes the business activities that direct the flow of goods and services from producer to consumer or users. On other words, it is the process of exchange of goods and services between the seller and buyer. Tourism, being the fastest growing and most popular industry should be marketed properly. It needs to be marketed systematically and rapidly according to the place of time and situations. It is the industry in which customer still has an immense verity of choice. There are number of other destinations completing with each other to get bigger hold share in the market. Despite that, the tourism central point of marketing should enhance the whole tourism activity. Today, all the direct and indirect promotional activities are related to tourism.

Suresh Dhaka (1991) attempts to study overall activities, functions and performance of Rajasthan Tourism Development Corporation (RTDC). The main thrust of the research is given to personnel management in the Rajasthan Tourism Development Corporation (RTDC) and analyzing personnel policies and practices adopted by Rajasthan Tourism Development Corporation (RTDC) for direction and control of people in formal organization. The major problem found in this research is that Rajasthan Tourism Development Corporation (RTDC) face a problem of shortage of employees in all units, no timely recruitment and absence of proper selection method. Rajasthan Tourism Development Corporation (RTDC) also face a problem of lack of sound knowledge about tourism by top management officers and rate of transfer is more at highest post like chairman, managing director and executives. The major suggestions made by research is that Rajasthan Tourism Development Corporation (RTDC) should adopt effective policy and programme for personnel department, arrange training and refresher courses for their employees, formulate and implement effective wage and salary administration and deveiop incentive scheme and performance appraisal system. The researcher also suggests that proper working condition, labour welfare and benefits should be offered to all employees.

Ajay Tiwari (1992) conducted a study that cover all the activities of RTDC like accommodation, transportation, trains, tours and packages, hotels and bars and boating facilities. This study analyses financial data from the year 1979-80 to 1989-90 of RTDC and reviewed that financial performance of the corporation has improved and concluded that corporation has successfully reduced expenses and increased revenues. The main problem identified by the researcher is that corporation does not make any serious effort to develop any programme on hotel management and tourist guidance and RTDC units are not competitive to attract tourists and there is a lack of information network by RTDC. The major suggestion made by the researcher is that there should be a better coordination among RTDC, State Tourism Department and other related agencies. The researcher also suggest that Tourist Information Centres (TICs) should be well equipped and adequately staffed and proper decision making and policy-making required by the tourist experts.

Butler (1992) conducted that the term sustainable tourism development entails as "tourism which is developed and maintained in an area (community, environment) in such a manner and at such a scale that it remains viable over an indefinite period and does not degrade or alter the environment (human and physical) in which it exists to such a degree that it prohibits the successful development and well-being of other activities and processes."

Ross Kingston Dowling (1993) examines the relationship between the environment and tourism and argues for a new environmentally based regional tourism planning approach. The main aim of environmental planning is to foster environmental protection and conservatism, whereas goal of tourism planning are to engender tourism promotion and area development. In this study researcher identified environment tourism relationship and described that environment and tourism have symbiotic and even synergetic possibilities in which the relationship is mutually beneficial and identify conflict which are destroying tourism foundations. The major conclusion made that both symbiosis and conflict are present in the environment tourism relationship. Therefore, it is suggested that ideal view be tempered by the realistic acceptance of tourism and the environment potential and actual conflicts. This leads to an integrative approach which minimizes adverse impacts and enhances positive outcomes through integrated planning and management.

A.G. Krishna Menon (1993) found that in India, the importance of tourism is seen primarily from the economic angle such as earning which is needed for foreign exchange and providing employment. In this study researcher observes that tourism brings more complex changes from other economic development projects, because it necessarily gives effects to culture and economic attributes. Here researcher analyses that a major reason for social and cultural problems following the wake of tourism is because the tourism industry in India is operated in a disjointed manner. The study has found that there was excessive concern with fiscal and administrative control at the policy-level, but *laissez faire* attitudes to its implementation at the field level. The major findings of the study are that tourism industry in India is still at emerging stage of development. Its effect on the culture and environment has so far been marginal in relation to other forces of changes such as urbanization, industrialization and modernization which are operating simultaneously in the society.

WTO (1993) defines sustainable tourism as that which improves the quality of life of host communities, provides a high quality and good experience for the visitor and maintains the quality of the environment on which both the host community and the visitor depends.

Bhatia (1994) mentioned in his book that the Swiss Professor Walter Hunziker defined the concept of tourism and Kurt Krapf, in 1942 is more technical which the International Association of Scientific Expert in Tourism (IASET) accepted. According to them "Tourism is the totality of the Relationship and phenomenon arising from the travel and stay of strangers, provided the stay does not employ the establishment of a permanent residence and is not consulted with a remunerated activity". Similarly, the Britain has also attempted to clarify the concept in the year 1976, defined as "Tourism is the temporary short-term movement of people to destinations outside the places where they normally live and work and their activities during the study at these destinations; it includes movement for all purposes, as well as day visits or excursions".

Tewari (1994) conducted a study and mentioned 18 motivations under 4 groups and they are considered to be most important in finding why people travel. They are: Educational and cultural motives, Relaxation and pleasure, Ethnic and Others such as Weather, Health, Economy, Sport, Adventure, Conformity, To participate in history, One-up man ship, and Sociological motives.

Ratan Deep Singh (1994) mentioned in his study that tourism has certain basic components through which it operates. In order to understand, systematically, it is necessary to know the various components, which together make tourism a holistic form. Tourism consists of various components, four of these may, however, be considered to be basic. They are transport, locale, accommodation, food and cuisine. In his view, a tourist is according to achieve his destination, has to travel through mode of transport which is the major component of tourism. The holiday tourist offer natural destination like sunshine, scenic beauty or sporting facilities etc. Accommodation is another important component which is essential for providing food and also rest. Varieties of cultural features—way of life, there folklore, music, arts and good hospitality also provide valuable attraction to many tourists.

Subhasish Saha (1994) finds that accommodation units do not have a separate promotion wing, limited extent of tourism promotion through arrangement of sightseeing facilities and mostly in collaboration with Pondicherry Tourism Development Corporation or one or two private guided tours. Other findings of the research are that less impact of Government policies on tourism, no many facilities exist other than good rooms and the essential services, the majority of tourists who visit Pondicherry are the business tourists or the vacation tourists, no formal orientation or training is arranged for employee in most of the units, no permanent jobs for employees and lack of performance appraisal of employees. The major recommendation made by the researcher is that Government policies that affect hotel industry need to be communicated timely so that proper benefit of accommodation sector may be utilized, reduce political interference and pressure on Hotel Industry, efforts taken to promote business centres in Pondicherry, proper marketing of tourism products requires, proper coordination and sharing of information between hotel industry and Department of Tourism including Pondicherry Tourism and Transport Development Corporation, the formal training at inception and further ongoing programmes need to be undertaken to bring the best of services.

Brent Ritchie and Goeldner McIntosh (1995) defined tourism as "the sum of the phenomenon and relationship arising from the interaction of tourists, business supplies host, government and host communities in the process of attracting these tourists and other visitors."

Shreshtha (1995) mentioned in his study that a mountain is difficult to define, but racy to perceive. One of the most pronounced features of a mountain is its vertical shape, which is expressed in an altitudinal gradient and stratification of climate, soil, vegetation, and life zone. The search for fresh air, natural water, scenic landscape, natural wilderness, indigenous culture tourist use to visit to mountainous areas. Mountains support a number of important economic activities such as hydropower, mining, forestry, agriculture and tourism. In addition, others come to the mountains "because they are not there before".

M.V. Kamalakhi (1996) conducted a study on hotel industry to recommend that travel and tourism industry is worldwide growing industry and accommodation industry is the most important segment of tourism industry. This research makes main focus on tourism in Kerala. The study reveals that trends in the hotel industry in Kerala shows that number of hotel are less in Kerala therefore, old units increase their capacity and build comparatively large hotels. In this study, researcher also finds major problems faced by the hotel industry in Kerala such as multiplicity of product, shortage of skilled personnel, short duration of the cycle of operation, inadequate marketing, non-popularization of package tours to Kerala and excessive tax burden. Researcher suggests various remedial measures for hotel industry in Kerala such as joint venture agreement are to be made with the world's well known international hotel chains, constructing new hotels close to the airports in Kerala, coordination and cooperation in the functioning of the various departments of the government will help in supporting the entrepreneur in the various steps taken in the promotion of hotels, to grant subsidy on the loan for construction of hotels and to promote off season tourism by offering attractive packages to domestic tourists.

World Tourism Organization (W.T.O.) (1996) has defined tourist as "Any person who travels to a country other than in which he/she has their residence, outside usual environment, for a period of at least one night, but not more than one year and whose main purpose of visit is other than the exercise of an activity remunerated from within the country visited. This term includes people travelling for leisure, recreation and holiday; visiting friends and relatives, business and professional, health treatment and other purposes".

Kunwar (1997) conducted a study on the concept of cultural tourism emerged in 1970s. This form of tourism was recognized by UNESCO in 1976. Smith defined cultural tourism as "the absorption by tourists of features resembling the vanishing lifestyles of past societies, observed through such phenomena as house styles crafts farming equipment and dress".

Simad Saeed (1997) is to assess the impact of tourism on the environment of Maldives and explores the environmental management practices in the tourism industry of Maldives. This chapter helps to understand present status of tourism development in the Maldives, environmental impacts of tourism and discussing various environmental management practices adopted by tourism industry of Maldives. This chapter concludes that Maldives has developed a very suitable form of tourism which is appropriate for small island environment and mentions that present development of tourism has not generated various environmental impacts on Maldives. This chapter also conceived that government has developed appropriate policies, legislations, plans and enforce it strictly for maintaining regulations.

Kalidas Sawkar *et al.* (1997) study suggest that tourism is concentrated along the Coastal Zone in Goa and it has a number of positive benefits in terms of increased incomes and employment, added avenues for upward mobility for locals, increased revenues and increased foreign exchange earnings. This study identifies some socio-economic and environmental impacts that affect tourism in Goa such as growth of no controlled coastal tourism, no clear tourism policy in the state, the principles of sustainability and the norms related to the conservation of the environment and ecology are ignored, traditional fishing activities are declining, shortage of resources such as land and water pose a major affect to the environment and many more. From this study many actions are suggested to reduce the adverse impact on tourism such as adopting and monitoring management system to ensure the effectiveness of coastal and environmental regulations to frame policies which recognize the type of interconnections among tourism, local communities and the environment to ensure that tourism contributes to a sustainable development agenda, to adopt a systematic study of the environmental impact of tourism through a life cycle analysis and the evaluation of the environment to enable its integration into decision-making.

Shreshtha (1999) observed that some tourist destinations have attracted more tourist destinations. The potentiality to attract tourists to a particular destination depend upon following factors: Attractions, Accessibility, Amenities, Tourist Organization, and Marketing. The attraction of destination may be natural or manmade. Natural attractions are: flora and fauna, national parks, lakes, waterfalls, rivers, mountain, valley, village etc. a manmade attraction are: historical sites, buildings, archaeological sites, cultural attraction, fairs and festivals, museums, trade fairs, religious places, etc.

Iyata Maharana (2000) study the role of tourism is important for earning income, generating employment and developing infrastructure in Sikkim state, the eastern Himalayan region. This work analyses the dynamics of tourism growth, economic and environmental benefits and participatory conservation and protection of natural resources by different stakeholders in the Sikkim state of India. The chapter concludes that annual tourist arrivals increased by ten times over last ten years in Sikkim state and report that more than 65 per cent of total households income of the people comes from tourism related activities, which increased the income and consumption pattern of the community. The article suggest that Sikkim state has greater economic potential than it realized in earnings and therefore, more effort is needed to increase the level of conservation contribution to fulfil the goal of eco-tourism.

Konstantinos Andriotis (2000) focus on Island Crete and recognizes that existence of the necessary infrastructure, natural beauty, climate, culture and history have contributed to tourism expansion in the Island. Researcher concludes that Island Crete now attracting approximately 25 per cent of foreign tourist arrivals and 55 per cent of the total foreign exchange earnings of Greece. The main aim of research was to examine their views on tourism development, in an attempt to establish overall desired directions for tourism development and to suggest effective tourism strategies and policies to reinforce positive outcomes and alleviate problems resulting from previous unplanned tourism development. The study concludes that the expansion of tourism has brought economic gains, employment creation, increased population, enhanced community infrastructure and cultural and environmental preservation. However, there is limited co-ordination of tourism activities and insufficient collaboration between the public and private sector.

Maeta Chumni (2001) conducted a research work to identify and examine some major determinants affecting th demand for Thailand's international tourist receipts and also exami ed the situation and statistics of Thailand tourism industry. For this study researcher selected five counties *viz*. Australia, Japan, UK, Malaysia and USA which generates demand for Thailand's tourist receipts. The major findings of the research are that world political situation gives a negative effect on tourism in Thailand. This study found that Malaysia is a competitor for Thailand in case of income receipts from tourism and cooperation between the two countries would be an advantage. While high current income elasticity of Japan suggest that Thailand should found timely generate the highest demand possible when Japanese income increase and also tries to reduce negative impacts when it declines, in the case of UK, the marketing expenditure effect is lowest which should be advantageous for Thailand policy-maker to generate higher demand. In the case of US shows highest elasticity to changes in marketing expenditures which should be taken seriously and proper measures should be adopted timely. For Australia policy-maker should try to find ways of maintaining price competitiveness and take advantages of past raise income, therefore serious attention and careful management are essential in order to attract positive effects and to reduce negative effects.

M.K. Maru (2001) conducted a study which covers problems, prospectus and progress of tourism in Saurashtra and Kuttchh region. This study learn role of tourism sector in earning foreign exchange, contribution in import and export and generating employment opportunities. This study reveals that tourism industry in Saurashtra and Kuttchh face the problem of lack of transportation, safety and healthcare facilities, education and accommodation facilities. This study is based on field-work where researcher collects answer of many questions relating to tourism in selected region.

Satish Chandra and Dennis Menezes (2001) observes that tourism is increased exponentially since 1950 and with this growth this industry has become significantly more competitive and the marketing role of National Tourism Organizations (NTOs) has taken an added significance. With this respect research related to the marketing aspects of international tourism has increased. In this chapter researcher concludes that with the large number of NTOs involved in international tourism and the significant differences in the size and operating budgets of these NTOs, the marketing roles and tasks performed by these organizations is likely to vary significantly. Thus, many NTOs perform many marketing tasks which play significant role in enhancing tourism. In this chapter researcher concludes that NTOs perform various marketing strategies and these marketing strategies are enhancing the role of tourism in many countries of world such as US, China and Europe where the various international tourism market segments such as eco-tourism, cultural tourism, theme based tourism, adventure tourism and the cruise market growing in importance.

Final Report November (2002) highlight on development after the historic Constitutional change of April 1975, through which the state joined the mainstream of national life, becoming the 22nd State of the Indian Union. Switchover from a monarchial system to democratic government has naturally generated great enthusiasm and rising expectations in the people of the State. The back-log of development that has to be made up in order to reach the level of other similarly placed States in the Union has rendered the task of planned development extremely difficult and challenging, but at the same time an exciting adventure... Nevertheless, the rural population of Sikkim, who have fought bravely for the changing of the old order and who have sacrificed in the past, have to be provided at least the minimum national needs.

Gupta (2002) conducted a study on the process of tourism development, which is related with human evolution. To search for basic needs of life like food, shelter, clothing and safety human used to move from one place to another. Travelling in those days was difficult because of severe constraints of antiquated transport facilities, besides lack of safety and comforts. When permanent settlement started, slowly religious and business emerged due to which people started to travel.

Adrin Franklin (2003) defined the word tour is derived from the Latin word 'Tornare' and Greek word 'tornos' meaning a Lathe or circle; "the movement around a central or axis". This meaning changed in modern English 'One's Trun'. The suffix—it denotes "one that performs a given action". According to Theobald (1991), when the word 'tour' and the suffixes—ism and its are combined, they suggest the action of movement around a circle. One can argue that a circle represents a starting point, which ultimately returns back to its beginning. Therefore, like a circle, a tour represents a journey that it is a roundup trip that is the act of leaving and then returning to the original points, and therefore, one who takes such a journey can be called a tourist.

Annual Report, Sikkim Tourism (2003-2004) mentioned that, Sikkim is among the most fascinating regions of the world for adventures. The towering Himalayas stand, awesome and majestic with their snow capped peaks pose an open challenge to adventures, mountaineers and explorers from all around the world. Adventurs tourism has a big potential for Sikkim due to remoteness and inaccessibility apart from the inhospitable and often forbidden nature. Despite that, it is known as paradise for trekkers and it is also popular for river rafting, jungle safari, mountain bicycling, hot air ballooning, gliding and skiing. Sikkim's Himalaya and various natural panoramas provide an opportunity to every part of people to live adventurous dreams.

Chamling (2003) published a book and focused that natural resources should be managed on the basic principle of sustainability. It is, therefore, necessary to plan development activities in such a manner that our precious environment is conserved not only for the present but also the future generations. Further, he assure that "we are looking at ways and means which will help us to keep over-development out of the areas of biodiversity as far as possible. We are, therefore, giving much more emphasis to ecotourism". This is a concept that will attract tourists who are both sensitive and responsible to the environment. Some of the future plans have been sited here as follows:

- ➢ Bringing out a comprehensive State Environment Policy.
- ➢ Strengthen the institutions that are working towards the end.
- ➢ Use NGO movement as a valuable resource in our quest for sustainability.
- ➢ At school-level we introduce curricula with "Himalayan Ecology" as a subject.
- ➢ At school level teach Eco-Tourism.

This educational initiative should help promote a sense of purpose in our young so that they will grow-up with a clear sense of vision about sustainability.

Nepal (2003) said that the report of the World Commission on Environment and Development (1987) the concept of sustainable development is based on equity, ethics and quality of life and is a process to meet the needs of the present without compromising the ability of future generations to meet their own needs. It is defined by the achievement of specific social, economic and environmental objectives and not just by some national measurements of the health of the environment.

Sarath Divisekera (2003) analyses the economic determinants of demand for international tourism for a range of destination countries representing three of the World's major regions—United Kingdom, United States and New Zealand. The result of this study enables to draw broad inferences to be drawn regarding the preferences of foreign tourists for the products offered by different destinations and demand parameters of individual ones included in each model. The major suggestions made that, to receive the benefit of tourism services and to capture income from the tourists it should be directed for tourism services and marketing. The main findings of the study has generated new information on the effects and sensitivity of economic parameters and their influence over demand for international tourism, they should also assist in formulating broad national policy measures directed towards maintaining and enhancing relative competitiveness enjoyed by individual destinations and developing strategic policies to receive maximum gains from tourism.

S.S. Bisht (2003) conducted a study to examine tourism marketing practices currently being followed in India, to examine the marketing mix to tourism to access the present state of tourism promotion in India and to evaluate tourism with regard to product/ package of marketing mix such as price, product, promotion mix and product/ package distribution of tourism. The main suggestions made by the researcher are that proper tourism marketing strategies adopted for marketing of tourism, effective and efficient system of communication adopted, stable price structure of various tourist product/package which is important for effective tourism marketing adopting various channel of marketing the tourism product to its potential buyers such as the travel agents, tour operators, institutions and sport organizations.

P.O. George (2003) study is to investigate problems of tourism industry in Kerala and formulating solutions of them, to suggest the ways and means of coordination by which the Department of Tourism, Government agencies and other public and private entrepreneurs can effectively employed for the promotion of tourism in Kerala. The major findings done by author in his research work is that tourism products of Kerala do not attract large number of tourist and there is a lack of professional management in the tourism industry in Kerala. The major suggestion made by the researcher is that proper formulation and application of tourism policy required in Kerala, providing effective training and adopting professional attitude towards tourism, encouraging role of private entrepreneurs for tourism development in Kerala and increasing accommodation, transportation and other tourism facilities in relation to tourism in Kerala.

Anita Kumari (2004) study on problems faced by domestic and foreign tourists and what remedial measures were taken to solve these problems. Researcher conclude that to speed up the process of evolution of tourism from an occupation to industry, the first requirement is that leaders, businessmen and all other people of society come forward and support in increasing role of tourism in the state. The major suggestions made are, increasing transportation facilities, quality of food stuff, accommodation facilities, training for tourist guides and operators and increase entertainment and communication facilities.

A.K. Raina and Neelu Jain (2004) include various aspects of tourism industry like role of tourism industry in the economic development of the regions, income creation, employment generation and revenue effect on the state economy. The study also aims at forecasting the trends of international tourist traffic which may help the policy-makers to prepare effective plans for the development of all regions of the state. They studied role of planning and management in tourism industry in Rajasthan, role of various tourism organizations and functions of RTDC. They also studied components of tourism industry in Rajasthan and analysed economic and social impact of international tourism in Rajasthan. They also suggested improvement in transportation, recreational and accommodation facilities which needs to be modernised and restructured.

Manisha D. Thaker (2004) conducted a study on identifying and highlighting the problem areas in the field of tourism development. The main aim of this research work is to find the answer of problems like shortcomings in the field of infrastructure development, accommodation, entertainment, publicity and marketing and recreation facility. This study was conceived and executed in the above mentioned context to prove that utility-oriented regional empirical study will not only help us to meet the challenges of tourism in Saurashtra, Gujarat, but also contribute its humble mite to the formation of a national policy of tourism.

A.R. Rhodes (2005), conducted a study to compare the institutional arrangement of both countries New Zealand and Mexico and suggested experience lessons from New Zealand which can be applied to Mexican context. This study suggests the management strategies and practices applied to management issues like administrative structures, policies, customs and management techniques. This research concludes that New Zealand provides valuable information with regard to tourism and recreation management to present institutional arrangement of Mexico. Thus, major findings of this study is that Mexico get international experiences and improve its capability for better handling the growing development of tourism and recreation in its protected natural area system.

In 2005, International Consultants and Technocrats Pvt. Ltd., New Delhi, India conducted a survey and this report is useful in formulation of tourism strategies to improve the tourism performance through increased competitiveness. The main area covered in this study are product development, new innovative products, sustainability of resources, wildlife and national parks, security of tourists, marketing and promotional aspects, training and HRD, community participation and inter-state coordination. The report finds that most of the city face problems of shortage of water, lack of basic facilities, pressure on infrastructure due to large population size and wastage. The report suggest various measures to overcome from above problem such as developing a conservation of water project, project to avoid wastage, energy saving practices, sewage and sanitation system, conservation and protection of environment, eco-tourism development project, developing new innovative tourism products, maintenance of heritage centres, developing inter-state coordination by forming regional tourism, setting organizations such as Direct Tourism Promotion Councils (DTPCs) partnership with service providers, private sector participation, tax concessions, organizing culture fairs and festivals and ensuring safety and security of tourists.

Li Fung Mei Sarah (2005) conducted a research and finds that China introduced tourism in the 1984 where policy introduced for international tourism and approved by the Chinese Government and Chinese Government has an appropriate form of economic development that could contribute to the modernization of the country. The Researcher studies that development of tourism in China take place due to development and presentation of natural sights and sites, culture of China and natural landscape of China. One outcome of this research is the identification of a Chinese tourist gaze that has many elements which distinguish it from the western tourist gaze. Researcher observes that a significant component of a Chinese tourist gaze is "the harmony gaze" which strongly contrasts with current western nations, but wilderness and unspoiled nature. This thesis defines that development of tourism in China is due to its natural landscapes such as mountains, caves, rivers which is contemporary tourism in China.

J.P. Singh *et al.* (2006) study the tourism industry in Jaipur, which is the vibrant capital of Rajasthan, popularly known as "Heritage Pink City", due to the colour of buildings in its wonderful old city. The "Pink City" label, applies specially to the old walled quarter of the Rajasthan capital, glorious palaces and temples, spanning centuries are scattered throughout the predominantly urban area. Team opinions that lodging facility in Jaipur is fast developing and it offer different lodging facility like five star hotels, three star hotels and circuit house/ tourist bungalows. Team also study the inflow of domestic and foreign tourists in Jaipur from 1992 to 2007 where only 20 per cent tourist traffic is foreign tourist and remaining 80 per cent is domestic tourists. They also study duration of stay in Jaipur where more than 42 per cent tourists spend two days of their trip in Jaipur and the main reason of travel to Jaipur is holiday and sightseeing, business study and others. They also study that various modes of transportation which are used by tourists like rail, bus, taxi and air.

Kishor Singh (2006) made a study that covers tradition, language, art and culture, literature and folk dance of Rajasthan. It also covers various tourist products like national parks, desert, pilgrims and religious places, jewellery and design which attract major domestic and foreign tourists in Rajasthan. The main suggestions made in the study are state should frame appropriate tourism policy, to appoint and train more people about various tourism services, to make emphasis on hotel and accommodation sector, to provide more services like foreign currency converter, travel, communication and healthcare in the state.

Lane (2006) wrote about the sustainable tourism in rural areas. The concept of sustainability in rural tourism must be a multipurpose one to get success. It should aim to sustain the culture and character of host communities, sustain landscape and habitats, sustain the rural economy, sustain a tourism industry, which will be viable in the long term and this in turn means the promotion of successful and satisfying holiday experiences and develop sufficient understanding, leadership and vision amongst the decision-makers in an area that they realize the dangers of too much reliance on tourism and continue to work towards a balanced and diversified rural economy.

Chamling (2007) speak Sikkim has varied vegetation with varied and rich fauna. There are number of varieties of species of wildlife in the forest of Sikkim. It includes the wild buffaloes, snow leopard, black bucks, bears, deers, red panda etc. He said Sikkim is also repository of many species of birds, fishes, amphibians and butterfly. Many migratory birds are seen in the slope and river bank of Teesta and Rangit.

Bahareh Pourafkari (2007) evaluates Iran's potential in the tourism industry and especially cultural tourism development and tries to compare it with Turkey because of their regional proximities and similarities in culture, attractions and religion. The problem identifies during this research is that there is a lack of promotion, training and funds for the development of cultural tourism. The suggestion made for these problems are that the government allocate more funds for safeguarding of cultural heritage as well as establishing the research centres for cultural and heritage studies. Researcher also suggests that proper training and recreation programme should be arranged for tourist guide and youth for increasing cultural and heritage tourism. The main conclusion made in this research is that both countries have the same resources with similar culture and tradition, however, Turkey gives more importance on highlighting some ancient tradition and arrange many fair and festivals and providing good hospitality and transportation which attract more tourists.

Roland Craigwell (2007) focus on primarily investigate both the nature and determinants of tourism competitiveness in Small Island Developing States (SIDSs) judging from the various calculated indices of tourism competitiveness as the competitive position of tourism in SIDS is a major issue. Writer suggests that there is a need to improve level of investment for the development of the technological infrastructure and more importantly to ensure that the economic gains from tourism are spread to the lower-income households. This study highlights major findings as some difficulties from a macro-economic perspective of designing appropriate policies and strategies to enhance tourism competitiveness in SIDS. Here researcher suggests a proper explicit policy framing which aimed at improving tourism competitiveness. In this study researcher observes that overall competitive position of SIDS is below that of developed countries, but slightly higher than the global level. In this chapter researcher suggests that for development of tourism in SIDS government must seek out every possible avenue to control. The price of key tourism inputs, most critically energy, as well as improve existing infrastructure and focus on human resource development.

Piali Haldar (2007) study measures the potential of rural tourism in India, to find out impact of rural tourism to our society, to identify the challenges and opportunities in rural tourism and to identify the essential elements for development of rural tourism. This chapter attempts to prove the impact of marketing of rural tourism in India, rural tourism can help in shaping our society. It can have both positive and negative impacts on rural as well as urban communities. Researcher suggests many measures for enhancing rural tourism such as the government should encourage private enterprises to promote tourism in rural areas. Here researcher suggests various remedial measures to overcome the problems such as investment in new technology, build confidence in safety and security, develop plan for sustainable growth of rural tourism, promote traditional tourism products, effective communication, improve quality, value of rural tourism, set environmental policy goals and give quality of services at all levels.

Tarannum Husain (2007) conducts a study to study tourism in India and its problem in general and Uttarakhand in particular, to focus on the scope of tourism sector in Uttarakhand and explore the new avenues of the tourism industry, to study tourist motivators, tourist profile and problem and opportunities with respect to accommodation, accessibility, attractions and amenities and to study the infrastructural facilities and tourism avenues in Uttarakhand. This study also aims to suggest measures to make tourism economically viable, ecologically sustainable and suggest appropriate and effective promotional strategy for promoting tourism in Uttarakhand. The main suggestions of the study are that to make tourism as a purpose activity in the state of Uttarakhand, it is necessary to develop and promote adventure tourism, sport tourism, wildlife tourism in addition to pilgrimage tourism.

A.P. Muhammed and V.P. Jagathyraj (2008) analyze the major challenges faced by Kerala tourism industry, to investigate the problems connected with the tourism industry and formulation of solution of problems to them, to suggest new and innovative strategies for tourism industry in Kerala, to ascertain the possibilities of implicating modern management techniques and methods in the formulation of plans, policies and programmes for the development of tourism in Kerala and to suggest means of integrating the function of the Department of Tourism with other local government agencies and private entrepreneurs for the promotion of tourism in Kerala. The major recommendation made in the study are to provide special attention and care to tourists, get feedback from tourists, start more tourist information centres, distribute tourism publicity material at airports, railway stations, conduct international fairs in Kerala, promote health tourism. In Ayurveda, give incentives to private entrepreneurs for arranging new tourism ventures and frame new laws and regulation to protect tourism industry and tourists.

Nafees A. Khan (2008) analyzes the HRD initiatives of tourism industry with special reference to Air India Ltd., to enhance and sharpen the capabilities of its employees. The study also identifies the need of Air India to incorporate the spirit of HRD in day-to-day functioning by utilizing the all possible human resource systems and mechanism to the organizations. The significance of the study is that India having a lot of tourism potentials, but share of India in global international tourism in relatively small in volume about 0.40 per cent of world tourism. The main finding of the study is that tourism industry faces various challenges in the field of human resources and one of them is quality of manpower, lack of trained human resources in tourism sector, lack of rewards in both monetary compensation and non-monetary recognition which feels individual inequality and inadequate infrastructure for Indian tourism. The major suggestions recommended by the researcher are: organize proper training, career planning, career development and career counselling to make employees aware for their growth and development. The researcher also suggests that the Government of India should form HRD Board, which should encourage researches upon increasing potentiality of human resources, more fund allocation on infrastructure development by Department of Tourism and Finance and the Ministry should formulate suitable policies and strategies for human resources development.

Anjan Bhuyan (2008) study reveals that Assam is one of the prominent states of the North Eastern region of India and enjoys a scope of destination tourist place because of its diversity and uncharted mysteries. But reality is far different and present that the share of Assam tourism in national tourism is very less over the years due to limited development of tourism entrepreneurship in Assam and poor development of accommodation industry especially hotels, cottages and midways in Assam. The researcher concludes that the major reason behind these problems is lack of availability of funds and limited role of government in planning efforts. The researcher suggests that this study will be helpful to solve a problem of poor entrepreneurship for tourism in Assam and government will formulate proper policies and strategies to overcome from these problems.

Eke Eijgelaar *et al.* (2008) studies the role of domestic and international tourism on 30 countries of the world and analyzes the impact of this on their economy and environment. This chapter first focuses the development of domestic visitor numbers over time per country. This chapter also studies the environmental impacts with a specific focus on Greenhouse Gas (GHG) emissions of domestic tourism compared to international tourism. The main findings of this research are that the tourism sector and tourism research community focus mainly on international and outbound tourism volumes and expenditures. Finally, researcher conclude that distance is the most important factor for high emission figures; per km emissions for example are actually a little lower for inter-regional air travel than for domestic air travel. Therefore, one conclusion is to start using distance classes instead of national border crossings in tourism statistics. These would cover the environmental impacts of tourism (trip sustainability) far more accurately, as they ignore differences in country size and include large domestic tourism volume.

Rohan Gawande and Sudhir Dethe (2008) studied the tourism statistics for the year 2006. The main problem found in this chapter is that the Indian tourism sector hit itself on its back with facts and figures that seem to be growing each passing year, but the fact is that in the year 2006, India represented a paltry 0.52 per cent of the world tourism market share. So, India still lags behind in tourism scenario. The major finding of this chapter is that The Travel and Tourism Industry in India is expected to grow and generate US $ 128 billion by 2016. The Total Demand is expected to grow by 8 per cent per annum, in real terms, between 2007 and 2016. The major suggestions made in this research is that India should give a due priority to niche tourism such as adventure tourism, medical tourism, eco-tourism, rural tourism, cruise tourism and MICE tourism. They also suggest that India should give due emphasis on increasing role of private players in manpower development and infrastructure facilities. The major conclusion of the study is that India is venturing into the second phase of its tourism branding and it is important at this stage to properly chalk out the plan for tourism development. This is because the competition for attracting major chunk of tourism is gearing up. Researcher suggest that it is time now for a committed effort by the governmental authorities with a co-ordination among various entities related to tourism along with participation of private players is of prime importance if India has to become a top priority for tourists.

Deepika Gupta (2008) made a study consider status of Tourism in Rajasthan, role of RTDC and various TRC (Tourist Reception Centres & Bureau), role of human resources, amusement parks, entertainment and leisure activities and national park and wildlife sanctuaries. The major suggestions made in this research are that to increase tourism facilities at railway stations, bus stand and airports, to encourage role of private sector in tourism, make a development of historical monuments, wildlife parks, pilgrim centres and historical sites. An attempt was made to find the solution of problems like dirtiness at restaurants, hotels and various pilgrim places like Pushkar. The researcher also recommends that State Government should enact legislation to curb the threat of touting, cheating, beggars and misguiding tourists and professional training should be provided to youth so that tourism services may be provided properly in the State.

Pradeep Trikha (2008) analyses cultural heritage of tourist interest, as suggested or claimed in tourist brochures, websites, travel guides, newsletters, advertisement and score of the sources. An attempt behind this study is to interpret the constituents of these products which enable a tourist to make-up their mind and in a way visit a place before the actual visit happens. In this chapter writer refer two main product manuals under consideration are—Rajasthan—A La Carte and Fodor's India. These both manuals provide valuable information regarding heritage places, desert, celebration of fairs and festivals, paintings and sculpture, shopper paradise, Rajasthani cuisine, village tourism and adventure sports. But the myth narrated gives rise to several queries and interpretation regarding information contained in these two brochures. This chapter defines that current scenario of Rajasthan Tourism is changed and many new organizations like Indian National Trust for Art & Cultural Heritage and State Level Commission for the conservation of Art and Cultural Heritage has been constituted, who are doing a commendable work to upgrade the neglected heritage sites of Rajasthan and develop them into new tourist destinations.

Neha Kala (2008) focuses on the community perceptions of the economic and socio-cultural impact of heritage tourism and examines the extent to which they coincide with the tourism impact literature. The chapter use city Jaipur as an example to illustrate the multifarious impact of tourism. The major finding of this chapter reveals that impact assessment of tourism is a complex matter and contains both positive and negative elements. The findings reinforce that the residents of Jaipur have a more optimistic perspective regarding the economic impact of tourism. It was found that not only the community benefits economically from as active tourism industry, but community pride is also enhanced. Writer points positive and negative impacts of tourism and viewed that positive impact of heritage tourism is that revitalization of traditional art, handicrafts, dance, music, fairs and festivals and various aspects of traditional life style were identified by respondents and points of negative impact such as adverse socio-cultural and environmental impacts of uncontrolled mass tourism. The writer's view is that careful management plans involving the calculation of environment and carrying capacities should be used without creating damage to the resource base, so that sustainable development of economic and environmental perspective is ensured.

V. Basil Hans (2008) traces the progress made by India's tourism industry in the planning era and the emerging issues (like alternative tourism) under globalization. This chapter examines the impact and challenges posed by GATS and the burgeoning service sector of the country as well as the pitfalls in tourism planning in India. This chapter also suggests some policy suggestions to address the constraints in promoting sustainable tourism in India. The writer identifies various problems which affect Indian tourism industry such as inadequate capacity of hotels, costly travel, lack of supportive infrastructure like roads, communication gaps, lack of information about tourist profile and lack of safety and security. The writer suggests that for sustainable tourism in India proper long-term plan requires for this industry with periodic evaluation and revision and suggest that tourism uniqueness should be clearly understood by India tourism.

Ester Kruk (2009) study the tourism in Himalaya region and argue that tourism is one of the most promising strategies to address these serious poverty concerns, creating innovative livelihood options in the rapidly changing social and economical context of the mountain area. The researcher conclude that tourism sector proved one of the promising strategy to remove poverty situation in the Himalaya-based regions comparative strength and advantages and by increasing links between tourism and local product system result in income retention from tourism for the poor regions of Himalaya. This chapter view that after coastal region tourism, mountain areas are second in global popularity as tourist destination and Himalaya region offers many adventure activities for mountain tourism such as hiking, camping, rock-climbing, mountain biking, wildlife viewing and other forms of recreation.

Anjan Chakrabarti (2009) contributed on primary sector towards Gross State Domestic Product (GSDP) is continuously falling while that of services is increasing. This trend resembles development pattern experienced by the so-called developed countries. However, a close look at real growth figures reveals that growth is more pronounced in the sectors where government is playing a direct role. The phenomenal growth of public administration and other services do suggest that government remains the sole provider of jobs in the State. However, a reversal of the trend is becoming prominent. Since 1996-97, the growth rate of trade, hotels and restaurants has started picking-up and is growing consistently. In addition to this, trade and commerce, banking and insurance are also growing very satisfactorily.

From 2000-01, transport and communication have also been consistently growing. This may be portrayed as the beginning of the end of government sponsored growth story and rapid expansion of tourism activities may be viewed as one of the prime contributors towards this positive turn around in sustaining overall growth of the State's economy.

Japan International Cooperation Agency (JICA), IC Net Limited (GOJ) (2009) conducted a supplemental study to verify the relevance of the Project and to recommend a detailed project design. In February 2009, the Department of Forest, Environment, and Wildlife Management, Government of Sikkim (Forest Department) agreed on the scope of work of the Preparatory Study for the Project (Study), which was launched in May 2009. The GOJ received an official request for an ODA loan to support the Project in June 2009. Sze Ming (2009) concerns how outbound tourists flow from China. This study used to identify the similarities and differences in policy and international tourist flow patterns in Japan, Taiwan and Korea and provide a benchmark for studying China's outbound tourism. This study identifies different forces in, macro-environment which affect China's outbound tourism namely demographic, economic, natural, political and competitive. This study identifies major challenges such as lack of consumer protection, widening income gap and wealth disparity among social groups are major considerations for the government, imposition of new regulation and control measures by government. Researcher suggested many areas for outbound tourist flow in China such as market driven economy and state control are the two main forces promoting and checking the outbound international tourist flow from China, therefore, more emphasis given to these two variables.

Forest Department, Government of Sikkim (2009) Archaeological and historical places, distinctive architectural style, local dance, music, drama, ceremonies, art and crafts, dress, customs and value system all comprise the culture of an area. This cultural heritage offer attractions for tourists and can either by selectively conserved and enhanced by tourism or degraded by it, depending on how tourism is developed and managed in a particular area. The cultural events, museums, monuments, historic places, shopping, entertainment, conference and conventions facilities attract many tourists. There are different cultures and many more attractive pilgrimage places. Among them most prominent places are Gangtok, Namchi, Rumtek, and

Aritar. That places are very rich in religious shrines, art and architecture which are described as the open air museums.

Ashok T. Patil and Kailash Choubey (2010) study the role of Goa tourism and identify problems faced by tourists while travelling in Goa. They conclude that now-a-days Goa has a positive tourism profile and silvery beaches, waterfalls, ancient temples and churches, greenery of cashew and coconut palm, friendly and hospitable people, all these geographical factors make a variable tourist paradise. The main objective of this chapter is to examine the location of tourist area and concentration of population related the tourist industry, to know the geographical features of the Goa, to examine the geographical environment and seasonal variation of tourist arrival in the area and to recommend that tourism is mostly developed the social as well as medical problems. The main findings of this chapter are that Government of Goa released various grants for the development of tourism industry, also give emphasis on enhancing several facilities to their citizens to travel within and outside the country, increasing number of domestic and foreign tourists, increasing development of historical and pilgrimage places especially Goa's largest churches.

Ashok Singh Rathore *et al.* (2010) analysed financial performance of RTDC for the period of 2002-03 to 2006-07 for research studies. In this study researcher analyzed profitability, liquidity, financial efficiency and financial position of RTDC during the selected period and analyzed the financial data with statistical and financial tools. They concluded that various profitability and liquidity ratios of RTDC are differ in accordance with period to period. The main result of this study indicated a high rate of fluctuations in profitability and liquidity ratios and indicated that financial efficiency and financial position of RTDC is not quite similar in a selected period and the financial performance of RTDC is not satisfactory to survive for a long-term.

Bhatia (2010) conducted a study that, there are different types of tourism organizations in local, national and international level for the development of tourism. Every country has a government like Ministry of Tourism and Civil Aviation (MoTCA). At the regional level many organizations have been formed to assist the development of tourism in the different regions of the world. Among them, the notable organizations are The Pacific Area Travel Association (PATA) and The European Travel Commission, The Caribbean Tourism Organization, etc. we have also commitee to develop tourism in South

Asia, especially SAARC region. At the international-level, The World Tourism Organization (WTO) based in Madrid, Spain, is the official tourism voice of United Nations. It was established in 1975 with the objective of promoting and developing tourism globally. Along with it, International Civil Aviation Organization (ICAO) was also established in 1994 to assist and promote travel and tourism. Marketing in tourism means the systematic and co-ordinate efforts exerted by the national tourist organization or the tourist enterprises at international, national and local levels to optimize the satisfaction of tourists, groups and individuals, in view of the sustainable tourism Growth.

Ghimire (2010) further characterized tourism as; individual has his own motive to travel. There are different factors that create the desire to travel and make them tourists. Different factors motive them to travel from one place to another. He has elaborated in following motivational factors, such as Physical motives, Pleasure, Relaxation, rest and recreations, Health, Participation is Sports, Curiosity, Ethnicity, Spiritual, Status and prestige, Profession or business, Participation in events/festival, Meetings, conference.

H. Lalnunmawia (2010) puts his views that tourism industry in India is growing and it has vast potential for generating employment and earning large amount of foreign exchange besides giving a fillip to the country's overall economic and social development. But writer put his opinion that still much more remain to be done such as eco-tourism needs to be promoted in India, increasing facilities of accommodation and entertainment for visitors, reducing adverse effect of environment pollution and giving more safety and protection to visitor. Writer suggests that all wings of Central and State Governments, private sectors and voluntary organizations become active partner in the endeavour to attain sustainable growth in tourism of India, so that India become a world player in the tourism industry.

Sikkim Tourism Policy (2010) focus on tourism one of the fastest growing industries in the world. The dynamic growth of this industry is evident from the fact that globally tourism accounts for more than 11 per cent of the global GDP and 8 per cent of the world trade employment. Nature has bestowed Sikkim with unique beauty, splendour with its lush green and undisturbed valleys, five climatic zones, peaceful, total sanitation, environment friendly, hospitable and smiling people and a rich cultural heritage—which is unparallel and would be hard put to create and find anywhere else. The most peaceful and crime free in the lap of Himalayas, "The land of Peace and Tranquility" Sikkim itself become its natural and unique USP with global appeal.

International Labour Office (2010) as a basis for discussions at the Global Dialogue Forum on new developments and challenges in the hospitality and tourism sector and their impact on employment, human resources development and industrial relations. The main purpose of this chapter is to study the structures and characteristics of the hotels, catering and tourism (HCT) sector and its general trends specifically on the hotel and restaurant subsector. The major findings of the chapter is that workers tend to have limited professional qualifications and except among large operators, opportunities for on-the-job training could generally be enhanced, in particular for women employees who have long been in the lower echelons of the industry. This chapter also studies that the tourism industry and its internationally operating enterprises are considered as actors of social development and poverty reduction in the destinations. This chapter suggests various measures taken to enhance the role of hotel, catering and tourism sector such as increasing the role of government for tourism marketing, more training and education for individual development, increasing technology development, involvement of public and private sector and increasing investment in tourism sector especially in accommodation sector.

Envis (2010) mentioned Sikkim has been projected as a naturalists paradise. A tourist visiting Sikkim is all praises for the richness in nature which no doubt has been the basic ingredient of tourism in Sikkim. It is here that Khanchendzonga—the third highest mountain in the world stands tall. Blessed with snow capped mountains, lakes, rivers and varieties of flora and fauna Sikkim is in par with other ecological hotspots of the world. Eco-tourism is the buzzword and Government, NGOs and individuals have all geared up for contributing to it. Eco-destinations of India "Sikkim Chapter" is an entire gamut of information about Sikkim—a humble attempt to showcase its rich bio-diversity. Through surveys and information through internet and books we have tried our best to bring-forth the rich natural wealth of Sikkim. We hope that this book will be found useful not only by those for whom it has been written—researchers and students, but also proves to be highly beneficial for the tourists visiting Sikkim.

In February 2010, the team of RTDC recommends that Indian tourism industry is highly competitive and it face many bottlenecks like inadequate facility and poor infrastructure. The team suggests that RTDC is a model for solution of above problems. The chapter recommends that India with its rich cultural heritage and numerous archeological monuments across its length and breadth can emerge as one of the most preferred tourist destinations in the world. However, problem of poor infrastructure and lack of promotion affect growth of tourism sector. Therefore, the team suggests that RTDC has shown the kind of growth and prosperity in tourism sector due to dedication and professionalism of the staff. The team of RTDC opinion that RTDC is an ideal body to get tourism in Rajasthan, which provides valuable services like arranging tours, fairs and festivals, providing comfortable and luxurious accommodation, operating trains such as Palace on Wheels and Rajasthan Royal on Wheels which give all the feeling of Rajasthan culture and tradition. Thus, the team of RTDC gives importance to all the activities of RTDC and suggests that due to more network of RTDC, domestic and foreign tourists enjoy many services of RTDC at a reasonable cost and in a short time.

Prakash Chandra (2010) studied that Rajasthan is a popular tourist hangout spot in North India. It is frequently visited by global tourists. The prosperous tourist attractions of Rajasthan includes numerous forts and palaces, monuments and structures, lakes and mountains, sand dunes and desert beauty, national parks and wildlife destinations. Writer recommends that Udaipur and Jaipur are the two most visited cities of Rajasthan. Udaipur is famous for silvery lakes. There are many lakes in the city and therefore, it is nicknamed as 'City of Lakes'. The capital Jaipur is most charming city of Rajasthan. The moods of city always remain pink and welcoming. Jaipur is also called as 'Shopper's Paradise'. Tourists enjoy window shopping in the city. The markets of Jaipur are famous for handicraft items, gems and jewellery and marble. The researcher also points that safari tour is the greatest adventure, to enjoy during Rajasthan tours. Tourists can enjoy camel safari, elephant safari, tiger safari and horse safari during their tours.

Ashok Aima *et al.* (2011) studies the leadership styles followed by the royal families to manage these properties. The study focuses on the HRH Group of Hotels in Udaipur. The Chairman and Managing director of this property continues to transform the past into the future to this day. In addition to providing leadership for the management of hotels the Managing Director has been instrumental in creating a brand that represents heritage hotels. The writer points that the "Land of Kings" Rajasthan is renowned world over for its heritage hotels. The state houses maximum number of heritage properties in the country. Many of these buildings were converted into heritage hotels, as much to maintain them as also a new means of livelihood. Despite the conversion however, most of these places have been able to retain the original flavour of medieval homes intact. This could be possible only because of the leadership styles followed by the royal ancestors. Leadership as researched can be categorized into two aspects: 'translation' and 'transformation'. 'Translation' is a leader's ability to communicate or frame the sustainability message so others understand it from their mindsets or points of view while 'transformation' is a style of enhancing the leader's own capabilities to take effective action.

Anamika Poonia (2011) is to study the availability of tourism facilities in terms of tourist arrival in the area. The area of this study is historical state Rajasthan because desert ecosystem is very fragile; continuously increasing number of tourist arrivals in some areas have created some environmental problems. Here researcher analyses the demand and supply side of tourism chain and identify that Rajasthan is not well prepared for this increasing number of tourist arrival because increasing arrival of tourists not leading to the increase in tourism services. The researcher suggests that government should develop policies and programmes to increase the availability of basic tourism facilities such as accommodation, transportation, tourist reception centres and communication which needed to increase sustainable tourism. Researcher concludes that tourism industry has a noticeable place in India, but also especially in Rajasthan economy. But, it is also possible that tourism is not governed properly and affects adversely the sustainability of the environment. Researcher analyses that Rajasthan is not well prepared for increasing number of tourist arrival and suggest that to reduce adverse effect on social, natural and economic environment, an adequate policy and planning needs for tourism industry.

P.K. Yadav *et al.* (2011) focus for making South-Asian region an unequalled identity through tourism globally. This chapter conclude that by implementation of tourism projects, development of integrated tourism circuits, rural destinations, forming new strategies for promotions and meeting the global standards will facilitate this region to develop. In this chapter writer mainly focus on SAARC countries, one combined vision of eight different countries of South-Asia like

India, Pakistan, Afghanistan, Bhutan, Nepal, Bangladesh, Sri Lanka and Maldives. The major finding of this chapter is that in terms of product diversification of South Asia having a unique 2500 year old cultural heritage and multifaceted natural splendor, in spite of being such a draw in tourist spots and destinations South-Asia fails to receive tourists in comparison to other regions such as New Zealand, US, Switzerland and many more because of lack of awareness about the tourists spots and destinations of South Asian region.

Adele Fondeux *et al.* (2011) conducts a survey that report displays the results of the Jaipur International Tourist Survey, 2011. This report is intended to form a sound basis for all the stakeholders such as government, retailers, restaurant and bars, tour operators and travel agencies and hotels in Jaipur tourism industry to improve service delivery and increase revenues through a better understanding of the expectations of international tourists. This research reports finds that Rajasthan attracts approximately one quarter of all arrivals in India, but as international tourists become increasingly aware of other regions and it has faced tougher competition. The report also views that Jaipur remains one of the major tourist destinations in the region. The key findings of research are that almost 60 per cent of international tourists come from Europe, France and the United Kingdom. The major shopping draws for international tourists are textiles, handicraft and jewellery and the majority of international tourists stay in 3 stars and guest house accommodation and price is the most important criteria in choosing a hotel which is followed by location and cleanliness.

Varun, Abhishek, *et al.* (2011) forecasting model for recommended is the multiple linear regression model. We need to ensure that we have the latest data available while generating the forecast. This is based on the assumption that the government agencies and other stakeholders of Sikkim preparing this forecast will have access to latest data which may not be published on the website. In case the data is not available then appropriate amount of error buffer should be built in while planning.

Saurabh Dixit and C.S. Barua (2011) present a chapter on tourism linkages that chapter takes a case of tourism linkages between India and Sri Lanka. Here researcher noticed that tourism forms an important link between India and Sri Lanka and India is the largest source of market for Sri Lankan tourism. Researcher concludes that India and Sri Lanka have a number of similarities and could promote tourism jointly to harness potential tourist's traffic in this region, i.e.

South Asia. The main conclusion of the chapter is that diplomatic relations catalyzed by informal relationship could help to promote Indo-Lanka tourism in positive direction and show potential linkages into tangible products.

U.P. Sinha and S. Kumar (2011) have been attempting to highlight the tourism development and marketing of tourist services in Bihar. The researcher made to suggest feasible and practicable plan for tourism development in the country. Study examine tourism marketing practices currently being followed in India, to examine the marketing mix to tourism to access the present state of tourism promotion in India in general and Bihar in particular and to evaluate tourism. The main suggestion made by the researcher is that proper tourism marketing strategies should be adopted for marketing of tourism, effective and efficient system of communication adopted, stable price structure of various tourist product/package which is important for tourism promotion in Bihar.

A.S. Rathore and L.S. Jodhana (2012) are to identify the guest satisfaction level of the guests who are using the services provided by the RTDC hotels. This chapter attempts to evaluate the satisfaction level of the guests who were staying in RTDC hotels. The results of the study reveal that the services of the RTDC hotels are not satisfactory. Therefore, it is the main cause of guest dissatisfaction. The major finding of the study reveals that the service standard of RTDC hotels is below average. The researchers also have given some major suggestions regarding the service operations of RTDC hotels such as adequate training to RTDC staff members, to improve security, dormitory as well as assembly hall in its hotels, improvement in housekeeping services of RTDC hotels and to improve food and beverage services.

N.M. Khatri (2012) study is to analyze the profitability of RTDC, for the financial year 2003 to 2008. The researcher concludes that the profitability is not a condition that exists and can be measured for a limited time only; it is a variable thing like the temperature and humidity of a day. For this study researcher calculated profitability ratios to measure the operating efficiency of organization. In this study, the researcher uses two types of Profitability ratios such as: (i) Profitability in relation to sales; and (ii) Profitability in relation to investment. The researcher's main findings are that the overall profitability of RTDC (Rajasthan Tourism Development Corporation) can be said to be satisfactory, but it can be increased if efforts are made to curtail the unnecessary expenses because there is wide gap between gross profit and net profit ratio.

The Steering Committee on Tourism of Planning Commission, Government of India studied role of tourism during the Eleventh Five Year Plan (2007-12). This committee reports that tourism is an important instrument for economic development and employment generation, particularly in remote and backward areas and which has been well recognized in the worldover. It is the largest service industry globally in terms of gross revenue as well as foreign exchange earnings. This committee recommends that tourism has also become an instrument for sustainable human development including poverty elimination, environmental regeneration, job creation, advancement of women and other disadvantaged groups. The committee opinions that tourism is insignificantly an industry of private sector service providers, although the public sector has a significant role to play in infrastructure areas either directly or through Public Private Partnership (PPP) mode. The committee recommends many strategies for the development of tourism during Eleventh Five Year Plan such as development of Infrastructure and Destination Management, publicity and marketing, developing heritage and cultural tourism, eco-tourism and wildlife tourism and domestic tourism, access connectivity by rail, road, air and other means, human resource development and capacity building.

Praveen Rizal and R. Asokan (2013) examine the impact of tourism industry on regional economic and health status in Sikkim state. Tourism industry is a largest contributor on the state economy and an important industry in Sikkim state. The growth and development in tourism has contributed in the socio-economic development in the state. Tourism is also resulting in the improvement in the health status of people in the region. The increase of inflow of tourists in Sikkim state resulted in the economic benefit in the region. The per capita Gross State Domestic Product (GSDP) is increasing along with the growth of the tourism sector. The average annual growth rate of Gross State Domestic Product was 10.7 per cent from 2004 to 2009 and the average annual growth rate of inflows of tourists was 18.4 per cent. In the year 2004-05, the population below poverty line was 30.9 per cent which decreased to 13.1 per cent in the year 2009-10. Tourism has its indirect impact on the health status. Tourism is providing the income and employment to the people and thereby making economically sound, which results in improving the health status. Tourism is helping in reducing poverty and boasts the regional economy, which indirectly leads to the better standard of living and improved health status of the people of Sikkim.

References

Abhishek, Varun, Prakash, Saurabh and Dipayan (2011): *Tourism Demand Forecasting—Sikkim*.

Aima, Ashok; Bhasin, Jaya and Gupta, Rachna (2011): "Heritage Tourism in Rajasthan: Study of Leadership Styles", Presented paper in Colombo Conference of India Tourism Congress, June 2011.

Andriotis Konstantinos (2000): "Local Community Perceptions of Tourism as a Development Tool: the Island of Crete", Ph.D. Thesis, Bournemouth University, Greece.

Annual Report, 2003-04. Department of Tourism, Government of Sikkim.

Bhatia, A.K. (1994): *International Tourism*, New Delhi: Sterling Publishers Private Limited.

Bhatia, A.K. (2010): *Tourism Development: Principles and Practice*, New Delhi: Sterling Publishers Private Limited.

Bhuyan, Anjan (2008): "A Study on the Development of Tourism Entrepreneurship in Assam, with Special Reference to Accommodation Industry", Ph.D. Thesis, Tezpur University, Assam: India.

Bisht, S.S. (2003): "Marketing Practices of Tourism Industry: A Case Study of Selected Organizations", Ph.D. Thesis, Jamia Millia Islamia University, New Delhi.

Butler, R. (1992): Alternative Tourism: The Thin Edge of the Wedge. In: V.L. Smith and W.R. Eadington (Eds.), *Tourism Alternative* (Vol. VI), New York: John Wiley & Sons Inc.

Chakrabarti, Anjan (2009): "Tourism in Sikkim: Quest for A Self-Reliant Economy," *The NEHU Journal*, Vol. VII, No. 1, pp. 89-104.

Chandra, Prakash (2010): *Rajasthan Tourism in India—Explore Its Attractions*, July, 2010.

Chandra, Satish and Menezes, Dennis (2001): "Applications of Multivariate Analysis in International Tourism Research: The Marketing Strategy Perspective of NTOs", *Journal of Economic and Social Research*, 3(1), pp. 77-98.

Chumni, Maeta (2001): "Tourism Demand Model: Determinants of Thailand's International Tourist Receipts", Ph.D. Thesis, Chulalongkom University, Thailand.

Cohen, E. (1979): "Rethinking the Sociology of Tourism," *Annals of Tourism Research*, January/March 18-35.

Craigwell, Roland (2007): "Tourism Competitiveness in Small Island Developing States", World Institute for Development Economics Research (WIDER), United Nations University, Finland: April, 2007.

Dhaka, Suresh (1991): "Personnel Policies and Practices in RTDC", Ph.D. Thesis, Jaipur: University of Rajasthan.

Divisekera, Sarath (2003): "A Model of Demand for International Tourism", *Annals of Tourism Research Journal*, Vol. 30, No. 1, Great Britain.

Dixit, Saurabh and Barua, C.S. (2011): "Tourism Linkages between India and Sri Lanka", Presented paper at India Tourism Congress—Colombo Conference, 14th June, 2011.

Dowling, Ross Kingston (1993): "An Environmentally Based Approach to Tourism Planning", Ph.D. Thesis, Murdoch University, Western Australia.

ENVIS Team : Ecodestinations of India "Sikkim Chapter", *Envis Centre Sikkim on Ecotourism* (online).

Eijgelaar, Eke; Peeters Paul and Pieter Piket (2008): "Domestic and International Tourism in a Globalized World", Presented Paper in International Conference "Ever the Twain shall meet—relating International and Domestic Tourism" of Research Committee RC50 International Tourism, International Sociological Association, Jaipur, Rajasthan, India.

Fondeux, Adele; Benisti, Antonin; Wanduragala, Gehan; Assedo, Maxime and Sharma, Shiv Kumar (2011): "Jaipur International Tourist Survey", *Survey Report*, Kanvic Management Consulting Firm, April, 2011.

Forest, Environment, and Wildlife Management Department (FEWMD), Government of Sikkim (2009): *Wild life Management Plan for the Maenam Wildlife Sanctuary South Sikkim 2008-2018*. Gangtok: Author.

Franklin, Adrian (2003): *Tourism: An Introduction*, London: Sage Publications.

Gawande, Rohan and Dethe, Sudhir (2008): "Branding Indian Tourism: Entering Second Phase" in *Conference on Tourism in India—Challenges Ahead*, Indian Institute of Management Kanpur.

George, P.O. (2003): "Management of Tourism Industry in Kerala", Ph.D. Thesis, Post-Graduate Department of Commerce, Kottayam, Kerala.

Ghimire, A. (2010): *Travel and Tourism*, Kathmandu: Ekta Books Distributers Pvt. Ltd.

Government of Sikkim (1991): *Master Plan for Gangtok*, 2020, Urban Development and Housing Department, Government of Sikkim.

Gupta, A. (2002): "Status of Primates in Tripura," *ENVIS Bulletin* 1(1), pp. 127-135.

Gupta, Deepika (2008): "A Study of Evaluating Economic Impact Assessment and Physical Carrying Capacity at Tourist Destination Areas of Rajasthan", Ph.D. Thesis, MDS University, Ajmer.

Haldar, Piali (2007): "Rural Tourism—Challenges and Opportunities", Presented Paper in *International Marketing Conference on Marketing and Society at Indian Institute of Management*, Kanpur: April.

Hans, V. Basil (2008): "India's Tourism Industry—Progress and Emerging Issues", Presented Paper in *State Level Seminar on World Tourism Day*, Srinivas College of Hotel Management, Pandeshwar: Mangalore and Karnataka, 27th September.

Husain, Tarannum (2007): "Promotional Strategies of Tourism Industry in Uttarakhand State of India", Ph.D. Thesis, New Delhi: Jamia Millia Islamia University.

Information and Public Relations Department, Government of Sikkim (2003): Sikkim Perspectives and Vision, Speeches of Chief Minister Pawan Chamling. Gangtok: Information and Public Relations Department, Government of Sikkim and New Delhi: Indus Publishing Company.

Information and Public Relations Department, Government of Sikkim (2007): Sikkim Perspectives and Vision, Speeches of Chief Minister Pawan Chamling. Gangtok: Information and Public Relations Department, Government of Sikkim and New Delhi: Indus Publishing Company.

International Consultants and Technocrats Pvt. Ltd. (2005): "Documentation of The Best Practices Adopted by the State Governments for the Development of Tourism", Survey Report, New Delhi, India.

International Labour Organization (2010): "Development and Challenges in the Hospitality and Tourism Sector", International Labour Office, Geneva, Switzerland.

JICA (2009): Study Team for Japan International Cooperation Agency (JICA) IC Net Limited (GOJ) Report, November 2009.

Jafari, Jafar (1983): "Anatomy of the Travel Industry." *Dirndl Hotel and Restaurant Administration, Quarterly*, Vol. 24, No. I, pp. 71-77, May.

Kala, Neha (2008): "Host Perception of Heritage Tourism Impact with Special Reference to the City of Jaipur", *South Asian Journal of Tourism and Heritage*, Vol. 1, No. 1.

Kamalakhi, M.V. (1996): "Hotel Industry in Kerala with Special Reference to Tourism", Ph.D. Thesis, Cochin University of Science and Technology, Cochin, Kerala.

Khan, Nafees A. (2008): "Human Resource Development in Tourism Industry in India: A Case Study of Air India Ltd.," New Delhi, in Elperiplo Sustentable No. 14, Faculty of Tourism and Gastronomy, Mexico State.

Khatri, Nitasha M. (2012): "Profitability Analysis of Rajasthan Tourism Development Corporation" in *Journal of Commerce and Management Thought*, Volume 3, Issue 2.

Kruk, Ester (2009): "Tourism in the Himalaya—Mountain of Opportunities in a Changing Climate", Nepal: International Centre for Integrated Mountain Development.

Kumari, Anita (2004): "Problems and Prospectus of Tourism Administration in Rajasthan", Ph.D. Thesis, Jaipur: University of Rajasthan.

Kunwar, R.R. (1997): *Tourism and Development, Science and Industry Interface*, Kathmandu: Laxhmi Kunwar.

Lalnunmawia, H. (2010): *Development and Impact of Tourism Industry in India.*

Lane, M. (2006): "Critical Issues in Regional Natural Resource Management." Paper Prepared for the 2006 Australian State of the Environment Committee, Department of the Environment and Heritage, Canberra: Australian State of the Environment Committee.

Leiper, Neil (1979): "The Framework of Tourism: Towards a Definition of Tourism, Tourist, and the Tourism Industry," *Annals of Tourism Research*, Vol. 6, No. 4, pp. 390-407, October-December.

Maharana, Iyata (2000): "Economic Benefits and Conservation Linkages from Tourism Development in the Sikkim-Himalaya".

Maru, M.K. (2001): "Progress, Problems and Prospects of Tourism Industry in Saurashtra and Kuttchh", Ph.D. Thesis, Rajkot: Saurashtra University.

Mathieson, A. and Wall, G. (1982): *Tourism: Economic, Physical, and Social Impacts*, New York: Longman, p. 208.

McIntosh, R.W. and Goeldner, R. (1990): *Tourism: Principles, Practices and Philosphies*, USA: John Wiley & Sons Inc.

Menon, A.G. Krishna (1993): "Case Study on the Effects of Tourism on Culture and the Environment: INDIA—Jaisalmer, Khajuraho and Goa," published in UNESCO Principal Regional Office for Asia and the Pacific, Bangkok.

Ming, Sze (2009): "Forces Shaping the Trends and Patterns of China's Outbound International Tourist Flows", Ph.D. thesis, Southern Cross University, Lismore, NSW.

Muhammed, Ajims P. and Jagathyraj, V.P. (2008): "Challenges Faced by Kerala Tourism Industry" in conference on *Tourism in India—Challenges Ahead* at Indian Institute of Management, Kanpur.

Negi, J. (1990): *Tourism and Travel Concepts and Principle*, New Delhi: Gitanjali Publishing House.

Nepal, S.K. (2003): *Tourism and the Environment: Perspectives from the Nepal Himalaya*. Lalitpur and Innsbruck: Himal Books and STUDIEN Verlag.

Ogilvie, F.W. (1933): *The Tourist Movement: An Economic Study,* London: Staples Press.

Patil, Ashok T. and Choubey, Kailash (2010): "Geographical Analysis of Tourism and Concerning Problems in Goa (India)", SSMRAE, *International Referred Research Journal*, Jaipur, Rajasthan, Issue-19, August, 2010.

Poonia, Anamika (2011): "Spatial Availability of Tourism Services in Rajasthan with its Sustainability Concept", *South Asian Journal of Tourism and Heritage*, *An International Referred Research Journal*, Vol. 4, No. 1.

Pourafkari, Bahareh (2007): "A Comparative Study on Cultural Tourism Development in Iran and Turkey", Ph.D. thesis, Iran: Lulea University of Technology.

RTDC (2010): "RTDC—A Model for Tourism Sector in India", The Team of RTDC, 20th February.

Raina, A.K. and Jain, Neelu (2004): *Dynamics of Tourism—Concept, Philosophy and Strategies*.

Rathore, Ashok Singh and Jodhana, Lokeshver Singh (2012): "An Empirical Analysis of the Service Operations of Rajasthan Tourism Development Corporation Hotels", *South Asian Journal of Tourism and Heritage, International Referred Research Journal*, January, Vol. 5, No. 1.

Rathore, Ashok Singh; Prasad, Hanuman and Jodhana, Lokeshver Singh (2010): "Financial Performance of Rajasthan Tourism Development Corporation (RTDC)—An Analysis", *South Asian Journal of Tourism and Heritage, International Referred Research Journal*, Vol. 3, No. 1, January 2010, pp. 129-135.

Rhodes, A. R. (2005): "Institutional Arrangements Study of the Recreation and Tourism Management on Protected Natural Areas of New Zealand and Mexico", Ph.D. thesis, New Zealand: Lincoln University.

Rizal, Praveen and Asokan, R. (2013): *An Overview of Tourism Industry and Its Impact on the Health Status in Sikkim State, Language in India*, ISSN: 1930-2940, Vol. 13:4, April, pp. 145-152, www.languageinindia.com

Ritchie, J.R. Brent and Goeldner, R. (1995): *Travel, Tourism and Hospitality Research*, second edition, New York: John Wiley & Sons Inc.

Saeed, Simad (1997): "Environment Impact Management in the Tourism Industry of Maldives", in EDI/SAARC Regional Seminar on "Economic Globalization and Environmental Sustainability" in Goa.

Saha, Subhasish (1994): "Tourism Development—Accommodation Sector: A Study of Pondicherry Accommodation Sector", Ph. D. thesis, Pondicherry: Pondicherry University.

Sarah, Li Fung Mei (2005): "Chinese Common Knowledge, Tourism and Natural Landscapes", Ph.D. thesis, Western Australia: Murdoch University.

Satyal, Y.R. (1988): *Tourism in Nepal—A Profile*, Varanasi: Nath Publishing House.

Sawkar, Kalidas; Noronha, Ligia; Mascarenhas, Antonio and Chauahan, O.S. (1997): "Tourism and the Environment Issues of Concern in the Coastal Zone of Goa", presented in EDI/SAARC Regional Seminar on "Economic Globalization and Environmental Sustainability", Goa.

Shreshtha, P. (1999): *Tourism in Nepal: Problems and Prospects*, Ph.D. Dissertation, Banaras Hindu University.

Shrestha, S.H. (1995): *Simple Geography of Nepal*, Kathmandu: Educational Enterprises.

Sikkim Tourism Policy (2010): Tourism Department, Gangtok, Government of Sikkim, Planting Seeds of Hope for a Greener Tomorrow.

Singh, J.P.; Mohanty, M.K.; Jena, S.N. and Mishra, Akhilesh (2006): "*Tourism Industry in Jaipur—Size and Status*", Vision R I, Connexion Services Private Ltd., New Delhi.

Singh, Kishor (2006): "A Study of Tourism Management and Organization in State of Rajasthan", Ph.D. thesis, MDS University, Ajmer.

Singh, Ratandeep (1994): *Tourism Today*, Volumes 1, 2, 3, New Delhi: Kanishka Publishers Distributers.

Sinha, U.P. and Kumar, Swargesh (2011): *Bihar Tourism : Retrospect and Prospect*, New Delhi: Concept Publishing Company (P) Ltd.

Tiwari, Ajay (1992): "Organization and Working of RTDC", for his Ph.D. Degree from University of Rajasthan, Jaipur.

Tewari, S.P. (1994): *Tourism Dimensions*, New Delhi: Atma Ram & Sons.

Thaker, Manisha D. (2004): "Problems and Prospects of Tourism Industry in Gujarat", Ph.D. thesis, Saurashtra University, Rajkot.

The Steering Committee on Tourism of Planning Commission, Government of India : Committee Reports, Role of Tourism during the Eleventh Five Year Plan (2007-12).

Trikha, Pradeep (2008): "Cultural Heritage of Rajasthan *vis-à-vis* Politics of Travel Information", *South Asian Journal of Tourism and Heritage*, Vol. 1, No. 1.

UNWTO (1998): *Guide for Local Authorities on Developing Sustainable Tourism*, Madrid: United Nations World Tourism Organization.

UNWTO (2003): *Sustainable Development of Ecotourism—A Compilation of Good Practices in SMEs*, Madrid: United Nations World Tourism Organization.

Yadav, P.K.; Singh P.B. and Saxena, R.K. (2011): "*Tourism Perspectives in South-Asian Region*", Presented paper in India Tourism Congress—Colombo Conference, 14th June, 2011.

4
Rural Tourism—Development Phenomenon

General Background of the Sikkim

The small but beautiful State of Sikkim is situated in the eastern Himalayas of India and geographically lies between 27°5' and 28°9' north latitudes and 87°57' and 88°56' east longitudes, and has an area of 7299 sq. km. It is bounded in the north by the vast stretches of the Tibetan Plateau and to its west lies the Kingdom of Nepal. In the east, it is bounded by Bhutan and the Chumbi valley of Tibet (China). The Darjeeling district of West Bengal stretches along its southern boundary. Its elevation ranges from 224 metres to over 8598 metres above the sea-level. Sikkim situated in the Eastern Himalayas spread below the world's third highest mountain Kanchenjunga (8585 m) revered by the Sikkimese as their protective deity.

Though measuring just 65 km by 115 km—the size of Switzerland, it ranges from sweltering deep valleys a mere three hundred metres above sea level to lofty snow peaks such as Kanchenjunga. On its west side is the massive 31 km long *Zemu* glacier. Various explorers and mountaineers have claimed to have seen *Yeti* or its footprints in the vicinity of the mountain and its glacier—"The abominable snowman" has its place in folklore.

Sikkim's botanical and zoological affluence is truly impressive. The varieties of birds and butterflies in Sikkim is matched only by incredible diversity in the animal and botanical world, nourished by unique and dramatic geographical features.

The lower altitudes are sub-tropical and abound in some of Sikkim's more than six hundred orchid varieties, sprays of cardamom fruit orchards and terraced rice paddies. To the Lepchas—this was "Nye-mae-el" (Paradise), to the Bhutias it is "Beymul Denzong"

(The hidden valley of Rice). Sikkim is commonly attributed to the Tsong's word "Sukhim" meaning (New or Happy Home).

The people of Sikkim are warm, simple and friendly with a natural gaiety. The custom and rituals of Sikkimese are as diverse as the ethnic groups that inhabit the land. They have an impressive repertoire of folk songs and dances. People of Sikkim love to celebrate with a gay abandon and their way of life is inextricably bound up with nature.

Just as Mt. Kanchenjunga is an indisputable part of the consciousness of the Sikkimese people, so too the rivers Tista and Rangitt with deep ravines and their valleys allowing monsoon to penetrate in the northernmost parts which nourishes this "Garden of the Himalayas".

At higher altitudes, monsoon mist cling to huge tracts of lichen covered forest, where every conceivable species of Rhododendron and giant magnolia trees, conifers and beautiful flowering plants as Primulas, Gentians, Blue poppies, Wild strawberry, Raspberry. All over Sikkim forest and wilderness areas are inhabited by the Snow-Leopard, Thar, Yaks, wild Ass in the Tibetan pleatue, Bharal or Blue Sheep, Shapi and the symbol of Sikkim—the endangered Red Panda.

The land of five Treasures—Mt. Kanchenjunga—the massive part of massive Himalayan range and other spectacular peaks of lives of Sikkimese people. The best known peaks are *Pauhunri* (7125 m), *Pandim* (6691 m), *Talung* (6147 m), *Tent Peak* (7365 m), *Jongsang* (7459 m), *Rathong* (6679 m), *Koktang* (6147 m) *and Sinioulchu* (6887 m) regarded by the mountaineers as the most beautiful peaks in the world.

Amidst the grandeur of the mountain peaks lush valleys, fast flowing rivers, Sikkim offers her visitors a rare and singular experience. Within a matter of hour one can move from its sub-tropical heat of the lower valleys to the cold of the rugged mountain slopes that reach up to the areas of perpetual snow.

The economy of Sikkim is mainly based on agriculture and animal husbandry. Approximate 11 per cent of the total geographical area is under agriculture. Agriculture is of the mixed type and still at the subsistence level rather than commercial level. The workforce participation rate as per 1991 census is 40.44 per cent. The female participation rate in Sikkim is also much higher than the national average. This is an important aspect of the hill economy, as productivity is low and hence, all the able-bodied people are employed in agriculture and other activities. Cultivators account for the greater majority of the people in the state. Their percentage is 57.84 per cent. Agricultural labourers as a whole constitute only 7.81 per cent of the workers in the state. Households and other industries are negligible, but other worker (Tertiary Sector) at the state-level represent a good percentage of population. The decreasing ratio of worker at the state-level indicates the low-level of economic diversification. The importance of agriculture can be judged by the high percentage of population approx. 65 per cent engaged in it. Animal husbandry is an integral part of the household economy of the region. There are certain household industries also which substantially adds to household incomes. The past one and half decade has witnessed a tremendous upward swing in various development programmes giving a new thrust to the Sikkim economy. This process has increased wage employment opportunities. Though most of the inhabitants are basically agriculturist, they have diversified into tertiary jobs such as Government services and recently they have shifting their jobs on Tourism Industry, keeping under consideration of higher earnings. All the persons from skilled to unskilled tourism starts creating employment opportunities.

Tourism in Sikkim

Sikkim, a former British Protectorate, became a part of India, as the 22nd State of the Indian Union on 16 May, 1975. It is located in the realms of the snow-clad peaks of the Himalayas, including the world's third highest peak, Mt. Kanchenjunga (altitude 8585 m). The state is a biodiversity hotspot and is inhabited by a mix of ethnic cultural groups with a great diversity of cultural traditions and practices. The congenial climatic conditions, rich biodiversity, panoramic view of mountains and valleys, villages in picturesque settings, pristine lakes and forests, cascading waterfalls, flower blooms and wilderness of trekking trails, Buddhist monasteries and religious artifacts, and cultural festivals of Bhutia and Lepcha tribes constitute the important elements of tourism in the state. Sikkim thus provides a varied experience ranging from urban mass tourism, to village tourism, nature tourism, religious and cultural tourism, and adventure tourism.

Tourism in Sikkim also developed spontaneously with the growth of infrastructure. However, the real efforts for development of tourism like consciousness building, awareness development and initiatives at the government and community-level started in the 1990s. The period also saw the development of tourism-related infrastructure and increasing emphasis on eco-tourism. A number of village tourism sites were developed and entrusted to community control. Sikkim, the ultimate eco-tourism destination, became the policy emphasis of the government and a tourism plan was developed. Development and marketing of at least one place in each of the 32 constituencies as an eco-tourism site/destination was envisaged.

Today, a number of tourist-related fairs and festivals are being organized in various tourist destinations to highlight the specific cultural characteristics and to popularize the important attractions of the concerned destination.

Some international events like the International Flower Show have also been initiated by the government to expose the visitors to the variety of floristic diversity of the state. Cultural festivals of the local ethnic groups and the various Buddhist monasteries also comprise tourist attractions.

Eco-tourism/nature tourism in the state is well supported by the institutional arrangements at village and community levels. Several capacity-building and awareness programmes are being continuously organized by NGOs and the State Tourism Department for the stakeholders to sensitize them on issues related to the environment and for better tourism culture and management in the state.

Entry Protocol

Travellers to Sikkim need to follow some rules and regulations as the state has few entry restrictions that falls under the restricted area regime due to proximity with neighbouring country China. So, in order to promote smooth tourism in the state, constraints on the entry protocols have been relaxed by the government for foreign nationals. They can visit the famous tourism spot like Gangtok, Rumtek, Pemayangste, Phodong, and the Yuksom only after obtaining the restricted area permit from any of the concerned departmental offices in India. Inner Line Permit is issued from Sikkim Tourism Offices at New Delhi and District Magistrate office of Darjeeling, Siliguri and Rangpo after you produce Indian Visa.

(i) Entry Protocol for Foreign Nationals

Foreign nationals intending to visit Sikkim for tourism can obtain a permit for an initial period of 15 days that is further extendable up to

30 days. Foreign tourist has to be in the group of two or more to visit restricted and protected areas of Sikkim like Yumthang Valley (for five days) as they are not allowed to club and go with Indian tourist.

A two days Inner Line Permit is also available at Rangpo. The same permit can be further extended from Home Ministry of Gangtok.

Foreigners can visit Rumtek, Gangtok, Phodong and Pemayangtse for a period of fifteen days after obtaining the restricted area permit. If they are intending to visit Yumthang Valley, Zongri, the rules are slightly tight.

Note: Re-entry into Sikkim is not allowed within 3 months after you leave the Sikkim. The gap of 90 days is necessary as per the instruction of Ministry of Home Affairs.

(ii) Entry Protocol for Indian Nationals

For Indian Nationals: Indian nationals willing to visit Sikkim do not require any special permit. They can visit some of the unrestricted areas of Sikkim like Gangtok, Yuksom, Rumtek, Pemayangtse, Phodong, etc. But for the following restricted areas in North Sikkim, Inner Line Permit is necessary to enter areas of north Sikkim like Yumthang Valley, Chungthang, Lachung, Yumesamdong, Lachen, Thangu, Chopta and Gurudongmar Lake. It is mandatory for Indian nationals also to obtain the permit.

Today, the number of tourists visiting Sikkim has reached 5 lakhs per annum. Tourist-related infrastructure is being expanded in the state, and many new areas are being developed for tourism purposes. An environmental fee is also being charged on visit to some environmentally sensitive zones.

Eco-tourism in Sikkim

Most of the tourism resources in the area could be utilized to develop Eco-tourism. There are numerous Eco-tourism products available in this region. "Wildlife in natural setting" is the most important product while the nature based recreational activities like camping, rafting, hiking and trekking are also found to contribute towards promotion of Eco-tourism.

Adventure Tourism/Adventure Sports

It goes without saying that Sikkim has an immense potential for adventure tourism related activities. Some of the important adventure activities being promoted in the State are: Trekking, Mountain climbing and Mountaineering, Rock climbing, River crossing, Paragliding, Bungee Jumping, White water rafting, Angling and many other types of traditional adventures. Trekking and Mountaineering are by far the most vibrant and visible adventure tourism activities in Sikkim and have much wider marketing prospects along with other adventure activities. In order to ensure the safety of participants in such activities, there is a need to lay down the minimum acceptable standards in terms of equipment and human resources. The State Government is looking into the matter and the Basic Minimum Standards of safety will be notified at the earliest in consonance with the guidelines issued by the Ministry of Tourism.

Trekking

Trekking in Sikkim can be a wonderful experience—an antidote to the stress of daily life and a memory to cherish rest of life. While trekking, we relish the pure air and the silence of wilderness and feel the awakening of senses dolled by urban living. Though each and every nook and corner of the state is worth trekking, following trek routes are worthy will to be discussed here:

- Gangtok—Penlong—Tinjure—Rumtek
- Lachung—Yumthang—Yumey Samdong
- Damthang—Tendong—Ravangla—Maenam—Sirwani
- Ravangla—Maenam—Borong—Tashiding
- Yuksom—Dzongri
- Hilley—*via* Sombarey—Varsey—Soreng
- Hilley—Varsey—Dentam—Singalila—Chiwabhangang.
- Mangan—Lingzin—Sakyong—Royot Patam—Dzongri—Yoksum.

Mountaineering

The first European to explore Kanchenjunga area was Douglas W. Freshfield in 1899. Famous Sikkimese Everester Sonam Gyatso climbed the summit of Siniolchu. Though mountaineering activities now a days is not frequent yet the activities are usually taken by Sonam Gyatso Mountaineering Institute.

Adventure Tourism/Adventure Sports and Trekking/Mountaineering.

Rafting in Sikkim

Under the category of water sports, White River rafting is the latest adventure sport in Sikkim. Rivers Teesta and Rangit are the ideal rivers for rafting. The following two routes are the most desired by the rafters:

(i) *On River Teesta* : Chungthang—Dikchu—Singtam—Melli.

Rafting in Sikkim.

(ii) *On River Rangit* : Legship—Jorethang—Melli.

Mountain Biking

This class of adventure tourism is recently introduced in this hilly State of Sikkim. Since most of the roads of Sikkim are accessible by motorbikes, this sport can gain momentum in the near future. Following routes are advisable:

- Gangtok—Rumtek—Sang—Sirwani—Temi.
- Damthang—Rabongla—Kewzing—Tashiding—Yuksam—Khecheopalri.
- Jorethang—Sikip—Reshi—Rinchenpong—Bermiok—Dentam.
- Jorethang—Melli—Rangpo—Singtam—Gangtok.

- Gangtok—Phodong—Rangrang—Dikchu—Makha—Sirwani—Temi—Singtam—Gangtok.

Wildlife Tourism

Due to the variation of altitude from sea-level to the mountain tops, Sikkim possess a wide and varied spectrum of flora and fauna. It has one of the richest assemblages of habitat in the world. The zoological and botanical richness and diversity is excellent, boasting of more than 4000 species of plants, 300 species of fern and its allies, 11 species of Oaks, 8 species of tree fern, 30-40 species of primula, 20 species of bamboos, 144 species of mammals, 500-600 species of birds (30% of all birds found in Indian sub-continent), over 400 species of butterflies and moths, together with many reptiles, medicinal herbs and shrubs. The state can be broadly classified into three zones:

(i) Tropical (Sea-Level –1500 m)
(ii) Temperate (from 1500 m to 3500 m)
(iii) Alpine (above 3500 m)

The jungle of lower altitude harbor Jungle cuts, Mongoose, sparrow and has abundance of bamboos, trees firm, walnut and oak. More than 600 species of orchids are found in Sikkim, which are indeed the jewels in the crown. The most important of them are—*Cymbidiums, Vanda Cuttaleya*, *Haberina*, and *Paphiopedilum*. Nobile orchid (*Dendrobium nobile*) is declared as the State flower. The fauna of Temperate Zone comprises of common Langur, Leopard cats, Red Panda, Musk deer, Himalayan black bear and the flying squirrel. The arid cold alpine region of Sikkim harbors snow leopard and wild ass roaming amongst rhododendron, the state hosts around 30 species of Rhododendron. The Rhododendron Nevium is delivered as the state tree of Sikkim. Parks and sanctuaries play an important role in promoting Sikkim tourism.

Cultural Tourism in Sikkim

Cultural tourism is "The practice of travelling to experience historic and cultural attraction to learn about a community's culture in an educational and enjoyable way". It is not a new concept as even in ancient times it has been a motivation for travel. Sikkim has immense potential to promote cultural tourism because of presence of wide variety of customs and traditions, indigenous knowledge, folklores. In Sikkim near about 200 monasteries which can be symbol of cultural heritage and lifestyle of the people, where they practice ancient ethnic rituals. Some of the unique monasteries in Sikkim are Pemayangtse Monastery, Rumtek Monastery, Tashiding Monastery, Khechopari Monastery, Do-drul Chorten (Buddhist Stupa) which are evaluated as monasteries of extraordinary and great importance and scattered in different parts of Sikkim. Sikkim has its unique experience food habits and lifestyles, which they can sell to the whole world. Today a number of fairs and festivals are organized by all the ethnic communities (Lepchas, Bhutias, Limbus and Nepalese) in some parts of the Sikkim. Tourism department promote these festivals to highlight the rich culture of different communities to the domestic as well as foreign tourists. In west Sikkim since 2005, the "Hee-Barmiok Tourism Development and Heritage Conservation Society" organizes heritage festival every year in the month of May. The features of the festival are—exhibition of traditional items of domestic use, multi-ethnic cultural dances by all ethnic communities, exhibition of tradition huts, tradition of *dhinki*.

Village/Rural Tourism—Home Stay

Village/Rural tourism has emerged as a very new concept in the tourism industry. This concept is fast growing in Sikkim as a responsible and sustainable tourism product with critical social objectives through people's participation. The rural tourism can be a more effective tool in boosting the overall tourism scenario of Sikkim as its rural hinterlands are endowed with fabulous natural beauty, serene environment, heritage sites and unique cultural flavour. The endorsement of rural tourism will ensure the dispersal of tourists from city congestion to the villages so that they can have a glimpse of rural Sikkim, familiarize with unique village culture and heritage so that they are mentally rejuvenated, culturally enriched and spiritually elevated. The objective is therefore to harness vast un-tapped rural tourism potential of Sikkim so that their multiplier benefit reaches out directly to the rural communities. Some of the villages of Sikkim like Kewzing, Hee-Bermoik, Yoksum, Lachen, Tumin, Pastanga, Tinchim, Lunchok, Maniram, Rong, Jaubari, Darap have already taken up lead in home stay facilities for the tourists. However, more professional approach needs to be initiated with optimum government incentives for aggressive promotion of rural tourism market. For this to achieve, the modal approach devised by the Ministry of Tourism, Government of India under the hardware and the software programme has been initiated. However, the prevailing CFA slab of ₹ 50.00 lakh only for the hardware component and ₹ 20.00 lakhs for Software component need to be reviewed and revised in order to accommodate widespread necessary hardware activities in the village. Some other programme on this taken up by NGOs and other agencies also will be streamlined by bringing them under the single umbrella for convergence in the development and promotion of well regulated product.

Typology of Tourism in Sikkim

There are different classes of Tourism interests for both in the domestic and International tourism and the competition is very high, we have to catch up the new market and also to sustain the existing market and hence this aspect needs to be given highest priority, professional management along with updating the State of World market for tourism. The strategies and objectives for this will be as under:

- **Organic Tourism:** Sikkim has already been declared as Organic State. This will promote the wellness tourism along with traditional cuisines. The Chief Minister of Sikkim, Shri Pawan Chamling, made a declaration in the Budget session of Sikkim Legislative Assembly in February, 2003 to make Sikkim an Organic State with doing away with the use of synthetic fertilizers, pesticides, plant growth regulators and additives in the state. This decision has been arrived at with the objective to achieve an economically and environmentally sustainable production system of agriculture and to promote soil, plant, animal, human and environmental health and well-being. With so many benefits of organic farming, it becomes a policy seeking to promote technically sound, economically viable, environmentally non-degrading, and socially acceptable use of natural resources—land, water and genetic endowment to promote sustainable development of agriculture.

As a matter of fact, Sikkim grows most of its crops more or less in organic conditions. Whether its commercial large cardamom or exquisite orchids, sweet mandarin orange or trenchant cherry pepper, typical buckwheat or unique pulses, all are one hundred per cent organic produce. And with the initiative made by the State Government, Sikkim becomes one among the first states to opt for Organic Farming in the country.

- **Culture:** Sikkim has unique cultural heritage. But till now, it could not be projected as such a tourism product. The stake-holders in these areas need to be promoted in well-planned manner with well-defined and professional events/ programme so that tourists especially come to get the benefit of it. Entire programme needs to have its own calendar fixed.

Traditional Dresses of Sikkimese Women.

Monuments, Pilgrimage places, Historical sites and other cultural sites and programme shall be listed as annual events with fixed dates and their themes.

- **Rivers, Streams and Lakes:** For special interests tourists important river side's of Teesta, Rangeet and others needs to be developed in well managed forms for Water sports, Camping sites, Hydro-tourism and many more new concepts. Some of the manmade or natural lakes shall be promoted for

Rivers, Streams and Lakes.

water sports. River front development will be undertaken at select locations by developing embankments, parks, walkways, food and shopping points and open air theatres.

- **Traditional Cuisines:** It has unmatched world market and becoming increasingly popular. There is need to establish a Sikkim Culinary Institute (SCI) that will research and document ancient culinary traditions, create a highly skilled workforce of culinary professionals that can populate not only hotels and catering establishments in India, but also internationally, serving to promote Sikkim internationally. To promote entrepreneurs to establish restaurants of Sikkim Ethnic Cuisine, the Government may come up with an innovative incentive scheme. This will provide healthy food and employment.
- **Rural/Village Tourism and Home Stay:** This product has a huge potential in Sikkim as all the villages are being well developed to have all basic amenities and have the god gifted landscape which is unmatchable. The momentum has already picked-up and will be given the right motivation and direction. This will be promoted as Primary Tourism Product to spread tourism and its socio-economic benefits to the masses. It needs to be well regulated with suitable area specific rules and guidelines in place. The people have developed the desire to do it and all the stakeholders and Government will educate them how to do and manage it with the following:
    - The fruits of tourism must percolate down to country side in order to make it sustainable and responsible tourism.
    - All such areas will be identified and notified by the Department along with guidelines to regulate it in proper manner. All such areas will be covered by Tourism Development Committee or Village Tourism Development Committee or Cooperative Society or under concerned Panchayat.
    - To monitor and regulate, any agency doing any village tourism shall first submit the proposal and obtain the concurrence and approval of the Government through Tourism Department so that there is no duplication and

Rural/Village Tourism and Home Stay.

all information are update, authentic and its impacts can be monitored.

- The villages will have traditional architecture only and a MoU shall be signed with Department and Panchayat that this will be maintained along with no unwanted activity or action which will have the negative impact on socio-economic fabric will not be permitted.
- The villagers may modify their houses internally with traditional materials supported by modern one but they must maintain their traditional outer façade.
- The schemes of Central or State Government or any other agency will be used for development of roads,

streets, drainage, lighting, parking, reception point, water supply, sanitation, rural museum, open air theater, parks, nature trails, handicraft bazaar, culture related, floriculture, organic food, fairs and festivals, capacity building and skill development and some addition/ improvements in houses. Grants/loans, etc. will be part of the programme.

➢ **Forests and Wildlife Tourism:** This is an integral part of eco-tourism. Sikkim has the highest network of National Park, Wildlife Sanctuaries and Biosphere Reserve and the unique Forest areas that perhaps not have been fully explored to its potential for tourism.

- It needs to be integrated as integral part of Sikkim tourism product in well planned and regulated manner keeping the carrying capacities of each site without any negative impacts. The quality of tourists facilities available will be enhanced, improved with modern visitor information, interpretation centres, safety and security, guides and the entry will be regulated by charging entry charges/fees. The revenue generated shall be ploughed back to the same area for its management and upgradation. For this special eco-tourism guides will be trained and promoted.
- Tourism Department proposes to work closely and actively with the Forest Department to further develop and improve the areas and other public utility services without any compromise with the conservation programme on the principle of sustainability in well regulated manner.
- A reasonable fee shall be charged for management and maintenance of these areas.

➢ **Bio-diversity Tourism:** Sikkim is one of the hot-spots of the Biodiversity world and hence, it has a great potential for researcher, educationists, students and nature lovers' types of tourists both domestic and international. Since, this is our rich wealth; it will be well regulated with compulsory guide/ interpreters with each group and well watched entry and outlets to check the bio piracy.

➢ **Unique Adventure:** Sikkim is also a hot-spot for adventure tourism. Entire State being Himalayas is an Adventure State.

Though adventure activities are picking up fast but it could not be done in professional manner. It goes without saying that Sikkim has an immense potential for adventure tourism related activities. Some of the important adventure activities being promoted in the State are: Trekking, Mountain climbing and Mountaineering, Rock climbing, River crossing, Paragliding, Bungee Jumping, water sports, White water rafting, Angling, Skiing, Skating, Aerosports, Hot air balloon, and many types of traditional adventures. Trekking and Mountaineering are by far the most vibrant and visible adventure tourism activities in Sikkim and have much wider marketing prospects along with other adventure activities.

- The Indian Himalayan Centre for Adventure and Eco-tourism (IHCAE), Chemchey, South has become operational and it will now create a highly skilled manpower for all type of Adventure activities. It will also develop field practical points in all the four districts.
- A comprehensive adventure tourism plan will be prepared and will also lay down the regulatory frame-work and enforced along with minimum safety and security guidelines.
- In order to ensure safety of participants in such activities, there is a need to lay down the minimum acceptable standards in terms of equipment and human resources. The State Government is looking into the matter and the Basic Minimum Standards of safety will be notified at the earliest in consonance with the guidelines issued by the Ministry of Tourism, Government of India.
- For brand of adventure Experience Unique Sikkim Himalaya (EUSH) may be used.
- Skiing facilities will be created and established at Yumethang and Kupuk and in other feasible areas.

➢ **Domestic Tourism:** This class mostly prefers recreational pursuits and leisure and its growth is very high. And hence more spot in urban and nearby areas will be developed and nearby villages of urban areas will be promoted as Home Stay to provide this class a unique experience and other products of tourism. Weekend/day tourism will also be

Unique Adventure/Bio-diversity Tourism.

promoted for quick weekend retreats, picnic and cultural shows etc.

- **MICE Tourism (Meetings, Incentives, Convention and Exhibition):** For this product of tourism, Sikkim has very wide potential for many obvious reasons. The suitable venues along with all the facilities, transport, and communication will be developed. This will certainly promote the quality tourism and also bring the investment to Sikkim. Steps will be taken to promote corporate tourism and a directory for the same will be prepared. Tourism oriented expositions at landmark venues will also be the part of this activity.
- **Wellness Tourism:** This will be developed and promoted as

Sikkim's most unique tourism product. The State being peaceful, environmental friendly, rich in medicinal plants, it will provide the holistic healing and rejuvenation of the people from every dimension—physical, mental, emotional and spiritual. It will certainly capture the essence of the best of Indian philosophy and culture for domestic and international tourist. In doing so, it would render a great service to the humankind making them healthy and efficient. The Sikkim Himalaya represents extremely unique eco-system rich in medicinal wealth associated with Ayurveda, Folk, Homoeopathy, Siddha, Amchi (Tibetan) and Unani system of medicines. High in the land of snows, amidst melting snow-beds, steep screes, and glacial moraines grow some of the most valuable medicinal plants in the state. It is reported to have more than 424 species of various medicinal plants, which have a strong traditional system of medicines. The local inhabitants for treatment of various ailments use numerous herbal remedies. Further, more modern medicines owes to the flora of these mountains. Many species of Himalayan origin have revolutionized the allopathic system of medicine. Many of the medicinal plants, which are threatened and are on the verge of extinction at other places, are still well conserved in Sikkim.

- **Unique Lodging Products:** A varieties of accommodations having different taste and feelings such as Ekant Vas and Agyat Van Vas, River side, Hill top, Home Stay, Pilgrimage huts, Tea in Lodge, High Class Camping etc. which have Unique Selling Propositions (USPs) will be created in Government, private and PPP mode.
- **Shopper's Paradise:** The shopping is recognized as an integral part of the tourism experience and a most valuable contributor to employment, income and revenue. The development of dedicated shopping centres for traditional crafts, costumes, jewellery, etc. designed on the lines of ethnic village haat, Shilpbustee, will be developed and encouraged with incentives from the Government in the initial stage. The availability of information on where to procure is very important and it will be made available in form of Directory and "Made in Sikkim" shall be controlled through regulation and quality control.

- **Arts, Crafts and Souvenir:** Arts, crafts and souvenir are the integrated part of tourism industry and it will be developed and promoted on the top priority for generation of employment and income. It may be developed by Government undertakings and private sectors. Along with it, the standardized packing also needs to be taken up as its integral part. The items will be on all aspects of State such as culture, folk, pilgrimage, events, places, nature, landscape, forests and wildlife, mountains, monuments, history and many more.
- **Fairs and Festivals:** Sikkim is a land of fairs and festivals. In last one decade, its promotional aspect has been very encouraging. Now, there is need to make them more attractive, targeting the tourists on well defined theme and spread over all the seasons. Their time and dates will be fixed, organized in more professional manner and will be given wide publicity. Its calendar will be prepared with the concurrence of organizers and some of festivals would to be given review and rethought to make them more effective and purposeful. This is a major contribution in National Integration.
- **Pilgrimage Tourism:** Pilgrimage tourism has witnessed a growth of 20-25 per cent in the year 2008 in India and has very bright future in Sikkim as a major chunk of domestic tourists are pilgrims. Buddhists circuit is coming up very

Pilgrimage Tourism.

well with Guru Padma Sambhava Statue, Buddha Park, Chen-Regi Statue and a high network of world famous monasteries. New unique destinations like Chardham, many temples and other pilgrimage places, sacred lakes, sacred rocks and caves etc. offer a wide range of pilgrimages in Sikkim.

Top Tourist Destinations in Sikkim

Gangtok

Gangtok, the capital of Sikkim, is constructed on a cloudy ridge 5,500 feet above sea level. When the clouds clear, it's possible to see all the way to Kanchenjunga's soaring peaks (it's the world's third-highest mountain). The city is refreshingly clean and well organized, and most tourists spend a couple of days there to make travel arrangements and see the sights. It's a popular base for those heading off on treks. Unfortunately, Sikkim currently doesn't have an airport (one is being built in Pakyong near Gangtok and it's scheduled to open in 2016). Getting to Gangtok requires a four hour drive from Siliguri in West Bengal, where the nearest trains station is. The nearest airport, at Bagdogra, is about 45 minutes from Siliguri.

Monasteries

In testament to the fact that Sikkim is a marvelous place for meditation, almost 200 monasteries dot the divine hilltops. The most visited monasteries in Sikkim are *Rumtek* (overlooking Gangtok), *Pemayangtse* (near Pelling in West Sikkim), and Tashiding (also in West Sikkim). Other monasteries that are worth visiting include the *Karma Kagyu* monastery with its 200 year old murals (in Phodong in North Sikkim), the *Enchey monastery* (in Gangtok), and the old *Sanga-Choeling monastey* (only accessible on foot from Pelling).

The monasteries hold many festivals, particularly around Losar in February/March. *Tse Chu*, in July, features Buddhist dancing at Rumtek. Enchey also hosts a *Chaarm* festvial in December/January.

Nathu La

Nathu La, three hours east of Gangtok on the Chinese border, was a major passageway on the Old Silk Route between India and Tibet

Monasteries.

before it was closed in 1962. The border consists of a lone barbed wire fence, and you will get the strange thrill of seeing the Chinese soldiers on the other side. Unfortunately, only Indians are allowed to travel this far though, and only on Wednesdays, Thursdays, Saturdays and Sundays. A specia' permit is also required and can be obtained through a registered t' avel agency in Gangtok.

With a permit, foreigners can go up to *Tsomgo Lake*, also called *Changu Lake*, 27 kilometres (17 miles) short of Nathu La. This spectacular high-altitude (12,400 feet) glacier lake remains frozen until May. For a quirky experience, ride a yak there.

Nathu La.

Flora and Fauna Sanctuaries

Sikkim is renowned for its astounding variety of birds, animals, and flowers—over 450 species of birds, 400 species of butterflies, 450 varieties of orchids, and 40 species of rhododendron. Varsey Rhododendron Sanctuary, situated in the Singalila Range in the south-west corner of West Sikkim, is a must-visit place during late spring. You will find Maenam Wildlife Sanctuary near Ravangla in south Sikkim. The Shingba Rhododendron Sanctuary is also a highlight near Lachung.

Closer to Gangtok, there is the Deorali Orchid Sanctuary in south Gangtok (visit from March to early May and the end of September to early December), and Fambong Lho Wildlife Sanctuary around an hour west of Gangtok. Kyongnosla Alpine Sanctuary is located about an hour east of Gangtok, on the way to Tsomgo Lake and Nathu La (vist from June until October).

Yuksom and the Dzongri Trail

Sikkim is a trekker's paradise and historical Yuksom is the gateway for treks towards Mount Kanchenjunga. The trek from Yuksom to Dzongri Peak and Rathong Glacier, and further on to Goecha Peak if you are up for the challenge, is the most popular trek in Sikkim. It passes through the unspoiled forests, magnificent rhododendron gardens, and powerful rivers of Khangchendzonga National Park. Allow seven to 10 days from Yuksom to Goecha Peak and back. March to May is the ideal time to go. Additional permits are mandatory for foreigners. See what it's like to trek the Dzongri Trail in this *Dzongri trek photo gallery*. If you want to go on an organized trek, *Mountain Tours* gets *excellent reviews* and is recommended. It is run by the family of mountaineer Late Da Namgel Sherpa, who was part of the first successful Everest expedition team in 1953.

Lachung, Lachen and Yumthang Valley

In far North Sikkim, six hours from Gangtok and 9,000 feet above sea-level near the Tibetan/Chinese border, Lachung and the Yumthang Valley dazzle visitors with dramatic pristine scenery. Lachung served as a trading post between Sikkim and Tibet before Tibet was annexed by China. Now, it is the base camp for the renowned Rhododendron

Flora and Fauna Sanctuaries.

Valley Trek from Yumthang Valley to Lachen Valley. Other attractions in the area are Lachung monastery, *Yumesamdong (Zero Point)*, and the astonishing high-altitude *Gurudongmar Lake* (it is one of the world's highest lakes, at more than 17,000 feet above sea level). North Sikkim is a restricted area and it is necessary to obtain a special permit to visit it. You will need to make your travel arrangements through a registered tour company, which will also organize the permit for you. This can be done in Gangtok. [(**Note**: that the Yumthang Valley is closed from December to March due to heavy snow, and foreigners are only permitted as far as the Chopta Valley (they cannot visit Gurudongmar Lake).]

Pelling

Pelling, three to four hours drive west of Gangtok, may be a rather charmless small town but it's the place to go for unparallelled views of Mount Kanchenjunga at dawn. Apart from the views, monasteries are the main attraction, along with the *ruins of Rabdentse*. Previously, the royal capital of Sikkim from 1670 to 1814, not much remains of Rabdentse these days. However, its location on a ridge provides a spectacular viewpoint. Overnight and day tours depart from Pelling by jeep and cover the major sights in the area. It is also possible to do a three-day combination jeep and hiking trip from Pelling to Tashiding (which has an atmospheric monastery on a hilltop) *via* Khecheopalri Lake. Alternatively, jeeps run from Pelling to Yuksom *via* Khecheopalri Lake, and you can hike from Yuksom to Tashiding in a day.

Ravangla

On the way from Gangtok to Pelling, Ravangla is most notable for its *Buddha Park* with a towering 130 foot golden Buddha statue surrounded by manicured gardens. Palchen Choeling Monastic Institute (also known as the new Ralong Monastery) in nearby Ralong also houses a substantially sized golden Buddha. It is home to more than 100 monks, and you can hear them chanting in the early morning and mid afternoon. There are number of other monasteries that can be visited in the area as well. Halfway between Ravangla and Namchi, you will find picturesque Temi Tea Garden. It is only tea garden in Sikkim and the tranquil *Cherry Resort* is nestled amidst it.

Namchi

Namchi is also famous for its giant statutes. It currently has two of them—one Buddhist and one Hindu—and a third one is apparently being planned. The Buddhist statue, of Guru Padmasambhava (credited with introducing Tantric Buddhism to the Himalayan region), reaches around 140 feet tall. It has a commanding position on *Samdruptse Hill*, 7,000 feet above sea-level. Not quite as tall but perhaps more impressive is the white 108 foot high *Lord Shiva statue* at Solophuk Hill, five kilometres south of Namchi. The epic

Ravangla.

complex surrounding the statue contains guest houses and temples, including replicas of the holy *Char Dham.*

Teesta River Rafting

River rafting is the latest adventure activity to arrive in Sikkim, and the Teesta River offers some world class opportunities. The major route is Makha-Sirwani-Bardang-Rongpo. Grade II to IV rapids are interspersed with placid patches to float along, and plenty of white sandy beaches exist for overnight camping. High cliffs and gorges, along with bolder-strewn river beds, add to the thrill. The Rangeet river, with its more turbulent waters, also offers advanced rafting

Namchi.

Holy Char Dham.

opportunities from Sikip-Jorethang-Majitar-Melli. The best time for rafting in Sikkim is from March to May and October to December.

Zuluk

An unexplored destination for those who want to get off the tourist trail, Zuluk is a tiny village nearly 10,000 feet above sea level in East Sikkim. It was once part of the Old Silk Route for traders, connecting Kalimpong in West Bengal to Tibet. Now, it is the first village along this route to offer homestay accommodations for visitors. The main attraction is the sight of Mount Kangchenjunga from Lungthung and

Teesta River Rafting.

Thambi View Point. Those who get car sick might want to avoid it though, as the very winding road has more than 30 hairpin turns! The landscape varies greatly depending on the time of year. It is carpeted in wildflowers from August to September and covered in snow from January until April. After the snow clears, there is abundant bird life.

As Zuluk is a military-controlled area near the Chinese border, it is off-limits for foreigners. Indians require an Inner Line Permit to visit it, which needs to be obtained from the police station at Rongli in West Bengal. The permit will allow travel to Gangtok *via* Zuluk, Gnathang Valley, Kupup, Baba Mandir, and Tsomgo Lake. (If you want to visit Nathu La, a separate permit must be obtained in Gangtok). Travel agencies offer Old Silk Route tour packages.

"The kinds of tourism in Sikkim" is an entire gamut of information about Sikkim—a humble attempt to showcase its rich bio-diversity. Through surveys and information through internet and books we have tried our best to bring-forth the rich natural wealth of Sikkim. We hope that this book will be found useful information about Sikkim tourism resources. *"The land of orchids", "The land of tranquility"*, these are the few ways in which Sikkim has been described. Sikkim has been projected as a naturalists paradise. A tourist visiting Sikkim is all praises for the richness in nature which no doubt has been the

Zuluk Silk Route.

basic ingredient of tourism in Sikkim. It is here that Kanchenjunga—the third highest mountain in the world stands tall. Blessed with snow capped mountains, lakes, rivers and varieties of flora and fauna Sikkim is in par with other ecological hot spots of the world. Eco-tourism is the buzzword and Government, NGO'S and individuals have all geared up for contributing to it.

References

Badan, B.S. and Bhatt, Harish (2007): *Culture and Tourism*, New Delhi: Commonwealth.

Bhattacharyya, P. Kumar (1984): *Aspects of Cultural History of Sikkim*, Calcutta: K.P. Bagchi & Company.

Birundha, D.V. (2003): *Environmental Challenges Towards Tourism*, New Delhi: Kanishka Publishers & Distributors.

Chakrabarti, Anjan (2009): *Economic Development and Employment in Sikkim*, New Delhi: Authors Press.

Gupta, Das Ishwar (2008): *Trends and Resources of Cultural Tourism*, New Delhi: Adhyayan Publishers and Distributors.

Hall, C. and Page, Stephen (2001): *Tourism in South and South-East Asia*, Oxford: Butterworth-Heniemann.

Joshi, R. and Dhyani, P.P. (2009): "Environmental Sustainability and Tourism Implications of Trend Synergies of Tourism in Sikkim Himalaya," *Current Science*, Vol. 97, No. 1, 10th July, pp. 33-41.

Kadt, de Emanuel (1979): *Tourism-Passport to Development? Perspectives on the Social and Cultural Effects of Tourism in Developing Countries*, Oxford University Press.

Kala, Neha (2008): "Host Perception of Heritage Tourism Impact with Special Reference to the City of Jaipur," *South Asian Journal of Tourism and Heritage*, Vol. 1, No. 1, pp. 65-74.

Online International Interdisciplinary Research Journal (Bi-Monthly), ISSN 2249-9598, Volume II, Issue III, May-June 2012, www. oiirj.org ISSN 2249-9598, p. 139.

Sikkim Human Development Report (2001), Delhi: Government of Sikkim, Social Science Press.

Sikkim Tourism Policy (2010) : Government of Sikkim.

Sinha, U.P. and Kumar, Swargesh (2011): *Bihar Tourism: Retrospect and Prospect*, New Delhi: Concept Publishing Company (P) Ltd.

5
Trends and Data Analysis of Tourism Development
Regional, National and Global

Tourism is the fastest growing sectors in the State of Sikkim and holds tremendous potential for future economic growth with equity and employment generation. Realizing this potential of tourism sector, the State Government has accorded for most priority to this sector with adequate policy and financial support. Sikkim has been witnessing a steady and healthy rate of growth of 15 per cent per annum tourist arrival, both domestic as well as international. In this chapter, the inflow of tourist and trends of tourism sector for last ten years has been explained.

Tourist Arrivals to Sikkim

According to the figure, tourists trends has been compiled, so, there 31,698 foreign tourists and 5,76,749 domestic tourists visited the state in 2013 as shown in Table 5.1.

The figures for international arrivals are precise, as foreign visitors have to obtain a permit to enter Sikkim and are recorded. However, the figures for domestic arrivals are more dubious, as they are obtained from hotel registration of visitors. This method excludes visitors that stay with friends and relatives, stay at accommodations that do not register or report guests to the Tourism Department, or those accommodated at camp sites. To compensate, the department inflates the figures it has collected from the registration by 25 per cent. It is also likely that there are incidents of double and triple counting of visitors that travel around Sikkim and stay in several hotels during their trip. It is estimated that the number of domestic tourists is likely to be substantially higher.

Table 5.1: Tourist Arrivals (1999-2013)

Year	*Domestic Tourist Arrivals*	*Percentage Change*	*International Tourist Arrivals*	*Percentage Change*
2004	286678	5.69	13528	6.50
2005	347650	6.90	16518	8.02
2006	421943	8.37	18049	8.77
2007	465204	9.23	17837	8.67
2008	512373	10.17	19154	9.31
2009	615628	12.22	17730	8.61
2010	700011	13.89	20757	10.09
2011	552453	10.96	23945	11.64
2012	558535	11.08	26489	12.87
2013	576749	11.44	31698	15.40

Source: Tourism Department, Government of Sikkim.

The growth rate of tourist arrivals to Sikkim has been comparable to that of India as a whole. Since 1999, average annual growth rates have been 11.20 per cent for domestic tourist arrivals and 14.20 per cent for international arrivals. Sharp increases in foreign arrivals are directly related to political problems in neighbouring Nepal, which suggests that Sikkim is currently perceived as an alternative to Nepal.

Tourism Demand and Profile of Visitors to Sikkim

No visitor survey has been conducted in Sikkim. The Tourism Department estimates that 80 per cent of all visitors to Sikkim come for general sightseeing, principally to see its nature and the spectacular mountain views, and for many domestic visitors from the hotter states of India to experience snow. With Sikkim's exceptional mountains and rivers, visitors come to enjoy adventure tourism such as trekking and mountaineering. After general sightseeing, trekking is the activity that attracts the most tourists. The remaining tourists visit Sikkim for pilgrimage to Buddhist monasteries, to pursue special interests such as bird watching, for business purposes, and to visit friend and relatives, in more or less equal proportions.

Despite the current interest in developing eco-tourism in Sikkim, it is not identified as a specific motive for visiting the state by the

Tourism Department. This is probably because there is no real definition of the concept of eco-tourism in Sikkim, and different institutions and organizations use the term to suit their requirements. It is likely that there are some eco-tourists among the general sightseers as well as in the adventure tourism group. It is imperative that the internationally accepted definition for this form of tourism is well understood by all stakeholders in Sikkim.

Domestic Tourists

The neighbouring State of West Bengal is not surprisingly the main domestic market to visit Sikkim. The metro of Kolkata currently accounts for 40 per cent of all domestic visitors. However, it is reported by the Tourism Department that the share of domestic tourist traffic from other metros is increasing, with Delhi now accounting for 15 per cent of domestic visitors, Mumbai 15 per cent, Hyderabad 10 per cent, Bangalore 5 per cent, and Chennai and Ahmedabad 6 per cent, respectively, as shown in Table 5.2.

Table 5.2: Domestic Generating Markets to Sikkim—2010-2013

Market Source	*Share in Tourist Traffic to Sikkim (in %)*
Kolkata	40
Delhi	15
Mumbai	15
Hyderabad	10
Bangalore	5
Ahmedabad	5
Chennai	6
Others	4
Total	**100**

Source: Tourism Department, Government of Sikkim.

Marketing campaigns by the government and the private sector have succeeded in attracting domestic visitors from all-over India, but two factors have had a major impact on domestic tourism to Sikkim. The first is the improvement in air connectivity because of the increasing number of low cost airlines flying into Bagdogra Airport, and the second is the amendment to the Leave Travel Concession (LTC) rule by the Government of India, allowing employees of Central Government and Public Sector Undertakings

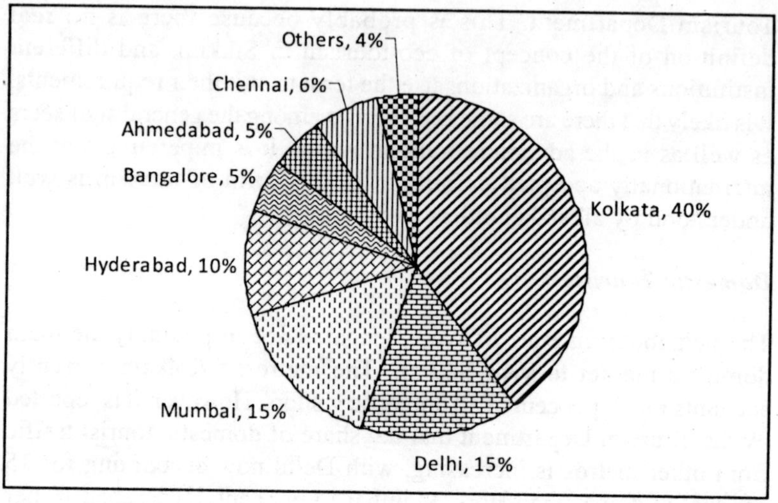

Fig. 5.1: Share in Tourist Traffic to Sikkim (in %).

(PSUs)—government-owned corporations—to travel by air free once a year with their entire family to North-east states, including Sikkim. These factors have given a real boost to the number of domestic arrivals in the last couple of years.

Sikkim is now directly connected *via* Bagdogra Airport to distant markets like Mumbai, Chennai, Bangalore, Hyderabad etc. The change in the LTC rule opens up a potential market of 10 million government employees from all-over India.

According to operators interviewed for this study and during the formulation of the Sikkim Tourism Development Master Plan in 2007, tourists from West Bengal are reputed to be enthusiastic travellers who particularly enjoy nature and the mountains. They tend to be budget travellers and low spenders. Visitors from Delhi, Mumbai, Hyderabad, Bangalore, and Chennai tend to be high spenders.

They look for cool weather, enjoying the snow, beautiful mountain sights, and good food. Their main purpose of travel is leisure. They usually demand good quality comfortable accommodation and will pay the price. They are interested in tasting local cuisine. Visitors from Gujarat are normally medium to high spenders. Like tourists from West Bengal, Gujarat are keen travellers and enjoys exploring new destinations.

Indian tourists usually travel in a family or group, which limits their activities. For instance, they may enjoy nature walks, but few tourists of this market segment will trek. They require a safe environment, enjoy trying out local food, and like shopping, particularly in Gangtok, which is their principal destination.

Many are interested in village tourism and the culture of indigenous people but are reluctant to stay at homestays and prefer hotels. While the majority are not 'eco-tourists' *per se*, they are attracted to natural sites and enjoy visiting national parks and sanctuaries, looking at plants and flowers, and trying to spot wildlife, seeing waterfalls, caves and rushing rivers, and generally like being in the natural environment.

Increasingly young Indian tourists are visiting Sikkim to participate in active vacations such as trekking. Tour operators report that Indian trekkers at the moment only make up 5 per cent of the market and that they tend to choose the easier routes, but it is a market that is increasing. A growing number of young Indians are choosing Sikkim for their honeymoon. They tend to be medium spenders.

Foreign Tourists

Sikkim attracts a relatively small number of foreign visitors, but international arrivals have increased steadily over the last few years. Europe and North America are the main international source markets for Sikkim. Table 5.3 shows that the UK is the largest generating market, followed by the USA, Germany, and France. The largest market from the Asia Pacific region is Australia, followed by Thailand and Japan. Sikkim accounted for just 0.4 per cent of total international arrivals to India in 2007, and efforts should be made to increase this market share. Eliminating the permit system or at least making it more straightforward as well as easing the restrictions within Sikkim would encourage more international arrivals to the state.

Foreign visitors mostly fall into two categories: backpackers and visitors on pre-booked arrangements from go trekking, take cultural tours, or pursue a special interest.

Backpackers will usually spend less on accommodation but, because they tend to deal directly with vendors such as suppliers of accommodation, guides, etc. rather than going through operators, their expenditure generally goes directly to the service providers. They tend to spend more locally than other market segments because they

Table 5.3: Top Ten Countries Generating Tourists for Sikkim in 2011-2015

Country	*Per cent of Arrivals 2011*	*Per cent of Arrivals 2012*	*Per cent of Arrivals 2013*	*Per cent of Arrivals 2014*	*Per cent of Arrivals 2015*
UK	21.29	20.83	20.52	20.19	20.16
USA	18.35	19.91	19.72	20.67	20.34
Germany	15.28	14.66	13.30	12.65	11.83
France	14.84	13.56	13.21	12.94	12.36
Australia	9.74	9.35	7.47	7.05	6.42
Thailand	4.03	5.38	6.01	6.44	6.06
Netherland	1.64	4.14	5.67	6.22	6.15
Canada	4.33	4.85	5.36	5.58	4.75
Japan	5.80	7.67	5.17	4.67	3.97
Italy	—	—	4.36	5.26	4.27

Source: Tourism Department, Government of Sikkim.

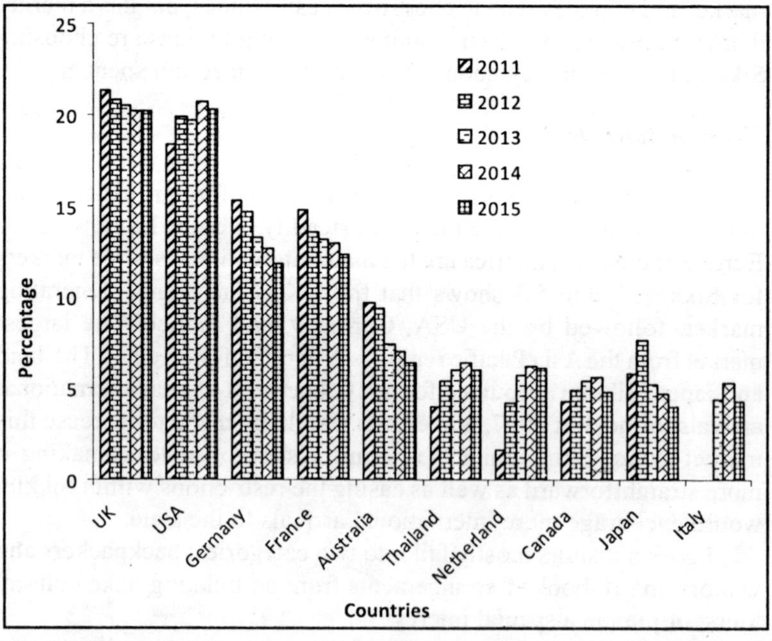

Fig. 5.2. Sharing in Top Ten Countries Generating Tourists for Sikkim in 2011-2015.

stay much longer in one place. A study in Australia shows that backpackers spend on average 2.4 times more than average tourists because of their length of stay (Tourism Tasmania, 2004). They are generally well-educated, interested in experiencing a different culture, enjoy social and adventure activities, and tend to travel independently or with a companion.

However, the benefits brought by this market are curtailed in Sikkim because of the time limits imposed by the permit requirements and the difficulty of travelling around the state independently. This is the market that would be most likely to choose homestays to experience living with indigenous people, but because of the restrictions, they have few opportunities to organize this. In Sikkim they may organize a trek through a local operator. Although no study has been carried out, anecdotal evidence suggests that the impact of this market segment is not being maximized.

Foreign tourists on organized tours have generally prepaid their holiday, and come on an all-inclusive basis. The majority come to Sikkim to trek. According to tour operators interviewed for this study, they are generally between 30 and 60 years of age, usually travel with friends or in a couple, or are from the expatriate market living in India. They are well educated and middle class.

Special interest tourists are usually high spenders willing to pay and put-up with difficult conditions to see something exceptional relating to their special interest. These include bird watchers, visitors interested in biodiversity, wildlife, and botany, and visitors interested in culture, religion, and anthropology.

Cultural tours to Sikkim are most often part of longer tours in the region in combination with other destinations. These tend to be focused on visiting the famous monasteries. Some tourists, mostly from Asia and also from other parts of the world, come to Sikkim for pilgrimage to the Buddhist monasteries.

Questionnaire for Tourists

This section is concerned with the response of Tourists, tourism entrepreneurs and tourism related persons, during 2014 in the study area. Altogether 600 respondents of different standard were interviewed. In the scaled questionnaire, mean value has been computed and analyzed on mean results. Besides simple percentage were computed to present and analyze the view and response of the respondents.

Table 5.4: Distribution of Domestic and International Tourists Visited in Study Area

Sl. No.	*Tourist Visited*	*Respondent*	*Percentage*
1.	Domestic	350	87.5
2.	International	50	12.5
	Total	**400**	**100**

Source: Field Survey, 2014.

Table 5.4 provides the information about the arrival of tourists from different parts of world. Out of 400 respondents, the proportionate share based on the region was 87.5 per cent from domestic and 12.5 per cent from international.

Table 5.5: Sex-wise Tourist in the Study Area

Sl. No.	*Sex*	*Respondent*	*Percentage*
1.	Male	254	63.40
2.	Female	146	36.60
	Total	**400**	**100**

Source: Field Survey, 2014.

Among the respondents 254 (63.40%) are male and 146 (36.60%) female.

In the Table 5.6, the respondents 240 (60%) were married and 160 (40%) respectively.

Table 5.6: Marital Status of Tourists

Sl. No.	*Marital Status*	*Respondent*	*Percentage*
1.	Married	240	60
2.	Unmarried	160	40
	Total	**400**	**100**

Source: Field Survey, 2014.

In the given Table 5.7, the respondents 123 (30.75%) were below 30 years and between 30-40 years is about 164 (41%) and over 40 years were 113 (28.25%), which shows that people used to visit Sikkim is of age about 30-40 years and they too are married, so Sikkim is also known to a honeymoon destination.

Table 5.7: Age-wise Distribution

Sl. No.	*Age Group*	*Respondent*	*Percentage*
1.	< 30 years	123	30.75
2.	30-40 years	164	41.00
3.	> 40 years	113	28.25
	Total	**400**	**100**

Source: Field Survey, 2014.

Table 5.8: Academic Status

Sl. No.	*Academic Qualification*	*Respondent*	*Percentage*
1.	School Education	104	26.00
2.	Under Graduate	160	40.00
3.	Post-Graduate	35	8.75
4.	Doctoral	52	13.00
5.	Others	49	12.25
	Total	**400**	**100**

Source: Field Survey, 2014.

From Table 5.8, among 400 respondents 104 (26.00%) are student below XII standard, 160 (40.00%) are undergraduate and 35 (8.75%) are postgraduate student, Doctoral 52 respondents that is 13 per cent and others 49 (12.25%) having professional qualification respectively.

Table 5.9: Number of Tourist have been in Sikkim Before

Sl. No.	*Yes/No*	*Respondent*	*Percentage*
1.	Yes	120	30
2.	No	280	70
	Total	**400**	**100**

Source: Field Survey, 2014.

From the total sample 120 (30%) respondents already visited Sikkim and 280 (70%) respondents were first time to visit Sikkim.

From Table 5.10, 216 (54.00%) were job holder both in the State and Central Government and other private organizations, out of 400 respondent 13 per cent people doing business followed by student 8.00 per cent and others 25.00 per cent respectively.

Table 5.10: Occupational Distribution of Tourists in the Study Area

Sl. No.	*Occupation*	*Respondent*	*Percentage*
1.	Job Holder	216	54.00
2.	Business	52	13.00
3.	Student	32	8.00
4.	Others	100	25.0
	Total	**400**	**100**

Source: Field Survey, 2014.

Table 5.11: Total Number of Visit by Tourists in Sikkim

Sl. No.	*No. of Visits*	*Respondent*	*Percentage*
1.	First time	282	70.50
2.	2-3 times	76	19.00
3.	4-5 times	23	5.75
4.	6-7 times	6	1.50
5.	8 times and more	13	3.25
	Total	**400**	**100**

Source: Field Survey, 2014.

The maximum number of respondents that is 282 (70.50%) tourist visited Sikkim for a first time, similarly, that is 76 per cent, 19.00 per cent, 5.75 per cent and 1.50 per cent tourist revisited Sikkim 2-3, 4-5, 6-7 and 8 times and above respectively.

Table 5.12: Length of Stay of Tourists

Total Number of Tourists	*Total Number of Days*	*Average Length of Stay of Tourists*	*Average Length of Stay in 2014*
400	**3600**	**9**	**9**

Source: Field Survey, 2014 and TAAS.

Table 5.13: Average Expenditure of Tourists

Sl. No.	*Expenditure per day (₹)*	*Respondents*	*Percentage*
1.	300—500 (₹)	120	30.00
2.	500—700 (₹)	123	30.75
3.	700—1000 (₹)	33	8.25
4.	1000 (₹) and above	124	31.00
	Total	**400**	**100**

Source: Field Survey, 2014.

Table 5.13 shows that 124 (31%) respondents spent about ₹ 1000 and above, similarly the average expenditure that is, ₹ 300 to ₹ 500 and ₹ 500 to ₹ 700 was made by 120 (30%) and 123 (30.75%) respondents respectively. Only 8.25 per cent of people spent in between ₹ 700 to ₹ 1000.

Table 5.14: Tourism Publicity Material Published by Government of Sikkim Tourism Department and Travel Agencies

Sl. No.	*Yes/No*	*Respondents*	*Percentage*
1.	Yes	172	43
2.	No	228	57
	Total	**400**	**100**

Source: Field Survey, 2014.

172 respondents that is 43 per cent tourists lead the publicity material relating to tourism published by Tourism Department, Government of Sikkim and Travel Agencies.

Hypothesis

Null Hypothesis (H_0): The publication of publicity material relating to Tourism by Government, TAAS, and travel Agencies is satisfactory.

Conclusion

Calculated Value of Z = 4.6

Now, the critical value of Z at 5% level of Significance one tailed test is 1.645. So, calculated Z > tabulated Z.

Therefore, publicity materials relating to tourism published by Government of Sikkim, TAAS and travel Agencies is not satisfactory.

Cross-Sectional Analysis on the Level of Satisfaction and Importance

For analysis, Emery S. Borgodous model has been used to analyze the level of satisfaction and importance regarding facilities and services of different aspects of Tourism (Table 5.15).

Cross-Sectional Analysis on the Level of Satisfaction and Importance

Table 5.15: Response Regarding Air Services and Facilities

Sl. No.	*Index*	*Scale*	*Index*
1.	Unsatisfactory	–2	Not important
2.	Fair	–1	Less important
3.	Neutral	0	Neutral
4.	Good	1	Important
5.	Satisfactory	2	Very important

Here, total no. of Respondents is 400.
So, the total Range is – 800 to + 800.

Index:

+100 to +100 = Neutral
+100 to +400 = Moderately Positive
–100 to –400 = Moderately Negative
+400 to +800 = Highly Positive/Highly Important
–400 to –800 = Highly Negative.

Table 5.16: Level of Satisfaction and Importance from Facilities and Services Regarding Airlines and Roadways

Sl. No.	*Factors*	*Satisfaction Borgodous Value*	*Result*	*Importance Borgodous Value*	*Result*
1.	International Airlines	+80	Moderately Positive	+543	Highly Important
2.	Domestic Airlines	+98	Positive Natural	+237	Moderately Important
3.	Roadways	+232	Positive Natural	+500	Highly Important
4.	Tourist Information Centre	+23	Positive Natural	+700	Moderately Important
5.	Customs	+34	Positive Natural	+600	Moderately Important

Source: Field Survey, 2014.

International Airlines

Table 5.16 shows the satisfaction from the international airlines to the trekkers and mountaineers is moderately positive whereas, the importance of international airlines is moderately positive and it is very important for tourism development in Sikkim.

Domestic Airlines

The satisfaction from the domestic airlines to the trekkers and mountaineers is positive natural, i.e. it must improve the facilities and service of domestic airlines existing in Sikkim. The importance of domestic airlines is moderately positive for tourism development in Sikkim.

Roadways

The satisfaction from the Roadways is positive natural, i.e. it must be improved in mechanism of tourism. The importance of Roadways is moderately high showed by the respondents.

Table 5.17: Level of Satisfaction and Importance of Location, Facilities and Services Regarding Hotel

Sl. No.	*Factors*	*Satisfaction Borgodous Value*	*Result*	*Importance Borgodous Value*	*Result*
1.	Location	+789	Highly Positive	+789	Highly Positive
2.	Cleanliness	+500	Highly Positive	+500	Highly Positive
3.	Quality of Food and Drinks	+600	Highly Positive	+756	Highly Positive
4.	Behaviour of Staff	+708	Highly Positive	+700	Highly Positive

Source: Field Survey, 2014.

- *Hospitality* : Table 5.18 revels the satisfaction from the hospitality. It is highly positive, i.e. the trekker and mountaineers are fully satisfied from our hospitability. It also shows that importance of hospitality is very important for mountain tourism development in Sikkim.

Table 5.18: Level of Satisfaction and Importance of Facilities and Services Regarding Tourism Activities

Sl. No.	*Factors*	*Satisfaction Borgodous Value*	*Result*	*Importance Borgodous Value*	*Result*
1.	Hospitability	+768	Highly Positive	+780	Highly Positive
2.	Banking Services	+67	Positive Neutral	+608	Highly Positive
3.	Transportation and Communication	+102	Positive Neutral	+546	Highly Positive
4.	Shopping Facilities	+300	Moderately Positive	+356	Positive Neutral
5.	Health Services	–123	Negative Neutral	+567	Highly Positive
6.	Currency Exchange	+306	Moderately Positive	+358	Positive Neutral
7.	Language Communication	+500	Highly Positive	+300	Positive Neutral
8.	Extension of Visa	–103	Negative Neutral	+121	Positive Neutral
9.	Agencies Services	+401	Highly Positive	+465	Highly Positive
10.	Guide	+508	Highly Positive	+788	Highly Positive
11.	Solid Waste Collection and Disposal	+352	Moderately Positive	+765	Highly Positive
12.	Security Arrangement	+698	Highly Positive	+567	Highly Positive
13.	Behaviour of Locals	+700	Highly Positive	+232	Positive Neutral
14.	Rescue	+123	Moderately Positive	+675	Highly Positive
15.	Entry Fee	+543	Highly Positive	+345	Positive Neutral

Source: Field Survey, 2014.

- *Banking Service*: The banking service is highly important for tourism industry. The satisfaction from our banking service is positive neutral. So, improvement in banking service is required.
- *Transportation*: Transportation is also highly important for tourism industry, but the level of satisfaction from transportation is positive neutral.
- *Shopping Facilities*: The importance and satisfaction of shopping facilities is moderately positive.
- *Health Services*: The trekkers and mountaineers viewed that

the importance of health services is highly positive whereas the level of satisfaction is negative neutral.

- *Currency Exchanges*: The importance of currency exchange service is highly positive but level of satisfaction is negative neutral.
- *Language Communication*: The level of importance and satisfaction of language communication is highly satisfactory.
- *Agency*: The level importance of agency service is highly important and highly satisfactory.
- *Guide and Sardar*: The importance of guide and *sardar* is highly important and the level of satisfaction and from it highly satisfactory.
- *Communication Facilities*: It is highly important aspect of tourism. Whereas, the level of satisfaction from Communication is positively neutral.
- *Solid Waste Collection and Disposal*: It is highly important aspect for tourism development but the level of satisfaction is less satisfactory.
- *Behaviour of Local People*: It is highly important and level of satisfaction is highly satisfactory.
- *Rescue*: It is highly important for adventure tourism, but level of satisfaction is moderately positive.
- *Entry Fee*: It is important but the level of satisfaction is Positive neutral.
- *Electricity*: It is also important for tourism industry. But the satisfaction from electricity is neutral.

Table 5.19: Sources of Information for Motivating Travel

Sl. No.	*Factors*	*Respondent*	*Per cent*
1.	Friends /Relatives	265	66.25
2.	Travel Agent	50	12.5
3.	Newspaper	67	16.75
4.	Magazine	23	5.75
5.	Television	12	3
6.	Tourist Office	12	3
7.	Guide Book	56	14
8.	Business Linkage	134	33.5
9.	Trade Fairs/shows	56	14
10.	Others	76	19

Source: Field Survey, 2014.

Sources of information on Sikkim—An attempt have been made to enquire about what factors influence trekkers and mountaineers to come to Sikkim. In this respect, the highest number 265 (66.25%) of visitors viewed that their friends/relatives are the main sources of information to come to Sikkim, followed by travel agent (12.5%), newspaper (16.75%) magazine 5.75% television/radio 3%, internet 33.5%, guidebook (32.6%) and business linkage (9.5%) respectively.

Table 5.20: Rating of Tourism Marketing of Sikkim

Statements	*Frequency*	*Per cent*
A	20	5
B	96	24
C	124	31
D	124	31
E	36	9
Total	**400**	**100**

Source: Field Survey, 2014.

Null Hypothesis (H_0): A : B : C : D : E = 1 : 1 : 1 : 1 : 1, i.e. each type of statement is uniformly distributed in the population.

Conclusion

Since, the computed value of x^2 is 43.7, which is greater than the critical value, *viz*. 9.488, it is significant at 5 per cent level of significance. Therefore, we do not accept the null hypothesis and concluded that each type of statement is not uniformly distributed among the population.

Table 5.21: Environmental Impact of Tourism Industry in Sikkim

Response	*Frequency*	*Per cent*
Yes	37	84.3
No	63	15.7
Total	**400**	**100**

Source: Field Survey, 2014.

337 (84.3%) tourists think of the environmental impact of tourism in study area, whereas 63 (15.7%) tourist did not think of the environmental impact of tourism in Sikkim.

Null Hypothesis (H_0): There is no environmental impact of tourism in Sikkim.

Conclusion

Calculated value of Z =11.4
Tabulated value of Z =1.645
Calculated value of Z > tabulated value of Z
Hypothesis rejected
Therefore, there is environmental impact of tourism in Sikkim.

Table 5.22: Kind of Environmental Impact of Tourism Industry in Sikkim

Sl. No.	*Factors*	*Response*	*Per cent*
1.	Degradation of Scenic Appeal	99	24.8
2.	Measures of Hold Population	56	14
3.	Erosion of Trekking Trial/Bridge	141	35.2
4.	Maintenance of Scenic Beauty/Landscape	78	19.6
5.	Deforestation/Destruction of Flora and Fauna	84	21
6.	Lack of Sanitation	20	5
7.	Narrow Road	200	50
8.	Police Protection	92	23
9.	Garbage/Litter/Pollution	274	68.6
10.	Others	68	17

Source: Field Survey, 2014.

From Table 5.22, it is clear that the highest proportion 274 (68.6%) of respondents perceived the occurrence of environmental impacts by way of garbage/litter/pollution. Similarly, other major environmental impacts pointed out by respondents were deforestation/distribution of fauna 84 (21%), erosion of trekking trails/bridges 141 (35.2%), lack of campsite with degradation of scenic appeal 99 (24.8%). However, some trekkers and mountaineers also observed that the tourism would generate Positive impacts like measure of hold pollution 54 (35.2%), cleanliness 51 (33.3%) maintenance of scenic landscape 78 (19.6%) and better protection 92 (23%).

377 (94.2%) trekkers and mountaineers accepted the economic impact of tourism in study area and 9 (5.8%) respondents rejected the impacts of tourism in Sikkim.

Null Hypothesis (H_0): There is no economic impact of tourism in Sikkim.

Table 5.23: Economic Impact of Tourism Industry in Sikkim

Sl. No.	*Response*	*Frequency*	*Per cent*
1.	Yes	377	94.2
2.	No	23	5.8
	Total	**400**	**100**

Source: Field Survey, 2014.

Conclusion

Calculated (Z) > tabulated (Z)
Hypothesis is rejected
Therefore, there is economic impact of tourism in study area.

An attempt has to find out the opinion of tourists regarding whether they perceive any economic impacts of tourism in the study area in Sikkim or not.

Table 5.24: Kinds of Economic Impact of Tourism Industry in Sikkim

Sl. No.	*Factors*	*Response*	*Per cent*
1.	Employment Opportunities	376	94
2.	Tax Income	80	20
3.	Foreign Exchange	23	5.75
4.	Souvenirs	40	16
5.	Improved Living Standard	123	30.75
6.	Business Opportunities	300	75
7.	Development of Infrastructure	125	31.25
8.	Others	50	12.5

Source: Field Survey, 2014.

Table 5.24 depicts that the highest 376 (94%) economic impact perceived by the tourists is on employment opportunities. Other impacts as indicated by the respondent are, local business opportunity 300 (75%), development of infrastructure 125 (31.25%), improved standard of living 123 (30.75%), souvenirs 40 (16%), foreign exchange 23 (5.75%), tax in income 80 (20%) and other 50 (12.5%) respectively.

An attempt has been made to find out the opinion of tourists regarding whether they perceive any socio-cultural impact of tourism to the inhabitant of study area. In this respect 332 (83%) respondents viewed that there might be economic impacts of tourism to the inhabitants of study area. Similarly small part 68 (17%) respondents viewed that there would be no economic impact of mountain tourism.

Table 5.25: Perceived Socio-cultural Impact of Tourism Industry in Sikkim

Sl. No.	*Response*	*Frequency*	*Per cent*
1.	Yes	332	83
2.	No	68	17
	Total	**400**	**100**

Source: Field Survey, 2014.

Null Hypothesis (H_0): There is no socio-cultural impact of mountain tourism.

Conclusion

Calculated (Z) =10.8
Tabulated (Z) =1.645
Calculated (Z) > Tabulated (Z)
Hypothesis rejected

Therefore, there is socio-cultural impact of tourism on inhabitants of Sikkim.

Table 5.26: Kinds of Socio-cultural Impact of Tourism Industry in Sikkim

Sl. No.	*Factors*	*Response*	*Per cent*
1.	Preservation of Folk Tradition	125	31.25
2.	People Begging for Money/Food	12	3
3.	Overcrowding	26	6.5
4.	Cultural Loss/Loss of Authenticity	282	70.5
5.	Change in Lifestyle	145	36.25
6.	Modernization of Facilities	167	41.75
7.	Increase in Urbanization	56	14
8.	Increase in Communication	300	75
9.	Preservation of Cultural Heritage	45	11.25
10.	Encourage Vocational Education/Knowledge	300	75
11.	Hygiene Problem	26	6.5

Source: Field Survey, 2014.

The number of respondents 125 (31.25%) perceive presentation of folk tradition followed by people begging for money or food (3%), overcrowding (6.5%), cultural loss of authenticity (70.5%), change in lifestyle/increase in western values (36.25%), modernization of facilities (41.75%), increase in urbanization (14%), increase in communication (75%), preservation of cultural monuments (11.25%), encourage education/knowledge (75%) and hygiene problem (6.5%) respectively. They are positive and negative socio-cultural impacts of tourism in study area.

Table 5.27: Garbage Management System

Sl. No.	*Factors*	*Borgodous Scale*	*Remarks*
1.	Strong Law and Effective Implementation	+600	Highly Positive
2.	Participation of Local Community	+756	Highly Positive
3.	Participation of NGO/INGO and Private Organization	+435	Highly Positive
4.	Increase more Deposit Fee for Garbage Management	+145	Neutrally Positive
5.	Public Awareness	+564	Highly Positive
6.	Others	+465	Highly Positive

Source: Field Survey, 2014.

In Table 5.27, almost all the factors of garbage management system in study area is highly Positive except increase more deposit fee for garbage management.

Table 5.28: Satisfaction Gain by Royalty/Fee by Sikkim Tourism

Response	*Frequency*	*Per cent*
Satisfactory	194	48.5
Unsatisfactory	206	51.5
Total	**400**	**100**

Source: Field Survey, 2014.

Majority of the respondents 206 (51.5%) are unsatisfactory with the present royalty fee regarding tourism in the study area and 194 (48.5%) respondent are satisfied with royalty fee.

Null Hypothesis (H_0): All the respondents are satisfied with the present royalty fee regarding Mountain tourism in Sikkim.

Conclusion

Calculated (Z) = 4.04
Tabulated (Z) =1.645
Calculated (Z) > Tabulated (Z)

So, Hypothesis is rejected. Therefore, not all the respondents are satisfied with the present royalty fee regarding tourism in the study area.

Table 5.29: No. of Skilled Persons Involved in Industry

Response	*Frequency*	*Per cent*
Skilled	194	48.5
Unskilled	206	51.5
Total	**400**	**100**

Source: Field Survey, 2014.

From Table 5.29, majority of the manpower 206 (51.5%) are not trained manpower in tourism industry of Sikkim and only (48.5%) manpower are trained in Sikkim tourism industry.

Null Hypothesis (H_0): There are trained manpower involved in tourism industry of Sikkim.

Conclusion

Calculated value of (Z) = 4.04
Tabulated (Z) = 1.645
Calculated (Z) > Tabulated (Z)

Therefore, there are no trained manpower involved in tourism industry of Sikkim.

Questionnaire for Tourism Entrepreneurs

To asses and evaluate impact, problem and prospects of tourism in the study area, and intensive interview with the travel/trekking agencies and hotels in the study area have been conducted. 100 respondents of tourism entrepreneurs, i.e. hotel and travel/trekking agencies were interviewed.

Table 5.30: Available Services of the Travel/Trade and Tourism Enterprises

Sl. No.	*Services*	*Number*	*Per cent*
1.	Guiding	86	86
2.	Tour Operating	70	70
3.	Ticketing	23	23
4.	Sightseeing	100	100
5.	Rafting	12	12
6.	Transportation	100	100
7.	Mountaineering	23	23
8.	Trekking	23	23

Source: Field Survey, 2014.

From Table 5.30, majority 86 per cent of entrepreneurs provided the guiding services. Similarly, by tour operating (70%), ticketing (23%), sightseeing (100%), rafting (12%), transportation (100%), mountaineering (23%) and trekking (23%) respectively.

Table 5.31: Types of Problem Facing by Tourism Entrepreneurs

Sl. No.	*Problems*	*Numbers*	*Per cent*
1.	Domestic Competition	50	50
2.	Foreign Competition	0	0
3.	Lack of Resources	0	0
4.	Lack of Skilled Personnel	68	68
5.	Unfavourable Government Policy	0	0
6.	Security Problem	13	13

Source: Field Survey, 2014.

Types of problems faced by tourism entrepreneurs were: unhealthy domestic competition (50%) and Lack of skilled persons are the main problems of the mountain tourism entrepreneurs contributing as 68 per cent of the total respondents. Similarly, the security situation (13%) foreign competition (0%) respectively.

Table 5.32: Performance of Your Agency in Providing Services to Consumer in Comparison to Other Agencies

Sl. No.	*Factor*	*Linker (Scale)*	*Result*
1.	The Rating of the Service Performance	—	—
2.	Satisfaction	150	Highly Positive

Source: Field Survey, 2014.

Rating the services performance of agency to customers
Highly satisfactory, satisfactory, so-so, unsatisfactory
4 3 2 1

Range 100 × 4 to 100 × 1
400 to 100
Index, 0 ± 100 neutral positive
+100 ± 200 moderately positive
+ 200 ± 400 highly positive

Table 5.33: Performance of the Travel Agent and Association of Sikkim (TASS) in Context of Tourism Promotion

Sl. No.	*Factor*	*Linker (Scale)*	*Result*
1.	Performance of the Travel Agent and Association of Sikkim (TASS) in Context of Tourism Promotion	—	—
2.	Satisfaction	400	Highly Positive

Source: Field Survey, 2014.

Conclusion

From Table 5.33, we can see that the rating performance of agencies in providing services to customers is highly positive.

Table 5.34: Satisfaction Level with the Present Tourism Products

Sl. No.	*Response*	*Number*	*Per cent*
1.	Yes	87	87
2.	No	13	13
	Total	**100**	**100**

Source: Field Survey, 2014.

Level of satisfaction from the present product
Only 13.0 per cent respondents are not satisfied (Table 5.34).

Null Hypothesis (H_0): They are satisfied with the present product.

Conclusion

Tabulated value (Z) = 1.645
Calculated value (Z) = 7.2
Calculated value (Z) > tabulated value
So, hypothesis is rejected.

Therefore, the entrepreneurs are not satisfied with the present product.

Table 5.35: Kind of Product should be Developed as Perceived from Entrepreneurs

Sl. No.	*Response*	*Number*	*Per cent*
1.	Preserve and Promote Our Product as it is	48	48
2.	Modify Product to Suit Target Market	36	36
3.	Combine Product Features	22	22
4.	Develop New Product	66	66
5.	Others	24	24

Source: Field Survey, 2014.

From Table 5.35, shows that majority of the respondents (66%) want to be developed new products (new areas, village tourism, rural tourism and eco-tourism, etc.). Similarly (48%) respondents want to preserve and present our products as it modify products to suites target markets (36%), combine product features (22.%) and others (allow to climb more other peaks and more new trekking routes (24%) respectively.

Table 5.36: Strength of Our Present Product

Sl. No.	*Weakness*	*Total*	*Per cent*
1.	Poor Preservation	50	50
2.	Congestion	21	21
3.	No Repeat Value	28	28
4.	Lack of Competitiveness	85	85
5.	Limited Products	88	88
6.	Poor Presentation	12	12
7.	Others	35	35

Source: Field Survey, 2014.

From Table 5.36, the majority of respondents (95.5%) expressed their view that the uniqueness is the major strength of Sikkim's present tourism product. Likewise other strengths of present product viewed by respondents were competitive (44.4%) location (42.2%) price (40%), repeat value (37.%), emotional value (35.5%), access (31.1%), mass appeal (28.8%), source of achievement (34.1%) and others like trust, friendship safety and friendly people respectively.

From Table 5.37, the highest percentage of respondents (88%) expressed their view that the limited products is the major weakness

Table 5.37: Weakness of Our Present Product

Sl. No.	*Weakness*	*Total*	*Per cent*
1.	Poor Preservation	50	50
2.	Congestion	21	21
3.	No Repeat Value	28	28
4.	Lack of Competitiveness	85	85
5.	Limited Products	88	88
6.	No Mass Appeal	12	12
7.	Others	35	35

Source: Field Survey, 2014.

of Sikkim tourism, (85%) lack of competitiveness, poor presentation (50%), no repeat value (28%), (21%) on congestion (12%) on no mass appeal and others (35%) respectively.

Table 5.38: Rating the Pricing Policies of Tourism Services in Sikkim

Sl. No.	*Factor*	*Borgodous Value*	*Result*
1.	Rating the Pricing Policies	—	—
2.	Satisfaction	95	Highly Positive

Source: Field Survey, 2014.

Conclusion

From Table 5.38, the pricing strategy of tourism services are generally rated satisfactory.

Table 5.39: Level of Competition of Tourism Industry in Study Area

Sl. No.	*Factors*	*Borgodous Value*	*Result*
1.	Rating the Level of Competition of Tourism	—	—
2.	Satisfactory	(–15)	Neutrally Negative

Source: Field Survey, 2014.

Result

In an attempt to know the level of competition in tourism business in Sikkim, respondents were asked about the level of their satisfaction. Satisfaction is neutral negative. It reveals that the level of competition of tourism business in Sikkim is unsatisfactory (Table 5.39).

Table 5.40: Level of Competition of Tourism Industry—National and International

Sl. No.	Factor	Borgodous value	Result
1.	Rating the Level of Competition of Tourism in National and International Level	—	—
2.	Satisfactory	–95	Neutrally Negative

Source: Field Survey, 2014.

Conclusion

In an attempt to know the level of competition in tourism business at international level respondents were asked about the level of their satisfaction. Table 5.40 shows that the level of competition in tourism business at international level is poor.

Table 5.41: Linkage with International Level

Sl. No.	Response	Number	Per cent
1.	Yes	45	45
2.	No	55	55

Source: Field Survey, 2014.

In Sikkim mostly tourism entrepreneurs have direct linkage with the international market. The largest proportion of respondents (55%) has indicated that there is no direct linkage with the international market and only about 45 per cent viewed the direct linkage of it.

Table 5.42: Medium of Link with International Market

Sl. No.	Medium	Number	Per cent
1.	Through Words from Mouth	45	45
2.	Direct Contact	64	64
3.	Through Internet	66	66
4.	Through Travel Trade Chain	25	25

Source: Field Survey, 2014.

From Table 5.42, about 66 per cent respondents were linked the informational market through internet, words of mouth, 45 per cent, direct contact (64%) and through travel trade chain (25%) respectively.

Table 5.43: Marketing Effort by the Government

Sl. No.	*Factors*	*Borgodous Value*	*Result*
1.	Marketing Effort by Government	—	—
2.	Satisfactory	–12	Neutrally Negative

Source: Field Survey, 2014.

In an attempt to know the level of marketing efforts of government of Sikkim, respondents were asked about the level of satisfaction. From Table 5.43, the level of satisfaction is neutral Negative. This clearly showed that substantial improvement is needed in this respect.

Table 5.44: Marketing Effort by the Marketing and Advertising Agencies

Sl. No.	*Factors*	*Borgodous Value*	*Result*
1.	Marketing effort by Marketing and Advertising Agencies	—	—
2.	Satisfaction	3	Neutrally Positive

Source: Field Survey, 2014.

Conclusion

From Table 5.44, it is clearly shown that level of satisfaction from the marketing efforts of the marketing/adv. agencies is Positive neutral. So, it must be improved.

Table 5.45: Response Regarding the Government's Efforts to Promote Sikkim as a Tourist Destination

Sl. No.	*Response*	*Number*	*Per cent*
1.	Yes	45	45
2.	No	55	55
	Total	**100**	**100**

Source: Field Survey, 2014.

Shows the majority of the respondents (95.6%) viewed that the government's effort is insufficient to promote Sikkim as a tourist destination.

From Table 5.44, the respondents expressed their views that the government be initiated to promote destination by 95 per cent, followed by development of infrastructure 87 per cent, special events

Table 5.46: Effort by the Government to Improve Sikkim as a Tourist Destination

Sl. No.	*Efforts*	*Response*	*Per cent*
1.	Destination Promotion	95	95
2.	Development of Infrastructure	87	87
3.	Developed New Product	12	12
4.	Marketing /Publicity	45	45
5.	Special Events	67	67
6.	Facilitating Tourism Industry	23	23
7.	Participation in Fairs and Exhibitions	34	34

Source: Field Survey, 2014.

(67%), marketing/publicity (45%) participation in festivals (34%), and facilitating tourism industry (23%), developed new products 12 per cent respectively.

Table 5.47: Cultural/Social Impact of Tourism on the Inhabitants of Sikkim

Sl. No.	*Response*	*Number*	*Per cent*
1.	Yes	95	95
2.	No	5	5
	Total	**100**	**100**

Source: Field Survey, 2014.

Tourism entrepreneurs were enquired whether they perceive any social/cultural impacts on Sikkim's tourism to the inhabitants of study area. Regarding this, the highest proportion (95%) observed that there are social/cultural impacts of mountain tourism and 5 per cent respondents viewed that there is no effect.

From Table 5.47, it can be seen that the highest number of 95 per cent respondents perceive the social/cultural impact on mountain tourism on the inhabitants on mountain region at study area by the change in life/imitation of best preservation.

Preservation of folk tradition (56%) people begging for money or food (12%), overcrowding (45%), cultural loss/loss of authenticity (85%), preservation of art or history (44%), urbanization (76%), increased communication (80%), encourage education/knowledge (87%) and hygiene problem (34%) respectively (Table 5.48).

From Table 5.49 an attempt has been made to find out the opinion of respondents regarding whether they perceived any environmental impacts of mountain tourism to the inhabitants of mountain region of

Table 5.48: Kinds of Cultural /Social Impact of Tourism on the Inhabitants of Sikkim

Sl. No.	*Impact*	*Response*	*Per cent*
1.	Preservation of Folk /Tradition	56	56
2.	People Begging for Money or Food	12	12
3.	Overcrowing	45	45
4.	Cultural Loss /Loss of Authenticity	85	85
5.	Preservation of Arts /History	44	44
6.	Urbanization	76	76
7.	Increased Communications	80	80
8.	Encourage Education/Knowledge	87	87
9.	Hygiene	34	34

Source: Field Survey, 2014.

Table 5.49: Any Environmental Impact of Tourism in Sikkim

Sl. No.	*Response*	*Number*	*Per cent*
1.	Yes	92	92
2.	No	8	8
	Total	**100**	**100**

Source: Field Survey, 2014.

Sikkim. In this respect, the highest number (92%) of respondents viewed that there may be environmental impacts of mountain tourism to the inhabitants of mountain region at Sikkim. Similarly, a small segment of (8%) respondents viewed that there would be no environmental impacts of tourism in the study area.

Table 5.50: Kinds of Environmental Impact of Tourism in Sikkim

Sl. No.	*Impact*	*Response*	*Per cent*
1.	Degradation of Scenic Beauty	67	67
2.	Measures of Hold Population	61	61
3.	Erosion of Trekking Trails	34	34
4.	Garbage/Litter/Pollution	45	45
5.	Maintenance of Scenic Landscape	55	55
6.	Deforestation /Destruction of Flora and Fauna	87	87
7.	Disturbances of Natural Resources	95	95
8.	Better Area Protection	55	55

Source: Field Survey, 2014.

From Table 5.50, Environmental impacts as indicated by the respondents were degradation of scenic appeal (67%), measures of hold population (61%), erosion of trekking trail (34%), maintenance of scenic landscape (55%), deforestation/destruction of flora/fauna (87%), disturbances of natural sources (95%), and Better area Protection (55%) respectively.

Table 5.51: Weaknesses of Our Present Product in Study Area

Sl. No.	*Weaknesses*	*Response*	*Per cent*
1.	Poor Preservation	50	50
2.	Congestion	23	23
3.	No Repeat Value	67	67
4.	Lack of Competitiveness	65	65
5.	Limited Products	98	98
6.	Poor Presentation	80	80

Source: Field Survey, 2014.

Table 5.52: Policies to Attract more Tourists

Sl. No.	*Policies*	*Response*	*Per cent*
1.	Government Policies	90	90
2.	Pollution Control	54	54
3.	Marketing	100	100
4.	Transportation	43	43
5.	Hospitality	97	97
6.	Communication	43	43
7.	Banking System	50	50
8.	Fairs and Festivals	90	90

Source: Field Survey, 2014.

The level of importance factor to attract more trekkers and mountaineers.

Conclusion

From Table 5.52, it is clear that the factors of Government Policy, Pollution Control, Safety and security, marketing and services are the highly important factor to attract more trekkers and mountaineers in Sikkim. Banking services are not satisfactory in major mountain tourism region. The majority (50%) respondents view that the banking services are not available in mountain region in Sikkim. Only 22.2 per cent respondents accepted that banking facility are available in mountain region.

Table 5.53: Factors to Increase the Length of Stay in Study Area

Sl. No.	*Factors*	*Response*	*Per cent*
1.	Enhancement of Infrastructure	100	100
2.	Improved Safety Measures	12	12
3.	Shopping Facilities	80	80
4.	Sustainable Development (Eco-tourism)	45	45
5.	Improve the Quality of Hotels	45	45
6.	Price Limiting	10	10
7.	Emphasis on Village Tourism	67	67
8.	Explore New Product	11	11
9.	Others	38	38

Source: Field Survey, 2014.

The important factors to increase the length of stay of tourists has been shown by above figure. In this attempt it is questioned to the entrepreneurs that how can we increase the length of stay of trekkers and mountaineers. Highest portion of (100%) respondents viewed about improved Enhancement of infrastructure followed by shopping facilities (80%), Emphasis on village tourism (67%), Sustainable development (eco-tourism) and Improve the quality of hotels (45% each), and other (38%) like diversification of services and peaceful environment developing new product in route (bulgy jumping) etc. respectively (Table 5.53).

Table 5.54: Training Required for the Development of Human Resources

Sl. No.	*Area*	*Number*	*Per cent*
1.	Language	54	54
2.	Hospitality	90	90
3.	Mountaineering	34	34
4.	Tour and Trekking Guide	67	67
5.	Education and Knowledge about Tourism	78	78
6.	Others	23	23

Source: Field Survey, 2014.

Training for Required Human Resources

In this respect, the questionnaire for the entrepreneurs is that area where it is necessary for the human resource for the tourism development. The highest portion (90%) of respondents emphasize on hospitality, education and knowledge (78%), tour/trekking guide (67%), language training (54%), similarly followed by mountaineering (34%) and others 23 per cent respectively.

Table 5.55: Economic Impact of Tourism Industry in Sikkim

Response	*Frequency*	*Per cent*
Yes	94	94
No	6	6
Total	**100**	**100**

Source: Field Survey, 2014.

In response to the query of economical impacts of tourism, the total number (100%) perceive that there might be economic effect of tourism in mountain region of Sikkim.

Table 5.56: Kinds of Economic Impact of Tourism Industry in Sikkim

Sl. No.	*Factors*	*Response*	*Per cent*
1.	Employment Opportunities	100	100
2.	Tax Income	45	45
3.	Foreign Exchange	45	45
4.	Souvenirs	67	67
5.	Improved Living Standard	50	50
6.	Business Opportunities	90	90
7.	Development of Infrastructure	45	45
8.	Others	23	23

Source: Field Survey, 2014.

From Table 5.56, the highest portion (100%) of respondents perceived the occurrences of economic impacts by way of employment opportunities. Similarly, the other major economic impacts pointed out by respondents are tax income (45%), foreign exchange (45%), souvenirs (67%), improved standard of living (50%), business opportunities (90%), better infrastructure (45%) and the gap between poor and rich increase (23%) respectively.

Questionnaire for Tourism Related Persons : (Driver/Potter/ Tourist Guide and Agriculturist)

Table 5.57: Distribution of Domestic and International Tourism Related Persons in the Study Area

Sl. No.	*Tourist Visited*	*Driver*	*Potter*	*Tourist Guide*	*Agriculturist*	*Total*
1.	Domestic	45	10	36	45	136
2.	International	0	35	9	0	44
	Total	**45**	**45**	**45**	**45**	**180**

Source: Field Survey, 2014.

Total 180 tourism related persons (Driver, potter, tourist guide and agriculturist) has been surveyed. Among them 45 sample from each tourism related respondent has been surveyed to draw the conclusion (domestic and international). Among 45 drivers all were domestic, potter 10 from domestic and rest are from out of nation especially from Sikkim, tourist guide 36 domestic and rest outsider, all the agriculturists are from within the country itself (Table 5.57).

Table 5.58: Sex-wise Tourism Related Persons in the Study Area

Sl. No.	*Sex*	*Respondent*	*Percentage*
1.	Male	120	66.66
2.	Female	60	33.34
	Total	**180**	**100**

Source: Field Survey, 2014.

Table 5.58 shows that 66.6 per cent of tourism related person are male and rest are female in the study area.

Table 5.59: Marital Status of Tourism Related Persons

Sl. No.	*Marital Status*	*Respondent*	*Percentage*
1.	Married	80	44.44
2.	Unmarried	100	55.56
	Total	**180**	**100**

Source: Field Survey, 2014.

As the fact from Table 5.59, that unmarried people are more

focusing in this industry about 55.56 per cent against 44.44 per cent married. It is depicted from the facts that more young people are focusing on tourism industry.

Table 5.60: Age-wise Distribution

Sl. No.	*Age Group*	*Respondent*	*Percentage*
1.	< 30 years	123	68.33
2.	30 – 40 years	40	22.22
3.	> 40 years	17	9.45
	Total	**180**	**100**

Source: Field Survey, 2014.

Table 5.61: Academic Status

Sl. No.	*Academic Qualification*	*Respondent*	*Percentage*
1.	School Education	124	68.88
2.	Under Graduate	25	13.88
3.	Post-Graduate	16	8.89
4.	Doctoral	0	0
5.	Others	15	8.35
	Total	**180**	**100**

Source: Field Survey, 2014.

Table 5.61 shows that about 68.88 per cent people who is engaged in tourism sector comes under school education followed by 13.88 per cent under graduate, 8.89 per cent post-graduate and others got have 8.35 per cent respectively. It is a fact that most of the people are unskilled workers.

Table 5.62: Nature/Types of Work

Sl. No.	*Items*	*Respondent*	*Percentage*
1.	Regular	0	0
2.	Ad-hoc	0	0
3.	Contractual	106	58.88
4.	Own	74	41.12
	Total	**180**	**100**

Source: Field Survey, 2014.

Table 5.62 depicts that 58.88 per cent of worker are doing their jobs on contractual basis. Beside it 41.12 per cent workers are doing their own business.

Table 5.63: Nature/Types of Wages

Sl. No.	*Items*	*Respondent*	*Per cent*
1.	Monthly	100	55.55
2.	Weekly	20	11.13
3.	Daily	30	16.66
4.	Annually	0	0
5.	Self Paid	30	16.66
	Total	**180**	**100**

Source: Field Survey, 2014.

Table 5.64: Nature of Job Prior to Present Job

Sl. No.	*Items*	*Respondent*	*Per cent*
1.	Wage Labour	60	33.33
2.	Farmer	20	11.13
3.	Contractor	20	11.13
4.	Government Employee	0	0
5.	Any Other	0	0
6.	Same Job	80	44.41
	Total	**180**	**100**

Source: Field Survey, 2014.

Table 5.65: Reason for Shifting the Job

Sl. No.	*Items*	*Respondent*	*Per cent*
1.	Interest	23	12.77
2.	More Earning	106	58.88
3.	Future Scope	45	25.00
4.	Any Other	6	3.33
	Total	**180**	**100**

Source: Field Survey, 2014.

Income Analysis

Lump-sum average income of tourism related persons (drivers, potter, guide and agriculture) is ₹ 52,000 and there is no saving against them as remaining amount will be invested on festivals and other purposes.

Table 5.66: Annual Investment Expenditure of Tourism Related Persons

Sector of Investment	*Amount of Investment (₹)*
Food, House Rent and Clothing	12000
Educational Expenditure	24000
Recreations	600
Sanitations	720
Orientation Programme/Training Programme	00
Others	12000
Total	**49320**

Source: Field Survey, 2014.

References

Annual Report— 2003-04, Department of Tourism, Government of Sikkim.

Annual Report— 2004-05, Department of Tourism, Government of Sikkim.

Annual Report — 2005-06, Department of Tourism, Government of Sikkim.

Annual Report— 2006-07, Department of Tourism, Government of Sikkim.

Annual Report—2008-09, Department of Tourism, Government of Sikkim.

Annual Report — 2009-10, Department of Tourism, Government of Sikkim.

Annual Report— 2010-11, Department of Tourism, Government of Sikkim.

Annual Report — 2011-12, Department of Tourism, Government of Sikkim.

Annual Report—2012-13, Department of Tourism, Government of Sikkim.

Sinha, U.P. and Kumar, Swargesh (2011), *Bihar Tourism : Retrospect and Prospect*, New Delhi: Concept Publishing Company (P) Ltd.

UNWTO (2009), *World Tourism Barometer,* Madrid: United Nations World Tourism Organization.

UNWTO (2010) *: UNWTO World Tourism Barometer,* Vol. 8, No. 1, January 2010. Madrid: United Nations World Tourism Organization.

UNWTO (2010), United Nations World Tourism Organization, www.unwto.org/index.php

6
Economic Impact of Tourism in Rural Perspective

For almost half a century the notion has prevailed and even gained ground that tourism is an economic panacea for developing countries. It is often referred to as a "white industry", "industry without chimney", "invisible export" with the implication that it could be a viable and powerful agent for development and an ideal economic alternative to more traditional economic sectors. Tourism to a developing country has always been considered as a source of foreign exchange earnings, which are essential for economic development. The role of international tourism in generating economic benefits has long been recognized in many developing countries. Therefore, tourism as a sector of developing countries economies deserves priority on the part of the governments and the business community. The importance of tourism to the development of national economy is now widely recognized. Although, the economic significance of tourism is primarily lauded in terms of its contribution to foreign exchange earnings, it also contributes towards generating employment opportunities (around 221 million people globally), utilization of human resources and growth and development of industries and services related to tourism. It is expected that in 2015 it will be providing some 269 million jobs. The tourism industry has grown rapidly worldwide, resulting in economic and social benefits; this industry may play a vital role in enhancing a country's trade performance. With proper interventions, such economic benefits can play a crucial role in the process of poverty alleviation. In general, tourism has become a significant industry in both poor and rich economies because of its important impacts on economics, livelihoods and socio-cultural development. India currently is a developing country, but it has a glorious past and can have a glorious future too if steps are taken in the right direction. One of the sectors where this country has a great future is tourism. According to the United Nations about 25,000 people die every day of hunger or hunger-related causes, yet there is plenty of food in the world for everyone. The problem is that hungry people are trapped in severe poverty. The Millennium Declaration of the United Nations identified poverty alleviation as one of the most compelling challenges the world is facing in the twenty-first century.

Tourism is already one of the most important sources of foreign exchange earnings and job creation in many poor and developing countries. The World Tourism Organization (WTO) is convinced that the power of tourism—one of the most dynamic activities of our time—can be more effectively harnessed to address the problems of poverty more directly. International targets aim to have the number of people living in poverty (defined as living on less than $1 per day) by 2015. Poverty reduction requires strategies on a variety of complementary fronts and scales, but a prerequisite of significant progress is pro-poor growth which benefits the poor. Tourism can be one source of such growth. To meet this objective, the UNWTO has concerned with advancing the development of the world's poorest countries, agreed in June 2002 to join efforts to implement a new framework to assist developing countries and LDCs in poverty reduction through tourism. The project, called ST-EP (Sustainable Tourism-Eliminating Poverty) seeks to refocus an intensive Sustainable Tourism—social, economic, and ecological—to make it a primary tool for Eliminating Poverty in the world's poor countries. The World Tourism Organization defines sustainable tourism in the following manner: "Sustainable tourism development meets the needs of present tourists and host regions while protecting and enhancing opportunities for the future". The study had investigated the benefits and use of "Pro-Poor Tourism" (PPT) as a mechanism for economic development in developing countries, especially in India. Pro-Poor Tourism (PPT) is tourism that results in increased net benefits for poor people. PPT is not a specific product or niche sector, but an approach to tourism development and management. It enhances the linkages between tourism businesses and poor people; so that tourism's contribution to poverty reduction is increased and poor people are able to participate more effectively in product development.

Links with many different types of "the poor" need to be suppliers, operators of micro-tourism businesses, craft-makers, other users of tourism infrastructure (roads) and resources (water), etc., there are many types of pro-poor tourism strategies, ranging from increasing local employment to building mechanisms for consultation. Any type of company can be involved in pro-poor tourism—a small lodge, an urban hotel, a tour operation in infrastructure developer. The critical factor is not the type of company or the type of tourism, but that an increase in the net benefits that go to poor people can be demonstrated.

The confluence of tourism and poverty, previously two separate domains, reflects an essential change in the philosophy of tourism development and poverty alleviation, which is illustrated by Figure 6.1. Traditionally, regional economic growth is predominantly set as the premier target of local tourism development, while poverty alleviation is either considered a sub-goal or a natural outcome of regional economic growth. In contrast, contemporary approaches, for example, pro-poor tourism and ST-EP, aim to establish a direct link

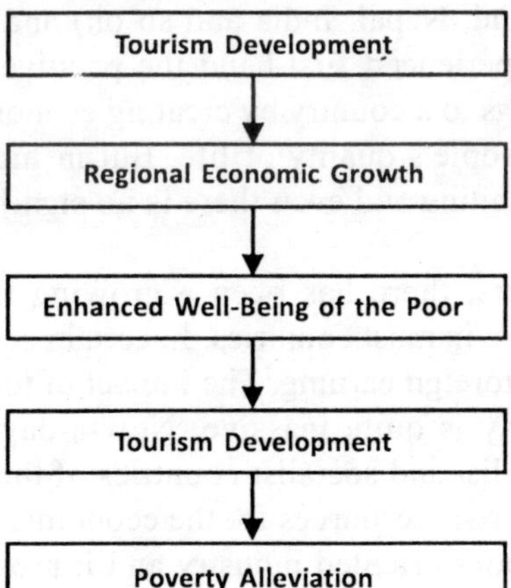

Fig.6.1: Philosophy of Tourism Development and Poverty Alleviation.

between tourism and poverty alleviation and emphasize the voices and needs of the poor in tourism development.

A change in the philosophy regarding tourism and poverty alleviation in contemporary approaches, the poor become the focus of concern; whether they can reap net benefits from tourism now is the primary criterion to justify any tourism-based development initiative. Such a new philosophy is believed to greatly enhance the chance of the poor to benefit from tourism.

This study had attempted to investigate the role of tourism in poverty alleviation. It is undeniable fact that mainstream tourism has contributed positively to national foreign earnings. India is a country which has many tourist attractions. These include archeological sites and monuments, resorts, hill tracts, the world's longest unbroken sea beach, the largest terracotta temple and historical and modern cities. For a lover of sports and outdoor activities, India offers opportunities for angling, water skiing, river cruising, rowing, surfing, etc. The country is rich in wildlife and game birds.

Poverty alleviation through tourism has been practiced by developing countries since the 1960s. There is growing recognition worldwide of the essential role tourism can play in reducing poverty and promoting sustainable development, especially in developing economies. Several Governments (Vietnam, Laos, Philippines, Africa, Sri Lanka, Thailand, Nepal, India and so on) and international aid agencies have experienced first-hand the positive impacts tourism development brings to a country by creating economic opportunities which improve people's quality of life. But in India still there is a lack of proper planning and even there is no significant research on it.

In recent years, there has been a growing realization of the potential of tourism in most countries. In certain countries tourism is the single largest foreign earning. The impact of tourism on the host country's economy is quite massive. Now-a-days developed and developing, capitalist and socialist countries of the world are trying to exploit their tourism resources for the economic development and growth. It is a labour-oriented industry and it provides many times more employment than any other manufacturing industry. Invested capital in adventure tourism in term gives employment in hundreds of different ways in hotels, restaurants, boarding, gift shops, transports companies and other utility centres. The employment generation capacity of adventure tourism increases in marginal areas, which are isolated and economically underdeveloped.

Tourism is a very useful means of earning much needed foreign currency and positive effect on the balance of payment. Many areas are characterized by fragile economies. This fragility is derived from various factors including overdependence on single industry, weak competitive firms and being remote far suppliers and markets. An important area of investigation concerning the role of tourism in the development of such areas—particularly from a policy perspective is the identification of types of tourism development that are most beneficial to local economies, particularly in generating sustainable income and employment.

A widely used technique for identifying the economic impact of tourist spending on income and employment is input-output analysis (I-O) which enables the estimation of income and employment multiplier effects of tourist spending can be divided into direct, indirect, and induced effect (Economic Multiplier).

From Tables 5.21, 5.22, 5.53 and 5.54, it becomes clear that 94.2 per cent tourist and 100 per cent tourism entrepreneurs viewed that there is economic impact of tourism in Sikkim. In our context, we summarize the economic impact of tourism in Sikkim as follows:

- The income of the local people continuously increasing.
- The government is earning hard currency and its balance of payment is improving.
- It creates jobs for hoteliers, travel/trekking agents, guide, porter etc.
- Some of the snow covered peaks, barren land-mass and stretches of water bodies are being utilized for economic gains.
- The economic activities of entire region are diversified.
- Multiplier effect is giving momentum to the economy.
- The existing infrastructure is improving and new infrastructure is coming up.
- Local art, craft, souvenir, handicraft and other small and cottage industries are developing.
- It starts improving the standard of living of the local.
- Tourism check the drainage of workforce towards plains and other cities.
- It is giving opportunities to the local people to become entrepreneurs by penetrating into travel and tourism business, adopt regular employment habits, and work for the thing they want.
- It is mobilizing the funds for regional development.

To address the above problems, time series data have been employed. The data on national income aggregates which represents Gross Domestic Product (GDP) were obtained from the published national income accounts and labour market statistic, Economic Survey of India, Ministry of Tourism, Government of India etc. The study has been decided to investigate more deeply sustainable tourism and pro-poor tourism and to establish economic benefit as a form of tourism which can produce direct benefits to the local people. Tourism has the potential of directly contributing to poverty reduction through creation of employment opportunities for local people and markets for products made locally in rural areas. The data related with tourism sectors, Total Tourist Arrival (TTA), Total Earning from Tourism (EFT), Foreign Exchange Earnings (FEE), Employment Generation through Tourism (EGT) and Economic Multiplier (EM) were compiled from various issues.

Before empirical tests are carried out, it is plausible to say about the data problems associated with the estimation of tourism on role of tourism for poverty eradication process. Either some data are available in Indian fiscal plan or in some areas tourism is a recent phenomenon. Along with the absence of quarterly series on GDP data, the national figures from expenditure side are available for 2006-2007 only.

In this study, nominal GDP were converted into real term by using implicit GDP deflator has been used. To examine the foreign earning through tourism termed as FEE effect and Economic Multiplier has been used to explain employment and income earning. The model as applied in this section are given below:

GDP Measurement Method

The simple model as applied in this study is in linear form and can formulate the following simplified version of the linear model as:

$$GDP_t = a_t + a_2 \, EFT \quad (1)$$

where, it is expected that $a_2 > 0$, EFT is total earning from tourism.

Similarly, the same model is being applied for the data relating to the constant price by deflating with the deflator used by Government of India. The model is expressed as:

$$GDP_t = a_t + a_2 \, EFT_t \quad (2)$$

where, a_2 is to be greater than zero.

Table 6.1: Share of Tourism Sector in India in GDP of the Nation and Share of GDP from Tourism Sector in Sikkim

Year	*Total Share of Tourism in GDP (%)*	*Total Share of Tourism in GDP (%) of Sikkim*
2002-05	5.83	20.00
2006-10	5.90	43.00
2011-13	6.58	69.00

Source: Ministry of Tourism, Government of India; Annual Report 2002-2013, Government of Sikkim.

Table 6.2: India's Share in World Arrivals and Sikkim's Share in Indian Arrivals

Year	*Arrivals India (Million)*	*Sikkim's Share in India's Arrivals (Million)*
2009	2.38	0.9
2010	2.73	0.95
2011	3.46	0.1
2012	3.96	0.11
2013	4.51	0.16

Source: Ministry of Tourism, Government of India; Annual Report 2009-2013, Government of Sikkim.

Total Contribution of India's Tourism Industry to GDP

Visitor exports are compared with exports of all goods and services, Domestic Travel and Tourism spending is compared with GDP Government individual Travel and Tourism, spending is compared with total government spending, Internal Travel and Tourism consumption is compared with total internal consumption (i.e. total domestic spending plus total export), Leisure Travel and Tourism contribution to GDP is compared with total GDP Business, Travel and Tourism contribution to GDP is compared with total GDP Travel and Tourism capital and investment spending is compared with all fixed investment spending.

Following are the few benefits ensured by the tourism industry in India in order to boost up the GDP of India:

- The Indian tourism industry offers online booking system, one of the basic proofs of technological advancement in this sector. These online bookings are applicable for booking the air tickets *via* Internet by logging on to the website and also booking the hotel room of the place to be visited.

Table 6.3: Tourism Industry—Total Contribution to GDP in India

Years	*GDP Share (%)*	*Marginal GDP (%)*
2003	8.8	—
2004	8.7	–1.14
2005	7.0	–19.54
2006	7.1	1.43
2007	7.2	1.41
2008	7.2	—
2009	6.7	–6.94
2010	6.5	–2.99
2011	6.6	1.54
2012	6.5	–1.54
2013	6.6	1.54
2014	6.8	3.31

Source: National Income Accounting and Statistics, 2014-15.

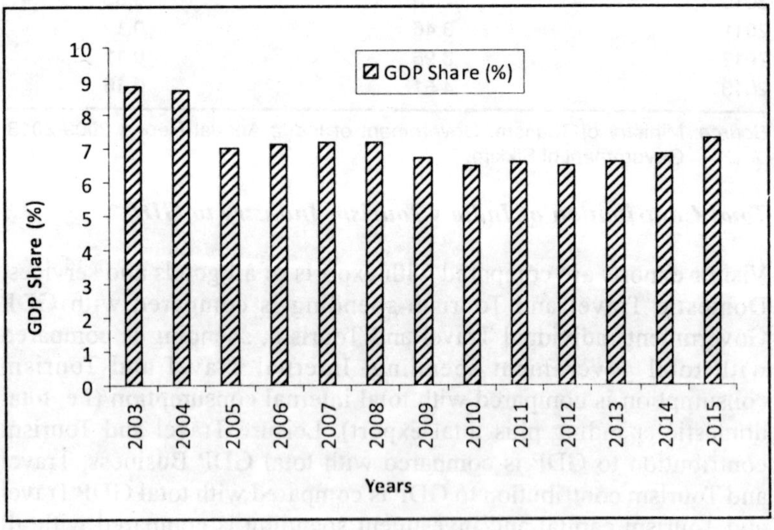

Fig. 6.2: Tourism Industry—Total Contribution to GDP in India.

- The online tourism industry has accounted for a turnover of US$ 800 million which is apparently 14 per cent of the entire travel and tourism industry.
- The Role of Tourism Industry in India GDP also features medical tourism that includes traditional therapies like *Yoga*, meditation, Ayurveda, allopathy and other conventional

systems of medicines is currently estimated at US$ 333 million and is most likely to reach US$ 2.2 billion by the year 2012.

International Tourism Receipts

In 2000, the receipts registered for international tourism amounted to over US$ 1 billion per year in 59 countries and territories out of approximately 200.

- The United States is unchallenged leader with US$ 82 billion in international tourism receipts in 2000. The United States has been able to maintain its first rank since a long time. However, the amount of receipts fluctuated each year such as US$ 82 billion in 2000, US$ 110 billion in 2012 and again declined to US$ 94 billion in 2013.
- Three important Mediterranean destinations Spain, France and Italy—had been holding 2nd, 3rd and 4th rank respectively from 2000 to 2013. However, international tourism receipts of Spain ranged from US$ 32 billion in 2000 to US$ 62 billion in 2012 and declined to US$ 53 billion in 2013. The same pattern of growth is discernible in the case of France and Italy also.
- The growth of international tourism receipts of China is highly encouraging. It increased from US$ 16 billion in 2000 to US$ 41 billion in 2012. China took 5th position from United Kingdom, which was also eclipsed by Germany. The United Kingdom suffered substantial decline. On the other hand, the tourism income of Turkey increased from US$ 8 billion in 2000 to US$ 21 billion in 2013. The growth was by 300 per cent (Table 6.4).
- Germany, the United States, the United Kingdom, China and France top with spending ranging from US$ 39 billion to US$ 81 billion in 2013. They are followed by Italy, Japan, Canada, Russia and Netherlands respectively. Each of these countries spent between US$ 21 billion to US$ 28 billion in 2013.
- The first, the second and the third rank of Germany, United States and the United Kingdom respectively remained

Table 6.4: Top Ten World's Tourism Earners (Receipts)

Rank							*Country*	*International Tourism Receipts (in billion)*						
2000	*2006*	*2011*	*2012*	*2013*	*2014*	*2015*		*2000*	*2006*	*2011*	*2012*	*2013*	*2014*	*2015*
1st	1st	1st	1st	1st	1st	1st	United States	82.2	85.8	97.1	110.0	93.9	92.9	89.9
2nd	2nd	2nd	2nd	2nd	2nd	2nd	Spain	31.5	51.1	57.6	61.6	53.2	52.2	51.2
3rd	3rd	3rd	3rd	3rd	3rd	3rd	France	30.8	46.3	54.3	55.6	49.4	46.4	45.4
4th	4th	4th	4th	4th	4th	4th	Italy	27.5	38.1	42.7	45.7	40.2	39.2	37.2
7th	6th	6th	5th	5th	5th	5th	China	16.2	33.9	37.2	40.8	39.7	34.7	33.7
6th	7th	7th	6th	6th	6th	7th	Germany	18.5	32.8	36.0	40.0	34.7	29.7	25.7
5th	5th	5th	7th	7th	7th	6th	United Kingdom	19.5	34.6	38.6	36.0	30.0	29.0	26.0
9th	8th	8th	8th	8th	8th	8th	Australia	8.4	17.8	22.3	24.8	25.0	24.0	23.0
10th	9th	10th	9th	9th	9th	10th	Turkey	7.6	16.9	18.5	22.0	21.3	18.3	13.3
8th	10th	9th	10th	10th	10th	9th	Austria	9.9	16.6	18.9	21.6	19.4	15.4	14.4

Source: World Tourism Organization (WTO).

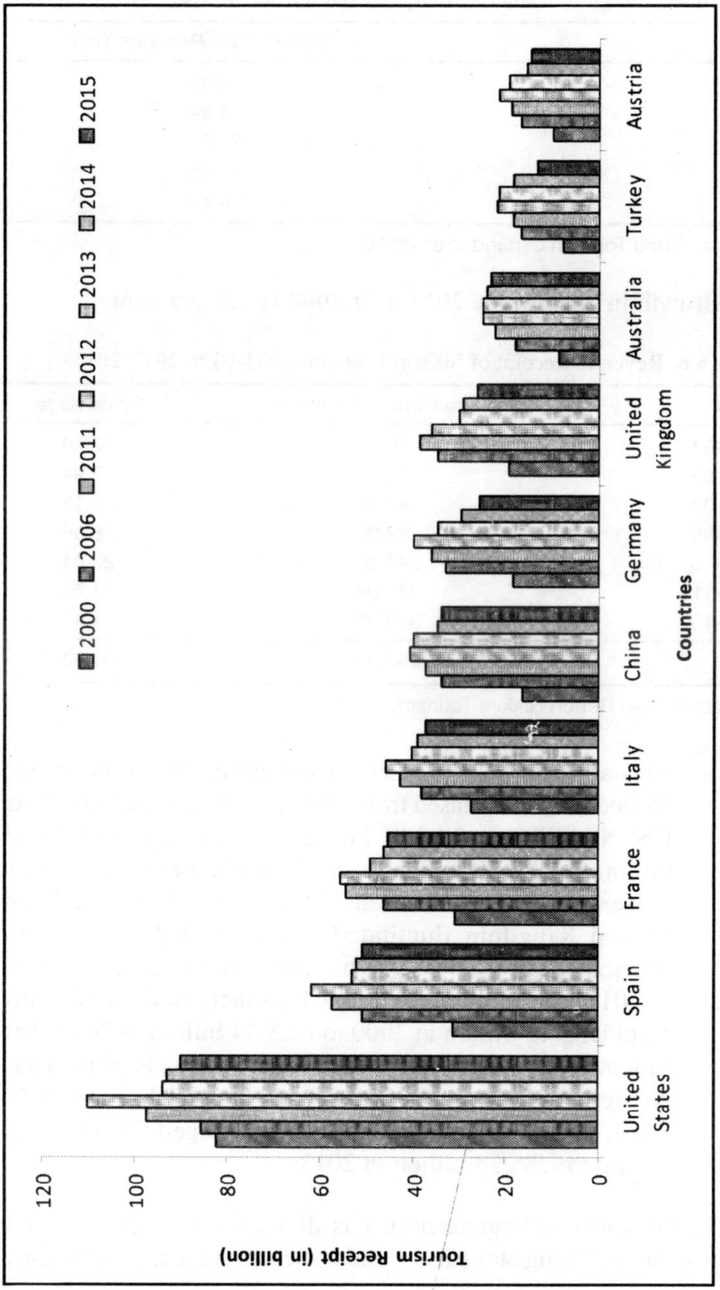

Fig. 6.3: International Tourism Receipt (in billion).

Table 6.5: Foreign Exchange Earnings by India from Tourism

Years	*% Change Over Previous Year*
2002	–3.09
2010	19.99
2011	35.00
2012	21.06
2013	25.23

Source: World Tourism Organization (WTO).

Growth in one decade 2013 over 2002 is 122 per cent.

Table 6.6: Revenue Receipt of Sikkim Tourism (2003-04 to 2012-2013)

Years	*Annual Income (Lakhs)*	*Percentage*
2003-04	70.69	7.40
2004-05	75.80	7.94
2006-07	87.38	9.15
2007-08	82.00	8.58
2009-10	227.00	23.81
2010-11	111.04	11.63
2012-13	300.00	31.42
Total	**953.91**	**99.93**

Source: Annual Report Sikkim Tourism.

constant from 2006 to 2013. Expenditure by Germany and United States increased from 2000 to 2012 significantly from US$ 48 billion to US$ 91 billion for Germany and US$ 65 billion to US$ 80 billion for USA. But expenditure of both these countries declined in 2013. Expenditure made by United Kingdom fluctuated largely and declined over previous years from US$ 71 billion in 2011 to US$ 50 billion in 2013. Expenditure done by China increased significantly from US$ 13 billion in 2000 to US$ 44 billion in 2013. The rankings of other countries such as Italy, Canada, Russia and Netherlands remained virtually unchanged from 2006 to 2013. The expenditure made by them ranged from US$ 21 billion to US$ 28 billion in 2013.

World Tourism Organization has divided the world into five regions for analyzing statistical trends, such as Africa, Middle East,

Table 6.7: Top Ten World's Tourism Spenders

Rank					*Country*	*International Tourism Expenditure (billion)*				
2000	*2006*	*2011*	*2012*	*2013*		*2000*	*2006*	*2011*	*2012*	*2013*
2nd	1st	1st	1st	1st	Germany	47.6	73.9	83.1	91.0	81.2
1st	2nd	2nd	2nd	2nd	United States	64.5	72.1	76.4	79.7	73.2
3rd	3rd	3rd	3rd	3rd	United Kingdom	36.3	63.1	71.4	68.5	50.3
7th	7th	5th	5th	4th	China	13.1	24.3	29.8	36.2	43.7
5th	4th	4th	4th	5th	France	17.8	31.2	36.8	41.4	38.5
6th	6th	6th	6th	6th	Italy	15.7	23.1	27.3	30.8	27.9
4th	5th	7th	7th	7th	Japan	31.9	26.9	26.5	27.9	25.1
8th	8th	8th	8th	8th	Canada	12.1	20.6	24.7	27.2	24.2
10th	9th	9th	9th	9th	Russia	—	18.1	21.2	23.8	20.8
9th	10th	10th	10th	10th	Netherlands	12.2	17.1	19.1	21.7	20.7

Source: World Tourism Organization (WTO).

Americas, Asia and the Pacific and Europe. Each region is sub-divided into sub-divisions. Table 6.8 shows regional share of international tourist arrivals (1950-2013). The data reveals that percentage share of Asia and the Pacific has increased tremendously from 0.8 per cent in 1950 to 34.6 per cent in 2013. The Asia and the Pacific is followed by Middle East and Africa respectively. The percentage share of Europe and Americas have declined significantly. The percentage share of Europe has decreased from 64.9 per cent in 1950 to 64.0 per cent in 2013. Similarly, the percentage share of Americas has declined from 29.3 per cent in 1950 to 25.7 per cent in 2013.

Table 6.8 : Regional Share of International Tourist Arrivals

Region	*Share of Regions (%) (1950-2013)*							
Periods	*1950*	*1960*	*1970*	*1980*	*1990*	*2000*	*2010*	*2013*
Africa	1.9	1.2	1.4	2.6	3.3	4.2	4.35	6.2
Americas	29.3	24.1	25.5	22.4	20.3	18.7	18.25	25.7
Asia and the Pacific	0.8	1.3	3.7	8.5	12.8	16.8	20.02	34.6
Europe	64.9	72.2	72.2	63.9	61.5	56.9	50.78	64.0
Middle East	0.8	0.9	0.9	2.6	2.2	3.5	5.87	6.8
World	**25.9**	**69.3**	**69.3**	**278.2**	**445.8**	**685.5**	**880**	**991.9**

Source: United Nations World Tourism Organization.

Similarly, Table 6.9 reveals the regional share of international tourism receipts (1950-2010). The data reveals that percentage share of tourism receipts of Asia and the Pacific increased very significantly between 1950 and 2010, which was from 0.9 per cent to 23.0 per

Table 6.9: Regional Share of International Tourism Receipt, 1950-2010 (World Receipts in US$ billion)

Region	*Share of Regions (%)*						
Periods	*1950*	*1960*	*1970*	*1980*	*1990*	*2000*	*2010*
Africa	4.8	2.9	2.8	2.4	2.1	2.2	4.9
Americas	52.4	36.2	26.8	23.8	25.4	27.5	45.3
Asia and the Pacific	0.9	2.9	6.7	10.6	17.2	18.7	23.0
Europe	42.9	56.5	61.5	59.8	53.4	48.4	67.5
Middle East	1.4	1.4	2.2	3.3	2.1	2.8	8.9
World	**2.1**	**6.9**	**17.9**	**106.5**	**272.7**	**476.4**	**675.0**

Source: United Nations World Tourism Organization.

cent. Percentage share of tourism receipts of the Middle East increased very insignificantly. Similarly, percentage share of tourism receipts of Europe also increased from 42.9 per cent in 1950 to 67.5 per cent in 2013. On the other hand, the percentage share of tourism receipt of Americas decreased very tremendously. The percentage share of tourism receipts declined from 52.9 per cent to 45.32 per cent in 2010. Similarly, percentage of tourism receipts of Africa also decreased during same period. The decrease was from 4.8 per cent in 1950 to 4.9 per cent in 2010.

- The latest scenario of region-wise growth of tourism is quite encouraging. The recent trend is that all regions posted growth in international tourist arrivals, but emerging economies remain the main driver of this recovery. This multi-speed recovery—lower in advanced economies (+5%) faster in emerging ones (+8%) is a reflection of the broader global economic situation.
- Asia (+13%) was the first region to recover and the strongest growing region in 2010. International tourist arrivals into Asia reached a new record at 204 million last year (2010), up from 181 million in 2009. Africa (+6%) to 49 million, the only region to show positive figure in 2009, maintained growth during 2010, benefitting from increasing economic dynamism and hosting of events such as the FIFA CUP in South Africa. Results returned to double digits in the Middle East (+14% to 60 million) where almost all destinations grew by +10 per cent or more.
- In Europe (+3% to 471 million) recovery was slower than in other regions due to the air traffic disruption caused by the eruption of the Eyja Falla Jokull volcano (Iceland) and the economic uncertainty affecting the Euro zone.
- The Americas (+8% to 151 million) rebounded from the decline in 2009 brought on by the economic hardship suffered in North America and the impact of the influenza (H1-N1) outbreak. The return to growth in the US economy has helped improve the region's results as a whole as did the increasing regional integration in Central and South America and the vitality of Latin American economics. The growth was strongest in South America (+10%).

Balance of Payment Effects

Tourism is one of the world's largest international industries. As such, it has a noticeable impact on the balance of payments of many nations. We have heard much about the balance-of-payments problems of the India in general and State of Sikkim in particular, and, indeed, tourism imports do affect the balance of payments and economic conditions generally. We define tourism imports as those expenditures made by Indian tourists in foreign countries. Our balance-of-payments situation directly affects the gross national product of the India (F). The formula is:

$$Y = C + I + G + (X - M)$$

where

Y = gross national product
C = consumer expenditures
I = investments
G = government expenditures
X = exports
M = imports

By looking at the formula, we çan see that if imports (M) exceed exports (X), then the difference ($X - M$) will be a negative number, and Y will thus be smaller. Thus, it is advantageous to us in our Indian economy to attract more visitors spending in the India. These "tourism exports" are like credits and help our economy. It is economically better to have foreign visitors come to the India than it is to have Indian citizen's travel abroad. However, this should be tempered with the realization that the situation is not entirely positive or negative.

Expenditures by Indian tourists abroad make possible purchasing power in foreign countries for those countries to buy Indian made products. For example, most airlines of the world use Indian made equipment. Purchase of these aircraft, parts, supplies, repair services, and so forth makes an important contribution to the export trade of the India; thus, we cannot charge the Indian international traveller with a total negative balance of payments. The purpose of the foregoing discussion is simply to point out the relationships.

Tourism exports become very desirable as far as the gross national product and the prosperity of the country are concerned. Efforts on the part of national tourism offices to attract foreign visitors have a great impact on the balance-of-payments situation. Business firms that serve the foreign visitor, provide desired services, and stimulate sales materially help our national economy. However, during periods when the Indian rupee is high against foreign currencies, a dampening effect occurs on our tourism exports because this situation is seen as unfavourable by prospective foreign visitors. Conversely, if the dollar is low, more foreign tourists will visit the India. This increases our tourism exports, improves our balance-of-payments, and raises the gross national product. These same relationships of comparable currency values exist between any country that exports tourism and the countries of its tourists' origin.

For example, in 1998, the value of the Canadian dollar was low in comparison to the U.S. dollar and illustrated this principle. The number of Americans visiting Canada to take advantage of the exchange rate increased dramatically. This contributed positively to Canada's balance-of-payments.

Investment Stimulation

The tourism industry has a unique structure. It is characterized by and, in fact, is an agglomeration of a large number of very small units, covering a variety of different service trades—the small restaurants, motels, guest houses, laundries, arts and crafts shops, and others. Thus, investment in infrastructure and sometimes expensive superstructure by the government stimulates investment in numerous smaller businesses. Because of the small size of these businesses, capital requirements are relatively low and investment generally proceeds at a rapid pace. In this respect, too, governments view tourism rather favourably. The initial investment in tourism brings forth a large investment in supporting and tertiary industries. This also includes large investments in major hotels, restaurants, shopping centres, marinas, airports, and so on.

Tourism Increases Tax Revenue

Tourists must pay taxes like most other people. Because they come from other regions or countries, their expenditures represent an increased tax base for the host government. In addition to the usual sales tax, tourists sometimes pay taxes in less direct ways. Airport taxes, exit fees, customs duty, and charges assessed for granting visas are just a few examples of commonly used methods of taxing tourists. The wisdom of imposing such special taxes on tourists is questionable, because it merely serves to reduce demand. In some countries, for instance, the room rate at a hotel can be different for tourists (generally higher) than for residents. This is a questionable practice, because it leaves the tourist with a feeling that he has been "taken". Apart from these special cases, the usual taxes collected from both tourist and residents increase because of tourism expenditures.

Is tourism, then, a panacea for all the economic woes of a region or country? It has been claimed that tourism increases incomes, employment, investment, tax revenues, and so forth, so it might indeed appear to be one. However, constraints limit the extent to which governments can maximize the benefit from these aspects of tourism. These constraints are of two types: social and economic. The social constraints have already been discussed. The economic constraints are in the form of potential economic costs that the tourism industry may impose. These merit further scrutiny to gain a better understanding of the government's optimization problem.

Inflationary Pressure

Tourists inject money (earned elsewhere) into the destination economy. While this increases the income of the region (as discussed earlier), it also might cause inflationary pressures. Tourists typically have a higher expenditure capability than the residents do—either because tourists have higher incomes or because they have saved for the trip and are inclined to "splurge" while on vacation. Hence, they are able to somewhat bid up the prices of such commodities as food, transportation and arts and crafts. This causes inflationary pressures, which can be detrimental to the economic welfare of residents of the host community. This is particularly true when inflation affects the prices of essentials such as food, clothing, transportation and housing. Land prices have been known to escalate rapidly in tourist destination areas. The prices that foreigners are willing to pay for "vacation homes" in the area can decrease the demand for "first homes" by residents.

Lundberg notes that as the tourist industry develops in an area, land prices rise sharply. In a particular underdeveloped area, the amount of investment in land constituted just 1 per cent of the total investment for a hotel project. By contrast, this ratio increased to 20 per cent in an area where tourism was overdeveloped. With such increases in land prices, it can be expected that local residents (with their lower incomes) are effectively "chased out" of the housing market in a tourism-developing section.

Economic Multipliers

Direct Effect

In addition to the direct impact of tourism expenditures on an area, there are also indirect impacts. The indirect or multiplier impact comes into play as visitor spending circulates and re-circulates. The direct effects are the easiest to understand because they result from the visitor spending money in tourist enterprises and providing a living for the owners and managers and creating jobs for employees.

Indirect Effect

This visitor expenditure gives rise to an income that, in turn, leads to a chain of expenditure-income-expenditure, and so on, until leakages bring the chain to a halt. Consequently, the impact of the initial income derived from the tourist's expenditure is usually greater than the initial income, because subsequent rounds of spending are related to it. For example, a skier purchases a lift ticket for ₹ 40. This money received by the ski area will be used to pay the wages of the lift operators. The lift operator spends the money on groceries; the grocer uses the money to pay part of his rent to the local landlady; the landlady uses it to pay for her dry cleaning; the dry cleaner spends it in a restaurant for a dinner; the restaurant owner spends it for steaks shipped in from Kansas City; and the cycle stops as the money is lost to the local economy. This last transaction is known as leakage ham the economy. The combination of the direct and indirect effects of an expenditure pattern determine the impact. In a typical situation, not all of the income generated in each round of expenditure is represent. Some portion tends to be saved, and some portion tends to be spent outside the local economy. The greater the proportion of income spent locally, the greater will be the multiplier.

The degree to which a local area is able to retain tourist income depends on how self-sufficient the local economy is. If the local economy is able to produce the goods and services tourists buy, the greater will be the multiplier effect. The more goods that have to be imported from outside the region, the smaller the multiplier will be.

From the discussion, it is clear that when a tourist's spending injects funds into the economy of a host area, an economic effect occurs that is a specified number of times what was originally spent. Initially, this effect is thought of as an income multiplier, as tourist expenditures become income directly and indirectly to local people.

However, there are additional economic phenomena. Increased spending necessitates more jobs, which results in an employment multiplier. Because money changes hands a number of times during a year, there is a transactions multiplier. This is of particular interest to governmental tax officials where sales taxes are imposed. As business grows in a tourist destination area, more infrastructure and superstructure are constructed. This results in a capital multiplier. Examples are provided here of how an employment multiplier and an income multiplier were determined.

Employment Multiplier

The employment multiplier varies from region to region depending on its economic base. In a study entitled 'Recreation as an Industry', by Robert R. Nathan Associates, county employment multipliers calculated for the Appalachian region provide a good illustration of what typical multipliers are and how they work.

The multipliers estimated in this study were based on county employment data. They represent the approximate measure of the direct and indirect employment associated with each addition of direct employment to the export sector of a county. Multipliers were estimated for 375 counties and three independent cities. The smallest multiplier was 1.13, and the highest was 2.63. Thus, the county with the smallest multiplier value would provide other employment opportunities for approximately 0.13 person for each person directly employed in servicing export demand, and the county with the highest multiplier value would provide other employment opportunities for approximately 1.63 persons for each person directly employed in servicing export demand. In general, county employment multiplies vary directly with the population or total employment size of the counties. As county population size grows, so does the multiplier value. This relationship is as might be expected, insofar as import leakages would tend to be less where diversity of occupations is greater, and diversity is positively associated with county population or total employment.

Income Multiplier

Jobs mean income, which stimulates the economy of the area in which the development occurs. How much stimulation occurs depends on several factors. The management of a hotel, for example, takes two actions with the revenue earned: It spends parts of the money on goods and services, and it saves part of such funds. Economists refer to such actions as marginal propensity to consume (MPC) and marginal propensity to save (MPS), removing funds from the local economy. Such removal of these marginal (extra) funds can be made in two ways: (1) they can be saved and not loaned to another spender, or (2) they can be used to purchase imports. In either case, so doing removes the funds and thus does not stimulate the local economy.

Economic research is needed in a tourist destination area to determine what these income relationships are. If the results of such economic research were made available, many beneficial results might be possible. For example, governmental bodies might be more inclined to appropriate additional funds for tourism promotion to their areas if they knew more about the income that was generated by tourist expenditures. Also, improved and added developments of facilities to serve tourists might be more forthcoming if prospective investors could have more factual data upon which to base decisions.

To understand the multiplier, we must first make some approximation as to what portion of the tourist rupees received in a community is spent (consumed) and what portion is saved (leakage). The findings shows that, the total tourist spending in a community on an average per day is ₹ 1,000 and that there MPC was about ½, and the expenditure pattern go through seven transactions per day in the tourist destination. The other formula for the multiplier is $1/MPS$. This is a simpler formula, because it is the reciprocal of the marginal propensity to save.

$$\text{Multiplier} = \frac{1}{1 - MPC}$$

So, in order to calculate multiplier, we have:

M = marginal (extra)
P = propensity (inclination)
C = consume (spending, MPC)
S = savings (money out of circulation, MPS)

Average daily consumption expenditure of tourist in study area is ₹ 1,000 of tourist expenditure and an MPC of ½. Then,

Rs. 1,000.00	
+	
Rs. 500.00	½ × 1,000
+	
250.00	(½)2 × 1,000
+	
125.00	(½)3 × 1,000
+	
62.50	(½)4 × 1,000
+	
31.25	(½)5 × 1,000
+	
15.63	(½)6 × 1,000
+	
7.81	(½)7 × 1,000

₹ 2000.00 (approx.)

Thus, the original ₹ 1,000 of tourist expenditure becomes ₹ 2,000 of income to the community.

"LEAKAGE"

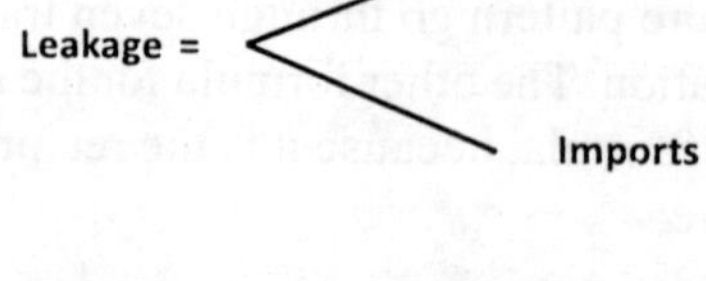

where,

Savings = not loaned to another spender
Imports = spending on tourism needs in sources outside country (state)

$$\text{Multiply} : \frac{1}{MPS}$$

Leakage, as defined, is a combination of savings and imports. If we spend the money outside our country for imports, obviously it does not stimulate the economy locally. If it is put into some form of savings that are not loaned to another spender within a year, it has the same effect as imports—not stimulating the economy. Thus, to get the maximum benefits economically from tourist expenditures, we should introduce as much of the tourist funds as possible into the local economy for goods and services rather than save the proceeds or buy a large amount of imports.

Here, also, more economic research is needed. Some studies have indicated that the multiplier might be as high as 3 in some areas, but economic research in other localities indicates that it may be more typically lower than this.

Employment

The World Travel and Tourism Council estimates that in 2005 employment in the travel and tourism economy was 22,15,68,000 jobs or 8.3 per cent of total employment, which is 1 in every 12.0 jobs. By 2015, this should grow to 26,95,56,000 jobs, 8.9 per cent of total employment or 1 in every 11.2 jobs. The 74,223,000 travel and tourism industry jobs accounted for 2.8 per cent of total employment in 2005 and are forecast to rise to 8,55,21,000 jobs or 2.8 per cent of the total by 2015.

Tourism provides both direct and indirect employment. Firms such as hotels, restaurants, airlines, cruise lines, and resorts provide direct employment because their employees are in contact with tourists and provide the tourist experience. Employees of firms providing goods and services to the direct employment firms, such as aircraft manufacturers, construction firms, and restaurant suppliers, create indirect employment.

The impact of this can be illustrated using a United States example. In 2003, the TLA published its annual study, Tourism Works for America, which contains employment estimates. Table 6.10, which illustrates employment by sector, shows that in 2002, travel and tourism directly generated nearly 7.2 million jobs in the U.S. economy.

Table 6.10: Direct Travel-Generated Employment by Industry Category, 2002 (Employees in thousands) World Wide

Items	*2002*	*Per cent of Total*	*Per cent Change from 2001*
Public Transportation	990.4	15.8	–8.9
Auto Transportation	251.8	4.0	–1.8
Lodging	1,165.1	18.6	–4.0
Food Service	2,340.9	37.5	–1.4
Entertainment/Recreation	987.1	15.8	–4.6
General Retail	331.7	5.3	–3.4
Travel Planning	183.3	2.9	–12.8
Total	**6,255.8**	**100.0**	**–4.1**
Generated by International visitors	908.9	—	–5.0
Grand Total	**7,164.7**		**–4.2**

Note: Data on employment generated by international visitor spending not available by category.

Source: Travel Industry Association of America, and Office of Travel and Tourism Industries.

Travellers in the United States produce secondary impacts over and above that of their original expenditures. These secondary outputs (sales) and earnings (wage and salary income) supported by this "indirect" and "induced" spending add an additional 9.7 million jobs to the U.S. economy. With the almost 6.3 million jobs in 2002 generated directly by domestic travel spending, and the 9,00,000 employment opportunities generated by international travel to the United States, total U.S. employment created by the travel and tourism industry was 16.9 million in 2002.

The complexity of accurately measuring the vast economic impacts of the tourism industry has created a movement to link tourism expenditure accounting with that used for the national system of accounting in most countries. Earlier attempts to include tourism in the Standard Industry Classification (SIC) codes proved unsuccessful because of the diversity and overlapping nature of many tourism expenditures. In order to overcome these difficulties, a system of tourism satellite accounting has been proposed and implemented.

The employment multiplier varies from region to region depending on its economic base. The multiplier estimates in this study were based on country employment data. They represent the approximate measure of the direct and indirect employment associated with each addition of direct employment to the export sector of a country. Multipliers were estimated for 375 countries and the study area. The smallest multiplier value was 1.13, the highest was 2.63. Thus, the country with the smallest multiplier value would provide

Table 6.11: Employment Generation through Tourism in India

Years	*Total Employment in Tourism Sector (million)*
2002	38.6
2003	41.8
2004	44.7
2005	47.8
2006	51.1
2007	52.8
2008	61.8
2009	65.6
2010	56.1
2011	59.6
2012	60.0
2013	69.6
2014	70.4
2015	71.6

Source: Ministry of Tourism, Government of India.

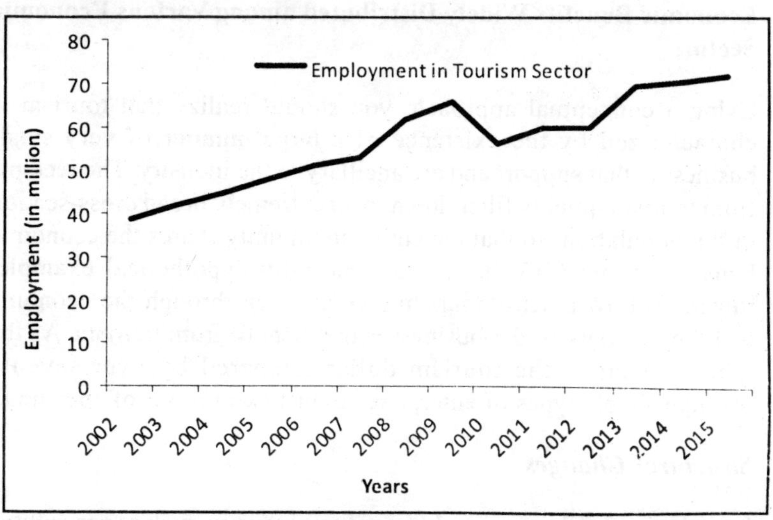

Fig. 6.4: Employment Generation through Tourism in India.

other employment opportunities for approximately 0.13 person for each person directly employed in serving export demand, and the country with the highest multiplier value provide other employment opportunities for approximately 1.63 persons for each person directly employed in serving export demand. In general, country employment multiplier varies directly with the population or total employment size of the country. Tables 6.11 & 6.12 represents the total employment through tourism sectors in India.

Table 6.12: Employment Generation by Tourism Sector in Sikkim, 2010-2013

Items	*No. of Local Employees (%)*	*No. of Non-local Employees (%)*	*No. of Trained Employees (%)*	*No. of Un-trained Employees (%)*
Hotels	52.20	47.8	65.11	34.89
Restaurants	19.54	52.2	—	—
Travel Agents	90.00	10.00	57.90	42.10

Note: Sikkim tourism industry has provide employment opportunities for almost 20 per cent of his population. No any official document has been made so far by the Sikkim Tourism, Government of Sikkim regarding employment provided by tourism sector Sikkim.

Source: Annual Report, Sikkim Tourism and Field Survey, 2014.

Economic Benefits Widely Distributed among Various Economic Sectors

Using a conceptual approach, you should realize that tourism is characterized by the existence of a large number of very small businesses that support and are ancillary to the industry. The receipts from tourism quickly filter down to an extremely broad cross-section of the population, so that the entire community shares the economic benefits. Table 6.13, based on a partially hypothetical example, illustrates how quickly tourism receipts seep through the economy and the diversity of the businesses that benefit from tourism. As the table indicates, the tourism dollar is shared by over seventy distinguishable types of enterprises in just two rounds of spending.

Structural Changes

In countries that primarily rely on a single industry, such as agriculture, the introduction of tourism has often led to a decrease in the

Table 6.13: Distribution of Tourism Expenditures

Visitors Spend for	*Travel Industry Spends for*	*Ultimate Beneficiaries*	
Lodging	Wages and Salaries	Accountants	Government
Food	Tips, Gratuities	Advertising and Public Relations	Education
Beverages	Payroll Taxes	Appliance Stores	Health
Entertainment	Commissions	Architects	Roads and Railroads
Clothing, etc.	Music and entertainment	Arts and Crafts producers	Utilities
Gifts and souvenirs	Administrative and general expenses	Attorneys	Development and others
Photography	Legal and professional services	Automobile agencies	Greengrocers
Personal care	Purchases of food, Beverages, etc.	Bakers	Grocery stores
Drugs and cosmetics	Purchases of goods sold	Banks	Financiers
Internal transportation	Purchases of materials and supplies	Beach accessories	Furniture stores
Tours and sight-seeing	Repairs and maintenance	Butchers	Importers
Miscellaneous	Advertising, promotion, and publicity	Carpenters	Insurance agencies
	Utilities — Electricity, Gas, Water, etc.	Cashiers	Landlords
	Transportation	Charities	Laundries
	Licenses	Chemists	Manufacturing agents
	Insurance premiums	Clerks	Managers
	Rental of premises and equipment	Clothing Stores	Motion picture theaters
	Interest and principal payments of borrowed funds	Clubs	Newspapers, radio etc.
	Income and other taxes	Confectioners	Night clubs
	Replacement of capital assets	Contractors	Office equipment suppliers
	Return to investors	Cooks	Painters
		Cultural organizations	Pastoralists
		Dairies	Plumbers
		Dentists	Porters
		Departmental stores	Printers, sign painters
		Doctors	Publishers
		Dry cleaning establishments	Real estate brokers and developers
		Electricians	Resorts
		Engineers	Restaurants
		Farmers	Room maids
		Fishermen	Shareholders
		Freight forwarders	Sporting events
		Garages and auto repairs	Transportation
		Gardeners	Travel brokers
		Gas stations	Taxi, limo services
		Gift shops	Unions
			Wholesale Establishments

Source: Pannell Kerr Forster and Belt Collins and Associates.

agricultural base of the country. Agriculture is an extremely low productivity industry in the developing countries. The promise of much higher wages in the tourism industry draws people away from farming. Agricultural output declines as a result, just when the demand for food increases because of the influx of tourists. The inflationary pressure on food prices is further aggravated and can lead to considerable social upheaval. In the mid-1970s, some Caribbean countries experienced a wave of protests and even direct attacks on tourists, as the resident population expressed its dissatisfaction over rising prices.

Another major implication of the structural change is that instead of diversifying its economic base, the country's tourism sector merely "cannibalizes" its other major economic sector. Diversity is the foundation of economic stability. When one sector (or industry) experiences a slump, another sector booms, thus reducing the probability of a severe depression and, indeed, reducing its impact if a depression does occur. Thus, tourism, instead of diversifying an economy, sometimes replaces agriculture as a "subsistence" sector.

Dependence on Tourism

Permitting tourism to become the subsistence industry is not desirable for a number of reasons. First, tourism is by its very nature subject to considerable seasonality. While seasonal fluctuations in demand can sometimes be reduced, they cannot be eliminated. Thus, when tourism is the primary industry in an area, the off-season periods inevitably result in serious unemployment problems. Such areas find that the seasonal character of tourism leaves severe economic and social effects on the host region.

Another very important reason relates to the source of demand for tourism. The demand for tourism depends largely on the income and the tastes of tourist, both of which are beyond the control of the host region. When the American economy goes through a slump, demand for travel to a foreign destination by Americans will fall off. A destination area can do precious little, in this case, to increase the level of demand. If the tastes of the people in the tourist-generating area change—that is, they decide to travel to a new destination—tourism in the old area will decline, causing economic and social problems. Again, the destination can do little or nothing to avoid this. In fact, as plug points out, there is reason to believe that such a decline in an area's popularity may be largely inevitable. Quite clearly then, tourism should not be allowed to grow to an extent that the destination area becomes totally dependent on it.

In other words, total dependence on a single industrial sector is undesirable. If it cannot be avoided, then dependence on domestic agriculture is in many ways preferable to dependence on tourism. The country has presumably adapted itself economically and socially to dependence on agriculture over several centuries. The demand for agricultural output is also unlikely to suffer from a secular decline, because people must eat. Also, it is the residents, not foreigners as in tourism, who directly benefit from agricultural production.

Investment Priorities

Sometimes, governments of developing countries take an overly optimistic view of tourism. They undertake aggressive investment programmes to develop tourism, assigning it top priority in their development plans. In extreme cases, such an approach can lead to the neglect of more fundamental investment needs of the country. For example, funds can be channelized into tourism development at the cost of education, health, and other social services—aspects of the social well-being of the population that should be of primary concern for a developing country. Not only is undue glamorization of tourism unwise because it usurps this position, but such a strategy only speeds up the process of dependence on tourism, which, as discussed earlier, is itself undesirable. Moreover, investment in tourism at the cost of health and education programmes also slows down the rate at which the local population is assimilated into the modern market economy of the country. Under certain circumstances, it may actually retard development rather than enhance it.

The conclusion is that although tourism has tremendous potential as a tool in economic development, it is no panacea. Governments should attempt to optimize (not maximize) the benefits that tourism provides, being ever mindful of the costs that it can impose. It should be noted also that the probability and the intensity of the economic costs of tourism are greater for developing nations (or regions) than for wealthy ones. Wealthy nations, by definition, possess robust economies that can more easily absorb the cost of tourism. Typically, such economies are well diversified, and government investment programmes are not so central to development efforts.

The social benefits and costs of tourism should be viewed similarly. While the host community seeks to maximize the benefits, it must weigh these against the social costs. The social costs are likewise higher in both probability and magnitude when tourism is being considered for development in an area that still possesses a traditional social structure.

Quantity Demanded and Price Elasticity

For some products, even a large change in price over a certain range of the demand curve results in only a small change in quantity demanded. In this case, demand is not very responsive to price. For other products, or for the same product over a different range of prices, a relatively small change in price elicits a much larger relative change in quantity demanded. Demand can be classified as inelastic or elastic on the basis of the relative responsiveness of quantity demanded to changes in price. Specifically, price elasticity of demand may be defined as the percentage change in demand resulting from a given percentage change in price. Most tourism products are price elastic. During 1992, when U.S. airlines began offering half fares, the number of air travellers increased to record-high levels.

Income Elasticity of Demand

As income rises, more travel is demanded at any given price. Thus, the relationship between income and demand is positive. The responsiveness of demand to changes in income is called 'income elasticity of demand'. It is defined as the percentage change in quantity demanded in response to a given percentage change in income, price remaining unchanged.

Table 6.14: Relationships Between Price Elasticity and Total Revenue (TR)

	Elastic Demand	*Unitary Elasticity*	*Inelastic Demand*
Price Rises	TR Falls	No Change	TR Rises
Price Falls	TR Rises	No Change	TR Falls

More Advanced Economic Concepts Related to Tourism

As can be seen from the beginning of this chapter, tourism makes a major economic contribution to the world economy. Despite this economic significance, tourism managers have for some time been met with complaints such as "All types about tourism's contribution to economic growth and job creation is a gross exaggeration". As well, members of the industry itself want to be sure that the economic impact figures are indeed accurate so that they can better plan their investments and improve their productivity and performance.

In an attempt to ensure the accuracy and reliability of the measures of tourism's economic impact, the World Tourism Organization (WTO) in collaboration with the World Travel and Tourism Council (WTTC), and with the support of the Canadian Tourism Commission (CTC), have undertaken to develop a tourism accounting system that is not only rigorous, but consistent with the national accounts of every country. This system has been named Tourism Satellite Account.

Tourism Satellite Account

A Tourism Satellite Account (TSA) is a system developed by the United Nations to measure the size of economic sectors that are not defined as industries in national accounts. Tourism, for example, is an amalgam of industries such as transportation, accommodation, food and beverage services, recreation, and entertainment and travel agencies.

Tourism is a unique phenomenon as it is defined by the consumption of the visitor. Visitors buy goods and services associated with both tourism and non-tourism alike. The key from a measurement standpoint is to associate their purchases to the total supply of these goods and services within a country.

The TSA is a new statistical instrument designed to measure these goods and services according to international standards of concepts, classifications, and definitions that will allow for valid comparisons with other industries and eventually from country to country and between groups of countries. Such measures will also be comparable with other internationally recognized economic statistics.

In addition, a TSA possesses the following characteristics:

- It provides credible data on the impact of tourism and the associated employment.
- It is a standard framework for organizing statistical data on tourism.

- It is a new international standard endorsed by the U.N. Statistical Commission.
- It is a powerful instrument for designing economic policies related to tourism development.
- It provides data on tourism's impact on a nation's balance of payments.
- It provides information on tourism human resource characteristics.

While it may be obvious, it is useful to stress why a TSA is needed. In brief, there is an acute shortage of information on the increasing role of tourism in national economies worldwide, hence the need for reliable data relative to the importance and magnitude of tourism, using the same concepts, definitions, and measurement approaches as other industries. With the TSA, governments, entrepreneurs, and citizens will be better equipped for designing public policies and business strategies for tourism and for evaluating their effectiveness and efficiency.

Development of a TSA framework has been fueled by the recognition that its implementation will serve to increase and improve knowledge of tourism's importance relative to overall economic activity in a given country. It will also provide instrument for designing more efficient policies relating to tourism and its employment aspects; and it will create awareness among the various players directly and indirectly involved with tourism of the economic importance of this activity and by extending its role in all the industries involved in the production of goods and services demanded by visitors.

The Nature of a TSA

A TSA is characterized by the manner in which it seeks to balance measures of tourism demand *versus* supply. Tourism measurements, in order to be credible and comparable with other industries in a country's economy, must follow concept and definitions consistent with internationally accepted macro-economic guidelines, such as the System of National Accounts.

The fundamental structure of the TSA therefore relies on the balance existing within an economy between, on one hand, the demand for goods and services generated by visitors and by other consumers and, on the other hand, the overall supply of these goods and services.

The idea is to analyze in detail all aspects of demand for goods and services that are associated with tourism within the economy, and to measure the relationship with the supply of such goods and services within the same economy. More specifically, a TSA measures:

- ➢ Tourism's contribution to Gross Domestic Product (GDP).
- ➢ Tourism's ranking compared to other economic sectors.
- ➢ The number of jobs created by tourism in an economy.
- ➢ The amount of tourism investment.
- ➢ Tax revenues generated by tourism industries.
- ➢ Tourism consumption.
- ➢ Tourism's impact on a nation's balance-of-payments.
- ➢ Characteristics of tourism human resources.

Because of its comprehensive nature, a TSA provides decision-makers with a valuable tool for planning and policy-making. In particular, it provides them with reliable data of tourism's impact on the economy and employment. As well, it permits the measurement of both domestic and non-resident tourism—and the employment associated with each. A TSA, however, can do much more. Following are some examples:

- A TSA can provide information on how much tourism is worth to the national economy, and how it compares to other industries and other countries. By demonstrating and using the size of tourism, tourism officials and private-sector businesses will have more influence on policy-makers at all levels of government. As well, it can make clear which industries benefit from tourism and by how much—in particular, industries not traditionally associated with tourism. For instance, business enterprises can identify the role tourism plays in their success and develop business strategies accordingly.
- A TSA is able to provide information regarding how much tax revenue is generated by tourism. This information is useful in convincing municipal, provincial, or federal levels of government to invest further in tourism.
- In addition, it provides data on visitor demand and how this demand is met by domestic supply. A TSA enables the establishment of a tourism economic impact model, which can be used to estimate the effect on the economy and on

employment of various tourism expenditure shocks. Such an impact model provides a better understanding of tourism employment and where each industry ranks compared to other tourism industries.

It should be emphasized that the ongoing development of TSAs as national promotion tools has been a process dating back to at least 1993. The most recent focus of this development was a major international TSA conference held in Vancouver, Canada, in 2001. This and other conferences have brought together the following organizations: World Tourism Organization (WTO), World Travel and Tourism Council (WTTC), Organization for Economic Cooperation and Development (OECD), United Nations (UN), Eurostat, and a number of government statistical agencies, national tourism administrators, and central banks.

The above collaboration demonstrates the general principle that in order to develop a national TSA, it is essential to involve a number of key actors within a country. The most significant of these are:

- National statistical offices, National Tourism Administrations (NTAs), central banks, and associations of national tourism enterprises.
- Information-producing units such as tourism enterprises and establishments, and other public departments.
- Users of the tourism information that is generated, the NTAs themselves, the units responsible for preparing the national accounts and the balance-of-payments, and others.
- The participation and collaboration of tourism enterprises and, more specifically, their corresponding national associations.

Tourism is one of the world's largest international industries. As such, it has a noticeable impact on balance-of-payment on many nations. We have heard much about the balance-of-payment problems of the India indeed, tourism imports do affect the Balance-of-payments and economic conditions generally. Tourism exports become very desirable as far as gross domestic product and the prosperity of the country are concerned. Efforts on the part of national tourism offices to attract foreign visitors have a great impact on the balance-of-payments situation. Business firms that serve the foreign visitor, provide desired service, and stimulate sales materially help our national economy. The increases in our tourism exports, improves our balance-of-payments and raises the gross domestic product. The main determinants of balance-of-payment through tourism are impact on foreign exchange earnings, increase in tax revenue, entry fee, per capita income etc.

This study mainly investigated the role of tourism in poverty alleviation in India in general and Sikkim in particular. The purpose of this study was to find out the contribution of the tourism in poverty alleviation in India and Sikkim, prove the belief that tourism is important to reduce the poverty rate in the developing world. From the outcome of the study it is very clear that tourism is the suitability tool for poverty alleviation and sustainable development. Several economic activities are practiced in the areas of the study area. But basically, tourism related activities are commonly practiced in the study areas. Specially, people mostly are related with tourism related activities. However, taking into account that all area are of rural setting, there is also significant participation in agricultural sector both farming and livestock in Sikkim. The people of the study areas do supply tourist related products such as tour guide, handicrafts, supply and sale of agricultural products. The main objective of this study was to analyze the direct and indirect livelihood impacts from tourism and their implications for poverty alleviation. The sector can be a very important part for the economic growth and poverty reduction in India. The study intended to investigate the benefits and cost as well of the tourism on the society in general and on the poor in particular. And there was another objective to analyze critically the pro-poor and its implications for sustainability. In order to achieve those objectives, the secondary data has been collected from various sources related to generation of foreign exchange earnings and employment, incomes, accessibility to assets and basic needs and their effects on the poor and the linkages of the tourism to the local economy. In the whole study both qualitative and quantitative information collected was subsequently used in the analysis of the data. Tourism is contributing to the national economy of India though the contribution is not so much through employment generation, foreign exchange earnings and public revenues. Especially, it has significant impact on the poverty reduction in the study area. However, the new tourism policy and regulation should be made immediately.

Tourism is an important economic activity in the areas of study particularly in activities such as tour operation, grocery shops and handicraft sales. However, agricultural activities are also practiced as study area people are fully depending on the tourism and other related field of activities. Tourism is significant on both direct and indirect employment opportunities. Directly, it is observed that there was substantial employment generation in hotels, restaurant, photo studios, and market and also in handicrafts industry. It is expected to support directly to increase in gross domestic product. In this study, GDP contribution through tourism has been taken as the main indicator for reducing the poverty. So, GDP has been quite alarming since the past few decades. Tourism industry has contributed enormously in the flourishing graph of India's economy by attracting a huge number of both foreign and domestic tourists travelling for professional as well as holiday purpose. The tourism industry in India witnessed a stupendous growth in 2006. The growth in the inflows in India's tourism industry is calculated both in terms of business and vacations. The number of foreign tourists arriving from all-over the world rose from 0.37 per cent to 0.53 per cent as has been stated by UN World Tourism Organization (UNWTO) in the year 2006. This remarkable growth in the graph of tourism industry in India popularized the entire South Asia as one of the most spectacular tourist terminal. Indian tourism industry contributes to around 5.9 per cent of the country's GDP and it provides employment to around 41.8 million of inhabitants. Some of the most significant features of India's tourism industry or the Role of Tourism Industry in India for alleviating poverty have been listed below:

- The percentage of foreign tourists in India has increased by 12.4 per cent in one year, that is, from 2006 to 2007. In 2006, Indian tourist industry witnessed a growth of 14.3 per cent, which reached around 3.89 million in 2007.
- The foreign tourists arrival led to a robust growth in the foreign exchange earnings that increased from US$ 5.03 billion during January-October 2006 to US$ 6.32 billion during January-October 2007, which is apparently a 25.6 per cent rise.
- Deeming the growing rate of the tourists arrival in the country, the Indian tourism industry designed a wide spectrum of holiday packages and cheaper airfares to attract more tourists.

- Nonetheless, the outgoing graph of tourism industry in India is in no way lagging behind from the inbound one. People travelling from India to abroad or states within India have increased by 25 per cent.
- The United Nations World Tourism Organization (UNWTO) has estimated the outgoing tourists to reach around 50 million by the year 2020.
- According to the European Travel Commission, the average expenditure per trip of Indian tourists travelling abroad has increased from US$ 611 in 2000 to US$ 822 in 2006.
- The booming success of Indian tourism industry has led to a drastic change in the hospitality department as well. The increase in the ratio of tourists resulted in the increase of room rates and also setting up of a wide range of hotels and other residing areas.
- A number of international hotels such as the Hilton, Accor, Marriott International, Berggruen Hotels, Cabana Hotels, Premier Travel Inn (PTI) and Inter Continental Hotels groups have professed about making some large-scale investments to append 65,000 additional rooms to suffice the needs.
- India is most likely to set-up forty hotels of global brands by 2011. The hospitality segment in India is assumed to reach US$ 11.41 billion in the coming two years.

The concept of "poverty alleviation through tourism" is very natural and meaningful in India. The concept should be included in tourism master plan. It has a huge opportunity to develop new products which can directly or indirectly alleviate poverty in India and to help to achieve millennium development goal where the first issue is poverty reduction. But it requires extensive preparations with a huge financial back-up for achieving this goal. For being successful in this industry, it may take some time. Government should take this very seriously and also to follow other countries project on same issues. On the other hand, an awareness campaign for pro-poor/sustainable tourism in Sikkim is also needed badly. Step-by-step, the seed of pro-poor/sustainable tourism concept will give birth to a sense of urgency, and consequently the tourism campaign across the country will be forceful and evocative. The principal motivation for a business or region to serve tourists are generally economic. An individual business is interested primarily in its own revenues and costs, while a community or region is concerned with tourism's overall contribution to the economy, as well as its social, fiscal and environmental impacts. A good understanding of tourism's economic impacts is therefore, important for the tourism industry, government officials, and the community as a whole.

References

Annual Report of Sikkim Tourism, 2002-2013.

Ashley, C.; Goodwin, H. and Roe, D. (2001): *Pro-poor Tourism Briefing No. 1*. Overseas Development Institute, April.

Ashley, C. and Jones, B. (2001) : *Joint Ventures between Communities and Tourism Investors*.

Ashley, C.; Roe, D. and Goodwin, H. (2001a): *Pro-Poor Tourism Strategies: Expanding Opportunities for the Poor*, Overseas Development Institute.

Ashley, C.; Roe, D. and Goodwin, H. (2001b): *Pro-Poor Tourism Strategies: Making Tourism Work for the Poor*, Overseas Development Institute.

Ashley, C. and Haysom, G. (2006): From Philanthropy to a Different Way of doing Business: Strategies and Challenges in Integrating Pro-poor Approaches into Tourism Business, *Development Southern Africa*, Vol. 2, No. 2, June.

Blamey, R.K. (1995): The Nature of Ecotourism, Occasional Paper No. 21, *Bureau of Tourism Research*, Australia.

Bolwell, D. & Weinz, W. (2008): Reducing poverty through tourism, International Labour Office, *ILO Sectoral Activities Programme*, Geneva, p. 22.

China National Tourism Administration (CNTA) (2003): *The Plan for the Investment in Western Regional Tourism*, Beijing: CNTA.

Crouch; Sunny Crouch, Matthew Housden (2003): *Marketing Research for Managers: The Marketing Series*; Chartered Institute of Marketing, Butterworth-Heinemann, p. 19.

Denzin, Norman K. and Lincoln, Yvonna S. (Eds.). (2005): *The Sage Handbook of Qualitative Research* (3rd ed.). Thousand Oaks, CA: Sage Publications.

Developing Asian Countries, *ESCAP Tourism Review*, No. 8, pp. 11-16, New York.

Dimoska, T. (2008): FACTA UNIVERSITATIS, *Economics and Organization*, Vol. 5.

Sinha, U.P. and Kumar, Swargesh (2011): *Bihar Tourism : Retrospect & Prospect*, New Delhi: Concept Publishing Company (P) Ltd.

7
Tourism Prospects

Future Potential of the Tourism

Tourism is a powerful economic force providing employment, foreign exchange, income, and tax revenue. The generators of economic impact for a city, a state, a province, a country, or a destination area are visitors, their expenditures, and the multiplier effect. The economic impact of tourism spending is a function of the numbers of domestic and international visitors and their expenditures. Because of the economic importance of tourism, the World Tourism Organization (WTO) maintains statistics by region and country on tourism arrivals (visitors) and both tourism expenditures (what a country spends) and receipts (what a country receives from visitor expenditures). Tourism destinations are becoming increasingly competitive as more and more destinations look at tourism to become the new economic generator replacing declining activity in agriculture, mining, and manufacturing.

The economic impact of tourism was dramatically demonstrated by the events of September 11, 2001. As a consequence of pervasive anxiety caused by these events, people cut back on their travel; economic forecasts were put on hold; airline, lodging, tour operators, and travel agent revenue declined; and widespread layoffs occurred throughout the industry. We realized very directly and in a personal manner the real economic impact of tourism. However, over the long-run, it is believed that travel will recover and the 2020 forecasts will be realized.

Negative factors such as the Iraq conflict, terrorism, SARS, and a weak economy made 2003 another difficult year for international tourism. SARS brought the steady growth of Asia and the Pacific to an abrupt halt in April and May, and while tourists quickly started to return after the virus was contained, the region could not make-up the losses in the remainder of the year. The war and the economy dampened tourism demand in other key regions. According to WTO preliminary results, the total number of international arrivals reached 991.69 million in 2013, a increase of 8.6 per cent from 2002.

Europe is the main tourist receiving region, followed by Asia and the Pacific, and the Americas. In 2013, Europe accounted for almost 58 per cent of the arrivals. Asia and the Pacific 17.2 per cent, and the Americas 16.2 per cent respectively.

International arrivals were most impacted by the unexpected drop of 12 million (–9.3%) in Asia and the Pacific due to the SARS panic. The Americas recorded a decrease of 2.5 million (–2.5%), while Europe was basically flat recording an increase of 0.4 per cent. The Middle East and Africa were the surprise regions in 2013 as they recorded healthy increases in tourism arrivals of 10 per cent and 5 per cent respectively.

Expectations for 2004 and Beyond

Prospects for 2005 and the future appear to be very positive as short-term data confirm the upward trend in arrivals that started in late-2003. Asia and the Pacific showing a strong rebound from 2003. United States international arrivals are recording monthly double-digit increases. Business travel is showing signs of recovery. Low-cost airlines are continuing to increase their capacity and expand their coverage. As expected, 2014 saw a return to growth in the travel industry with a record 1000 million international arrivals for a 10 per cent increase over 2003. However, rising oil prices are a major concern.

Tourism 2020 Vision is the World Tourism Organization's long-term forecast and assessment of the development of tourism through the first twenty years of the new millennium. An essential outcome of Tourism 2020 Vision are quantitative forecasts covering a 25-year period, with 1995 as the base year and forecasts for 2000, 2010 and 2020.

WTO's Tourism 2020 Vision forecasts that international arrivals are expected to reach over 1.56 billion by the year 2020. Of these worldwide arrivals in 2020, 1.18 billion will be intra-regional and 377 million will be long-haul travellers.

The total tourist arrivals by region shows that by 2020 the top three receiving regions will be Europe (717 million tourists), East Asia and the Pacific (397 million), and the Americas (282 million), followed by Africa, the Middle East, and South Asia.

East Asia and the Pacific, South Asia, the Middle East, and Africa are forecasted to record growth at rates of over 5 per cent, compared to the world average of 4.1 per cent. The more mature regions of Europe and the Americas are anticipated to show lower-than-average growth rates.

Europe will maintain the highest share of world arrivals, although there will be a decline from 60 per cent in 1995 to 46 per cent in 2020. By 2010, the Americas will lose its number-two position to the East Asia and Pacific region, which will receive 25 per cent of world arrivals in 2020, with the Americas decreasing from 19 per cent in 1995 to 18 per cent in 2020.

Long-haul travel worldwide will grow faster, at 5.4 per cent per year over the period 1995-2020, than intraregional travel, at 3.8 per cent. Consequently, the ratio between intraregional and long-haul travel will shift from around 82:18 in 1995 to close to 76:24 in 2020.

Comparing International and Domestic Expenditures

Despite the importance of international tourism (that is, tourists travelling outside of their country of residence), for many (if not most) countries, domestic tourism (tourists travelling in their country of residence) is even more important. As shown in Table 1.2, the World Tourism Organization (WTO) estimated (based on preliminary figures) that international travel involved receipts of US$ 514.4 billion in 2003. In contrast, the World Travel and Tourism Council estimated that in 2010, both international and domestic travel together generated about US$ 3,133.2 billion. As can be seen from these estimates of the magnitude of international and domestic travel, the latter is much greater than the former. This fact surprises many people who primarily think of tourism as being exotic, international travel.

In the United States, the travel industry received $ 545.5 billion from domestic and international travellers (including international passenger fares) in 2012. Of this total international visitors spent $112.6 billion travelling in the United States for 15.3 per cent of the total. Domestic travel expenditures were $462.0 billion for 84.7 per cent of the total.

Optimization of Tourism Industry

Economics is concerned with the attainment of an optimum return from the use of scarce resources. Whether it is a person seeking psychological benefit from travel, or a business interested in providing tourists goods and services at a profit, or a host community government viewing tourism in terms of the economic benefits fits resulting from tourist expenditures, the principle is the same. Economic agents seek to allocate the limited supply of tourism resources (both physical and financial) as they seek to meet the demands of tourists. The demands are the result of their physical/ functional needs (which, as a rule are limited) and their psychological wants (which can be virtually unlimited).

As such, the problem that economics attempts to solve is how to achieve an economical optimal allocation of scarce tourism resources, when facing the constantly shifting demand (generated by physical needs and psychological wants) for these resources.

Goals

As indicated, at least three major goals can be identified in tourism:

1. Maximize the amount of psychological experience for tourists.
2. Maximize profits for firms providing goods and services to tourists.
3. Maximize the direct (primary) and indirect (secondary) benefits of tourist expenditures on a community or region.

These goals are often compatible; maximizing psychological experience creates happy clientele, which causes them to return, to spend money, and to make everyone in the industry and the region satisfied. In certain situations, they can also be incompatible. A short-run profit-maximizing goal may cause the development of facilities beyond the capacity of the site, thus leading to overuse and a decline in psychological enjoyment. Extreme emphasis on tourism as an element in economic development might have the same result. There can also be clashes between the use of resources for tourism and for other kinds of development.

Constraints

The second half of the optimizing situation is occupied by those factors that place obstacles in the way of goal attainment. We assume that it is desirable to have unlimited amounts of psychological enjoyment, profits, and local impacts. But this is not possible, because something always gets in the way. Tourism, being extremely broad and diverse, must deal with a large number of constraints. To make an analysis of relationships, it will be necessary to classify them.

Demand

Every firm providing goods and services to tourists is constrained by the demand functions of its customers. These relate quantity purchased to price, wealth, and income.

Supply of Attractive Resources

Possibly one of the most important constraints faced by the industry as a whole is the limited amount of resources available for tourist enjoyment. This is particularly true when geographic distribution of these sites is considered. Some areas are simply better attractions for tourists than others are.

Technical and Environmental Constraints

Each particular site or situation has certain technical and environmental constraints. They involve such things as the relationship between sewage effluent disposal and the environment, numbers of fish and numbers of fishermen, number of people who can walk in a given area without causing unacceptable damage number of elephants supportable on a wildlife range, impact on lions' behaviour tourists observing them from a car, number of composites possible in a given area without harming the environment, and so on.

Time Constraints

The amount of vacation time available limits what the vacationer can do. The length of the tourist season influences profitability of tourist-oriented businesses and the impact of tourist expenditures on the local economy.

Indivisibilities

Many times it is necessary to deal either with all of something or with nothing. It is not possible to fly half an airplane, even though the seats are only half filled. It may not be profitable to build a hotel under a given size. A road has to be built all the way from one point to another.

Legal Constraints

Several types of legal constraints affect tourism. Activities of the government tourist bureau might be one. Laws concerning environmental problems could be another. Zoning and building codes may influence the construction of facilities. Laws concerning contractual relations may limit activities.

Self-imposed Constraints

Conflicting goals need to be reconciled, which leads to self-imposed constraints. The conflicts may arise within a firm or among firms, government agencies, and so on, that are seeking to develop a particular area or concept.

Lack of Knowledge

Many activities are limited because little is known about particular situations. Business people are used to living with a certain amount of uncertainty, but there are inevitable limits to the amount they are willing to countenance. Ignorance influences governmental operations as well.

Limits on Supportive Resources

There are always limits to the amount of money, managerial talent, workers, construction materials, social capital, and so on. And these, in turn, limit chances to provide psychological enjoyment, take advantage of profit-making opportunities, or develop local attractions.

Many times these individual constraints interact, creating compound constraints on given activities.

Optimizing the Experience

Maximization of the tourist experience is subject to a number of constraints and is manifested in the demand function. Demand for tourist experience is peculiar in the sense that the product being purchased is not easy to identify directly and is frequently purchased sight unseen.

The tourist is particularly constrained by time and budget. To optimize the experience, it is necessary to determine the combination of destinations preferred and then the possibilities within the money and time constraints. This explains some of the popularity of package tours, where both time and cost can be known in advance. There are some exceptions. Retired persons and young people often have time but limited resources. A few people have neither constraint.

Optimizing Returns to Businesses

Because goods and services provided to tourists are really inputs to the process of producing the experience, demand for them is derived from demand for tourism as a whole. Some goods and services are complementary, and their demand is interrelated in a positive fashion. Others are substitutes and are characterized by limited area competition.

Packaged tours have the characteristic of putting all parts and services together, so they become complementary. Competition occurs among tours. Tour operators can maximize profits by selling tours of different value and costs, in order to cater to as many people as possible along the demand curve. The number of people to be accommodated can be determined from the marginal cost of the tour and the marginal revenue to be derived from a given price level.

Goods and services sold to tourists are subject to severe peaking in demand. That is, the heaviest tourist season is usually limited. During that period, demand is intense and must be met with facilities that are excess in the off-season. This means that investment necessary to provide the excess capacity must be paid for from revenues received during the peak period. During off-peak periods, only variable cost is of interest, but because demand is low, some capacity will not be utilized.

As owners of the facilities, firms are concerned with providing adequate long-run capacity and with choosing those investments that will give optimum returns. In the tourist industry, a number of interrelationships must be considered. Sometimes, low benefit-cost investments are made so that higher-yielding investments can succeed. Consequently, it is not always true that investors choose the highest-yielding opportunities.

Generally, it is considered the long-run business of the firm to remove constraints on operations. But tourism has a number of constraints to expansion. These include demand for the tourist experience and environmental constraints.

Optimizing for the Local Economy

Tourism affects a region during periods of intense investment activity and afterward when the investments are producing. The effects depend on linkages among economic units. Money spent for investment will go to construction and a few other industrial sectors. These will have links to economic units varying from households to manufacturing plants. Money spent by tourists will also be introduced through a few sectors that will also be linked to the economy.

The multiplier effects in both cases are dependent upon the strength of the linkages. The multiplier reflects the amount of new economic activity generated as basic income circulates through the economy. Some sectors have strong links to other sectors in an economy and a large multiplier effect. Others have weak links and small multipliers. It is possible to have a thriving tourist industry and abject poverty in the local populace if there are no links. For example, linkages will be strong and the income multiplier high if the year-round resorts in a particular destination area hire all local labour; buy their flowers, fruit, vegetables, and poultry products from local farmers; hire local entertainers; and buy furnishings for guest rooms from local manufacturers. Linkages would be weak if most of these goods and services were imported from another state or country.

Tourism Exports and Imports

The host region is defined loosely as a county, a state, or a nation, depending on the level at which the problem is being considered. For a county-level government, the income of the county is of primary interest. A State Government would perceive the maximization of the combined income of the entire state to be its objective, and so on.

Regardless of which definition of host region is being considered, expenditures in this area by tourists coming from another region represent injections into the area's economy.

Japanese tourists travelling to India presumably earned their income in Japan. When spending money in the India as tourists, they are "injecting" money into our economy that was not here before. As such, expenditures by foreigners in this country (for travel purposes) represent tourism exports for the India. This may be somewhat confusing because we are accustomed to thinking of something leaving the country as an export. When we export computers or cars, for example, these commodities are sent out of the India. In the example of the Japanese tourists, the tourists are coming into this country. So, how is it an export? There seems to be a contradiction in terminology. As the astute student would note, however, when tourists come into this country, they are purchasing travel experiences. When they leave, they take these experiences back with them. Thus, we have exported travel experiences, which are, after all, what tourism is all about.

In tourism exports, the flows of tourists and payments are in the same direction, whereas in commodity exports, the two flows are in opposite directions. Therein lies the confusion. However, if one were to look at the *direction of payment flow* to determine what is an export, there is no contradiction between the two cases. When payment flows into the India, something has been exported—travel experiences, for instance, or commodities. Both payment flows are in the same direction.

Career Opportunities in Tourism Sector

Every student eventually must leave the college or university campus and seek career-oriented job. This is a difficult decision-making time, often filled with doubt as to what goals or ambitions should be pursued. Coming face to face with the problem of getting a first major career-oriented job is a challenging task. You are marketing a product-yourself—and you will have to do a good job of communicating to convince a prospective employer that you have the abilities needed and that you will be an asset to the organization.

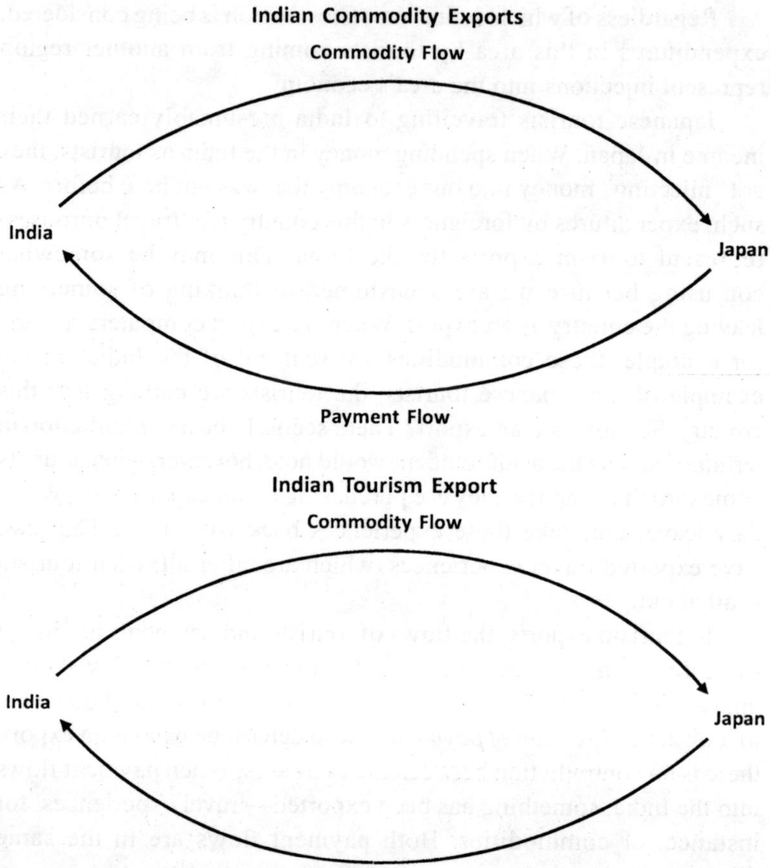

Fig. 7.1: Economic Comparison: Commodity Flows and Tourist Flows.

Job Forecasts

The World Travel and Tourism Council (WTTC) estimates that in 2005 there were over 221.5 million people worldwide, some 8.3 per cent of the total workforce, employed in jobs that exist because of the demand generated by tourism. While tourism contributes to Gross Domestic Product (GDP), capital investment, employment, foreign exchange, and export earnings, it is the job-creation capacity of tourism that is its most significant feature. By 2015, WTTC forecasts that there will be 269.5 million people around the globe having jobs created by tourism accounting for 8.9 per cent of total employment, or 1 in every 11.2 jobs.

Career Possibilities

Tourism today is one of the world's largest industries. It is made-up of many segments, the principal ones being transportation, accommodations, food service, shopping, travel arrangements, and activities for tourists, such as history, culture, adventure, sports, recreation, entertainment, and other similar activities. The businesses that provide these services require knowledgeable business managers.

Familiarity with tourism, recreation, business, and leisure equips one to pursue a career in a number of tourism-related fields. Tourism skills are critically needed, and there are many opportunities available in a multitude of fields.

Because tourism is diverse and complex and each sector has many job opportunities and career paths, it is virtually impossible to list and describe all the jobs one might consider in this large field. However, it depends on a person how interested he is in tourism.

Airlines

The airlines are a major travel industry employer, offering a host of jobs at many levels, ranging from entry level to top management, including reservation agents, flight attendants, pilots, flight engineers, aircraft mechanics, maintenance staff, baggage handlers, airline food service jobs, sales representatives, sales jobs, computer specialists, training staff, office jobs, clerical positions, ticket agents, and research jobs. Because airlines have to meet safety and other requirements, opportunities also exist with Payong International Airports. Other policy and air-safety-related jobs are available with associations such as the Air Transport Association.

Bus Companies

Bus companies require management personnel, ticket agents, sales representatives, tour representatives, hostesses information clerks, clerical positions, bus drivers, personnel people, and training employees.

Cruise Companies

The cruise industry is the fastest-growing segment of the tourism industry today. Job opportunities include those for sales representatives, clerical workers, market researchers, recreation directors, and CEOs. Because of its similarity in operations, the cruise industry has many of the same jobs as the lodging industry in Sikkim.

Railroads

Rail passenger transportation is much more developed and widespread, offering greater opportunities in Sikkim. Railroads hire managers, passenger service representatives, traffic analysts, marketing managers, sales representatives, reservation clerks, information specialists, conductors, engineers, coach and lounge car attendants, and station agents. Railroad is likely to be open for Sikkim as well. Otherwise nearest railways junction is at New Jalpaiguri.

Rental Car Companies

With increased pleasure air travel and the growth of fly/drive programmes, rental car companies are becoming an ever more important segment of the travel industry. This sector of tourism employs reservation agents, rental sales agents, clerks of various kinds, service agents, mechanics, and district and regional managers.

Hotels, Motels, and Resorts

The range of jobs in hotels and motels is extremely broad. The following list is representative: regional manager, general manager, resident manager, comptroller, accountants, management trainees, director of sales, director of convention sales, director of personnel, director of research, mail clerks, room clerks, reservation clerks, front-office manager, housekeepers, superintendent of service, bellhops, lobby porters, doormen, maids, chefs, cooks, kitchen helpers, storeroom employees, dishwashers, waiters, bartenders, apprentice waiters, heating and air-conditioning personnel, maintenance workers, engineers, electricians, plumbers, carpenters, painters, and laundry workers.

Resorts tend to have the same jobs as those mentioned for hotels and motels; however, larger resorts will have greater job opportunities and require assistants in all areas. Resorts also have a number of additional job opportunities in the areas of social events, entertainment, and recreation, such as for tennis and golf pros. At ski resorts there will be ski instructors, members of a safety patrol, and so on.

Travel Agencies

Travel agencies range from very small to very large businesses. The smaller businesses are very much like any other small business. Very few people carry out all the business operations, and jobs include secretarial, travel counselling, and managerial activities. In large offices, job opportunities are more varied and include branch manager, commercial account specialists, domestic travel counsellors, international travel counsellors, research directors, and advertising managers. Trainee group sales consultants, accountants, file clerks, sales personnel, tour planners, tour guides, reservationists, group coordinators, trainees, operations employees, administrative assistants, advertising specialists, and computer specialists are other possibilities.

Tour Companies

Tour companies offer employment opportunities in such positions as tour manager or escort, tour coordinator, tour planner, publicist, reservations specialist, accountant, sales representative, group tour specialist, incentive tour coordinator, costing specialist, hotel coordinator, office supervisor, and managerial positions. Often, a graduate will begin employment as a management trainee, working in all the departments of the company before a permanent assignment is made.

Food Service

Many job opportunities are available in Sikkim on the rapidly growing food service industry, such as headwaiters, captains, waiters and waitresses, bus persons, chefs, bartenders, restaurant managers, assistant managers, personnel directors, dieticians, menu planners, cashiers, food service supervisors, purchasing agents, butchers, beverage workers, hostesses, kitchen helpers, and dishwashers. In addition, highly trained managers having a strong background in this sector are required to oversee the development and performance of large restaurant chains.

Tourism Education

As global tourism continues to grow, the need for training and education grows. In Sikkim, many schools, colleges and universities have added travel and tourism programmes, existing programmes have expanded, vocational schools have launched programmes, trade associations have introduced education and certification programmes, and private firms have opened travel schools. There are job opportunities for administrators, teachers, professors, researchers, and support staff in Sikkim.

Tourism Research

Tourism research consists of the collection and analysis of data from both primary and secondary sources. The tourism researcher plans market studies, consumer surveys, and the implementation of research projects. Research jobs are available in national tourism offices, state/provincial travel offices, and so on.

Travel Communications

A number of opportunities are available in travel writing for editors, staff writers, and freelance writers. Most major travel firms need public relation people who write and edit, disseminate information, develop communication vehicle, obtain publicity, arrange special events, do public speaking, plan public relations campaigns, and so on. A travel photographer could find employment in either public relations or travel writing. Television is a medium with increasing opportunities.

Recreation and Leisure

Jobs in recreation and leisure are enormous. Some examples are activity director, aquatics specialist, ski instructor, park ranger, naturalist, museum guide, handicapped-programme planner, forester, camping director, concert promoter, lifeguards, tennis and golf instructors, coaches for various athletic teams, and drama directors.

Many recreation workers teach handicrafts. Resorts, parks, and recreation departments often employ recreation directors who hire specialists to work with senior citizens or youth groups, to serve as camp counsellors, or to teach such skills as boating and sailing. Management, supervisory, and administrative positions are also available.

Attractions

Attractions such as amusement parks and theme parks are a major source of tourism employment. Large organizations such as Disney World, Disneyland, Six Rags, Europa-Park, Tivoli Gardens, and Sea World provide job opportunities ranging from top management jobs to clerical and maintenance jobs.

Festivals and Events

Festivals and events are one of the fastest-growing segments of the tourism industry. Event management is emerging as a field, is becoming more professional, and is providing a new source of job opportunities. Events are creating offices and moving them to year-round operation. A study of the International Special Events Society showed that event managers earned between $ 25,000 and $ 75,000 per year and that the majority held baccalaureate degrees.

Sports Tourism

Sports are popular throughout the world, with many sports teams and enterprises becoming big businesses and offering job opportunities in the management and marketing areas.

Tourist Offices and Information Centres

Numerous jobs are available in tourist offices and information centres. Many chambers of commerce function as information centres and hire employees to provide this information. Many states operate welcome centres. Job titles found in state tourism offices are director, assistant director, deputy director, travel representative, economic development specialist, assistant director for travel promotion, statistical analyst, public information officer, assistant director for public and marketing coordinator, communications specialist, travel editor, media liaison, media specialist, photographer, administrative assistant, information specialist, media coordinator, manager of travel literature, writer, chief of news and information, marketing coordinator, market analyst, research analyst, economist, reference coordinator, secretary, package tour coordinator, and information clerk.

Convention and Visitors Bureaus (Destination Management Organizations)

As more and more cities enter the convention and visitor industry, employment opportunities in this segment grow. Many cities are devoting public funds to build convention centres to compete in this growing market. Convention and visitors bureaus require CEOs, managers, assistant managers, research directors, information specialists, marketing managers, public relations staff, sales personnel, secretaries, and clerks.

Meeting Planners

A growing profession is meeting planning. Many associations and corporations are hiring people whose job responsibilities are to arrange, plan, and conduct meetings.

Gaming

One of the fastest-growing sectors is gaming. Today, one is hard-pressed to find a state where gambling is not allowed or a gaming proposal is not in front of the State Legislature. From riverboats to Indian reservations to land-based casinos, new destinations are being created. Casinos provide job opportunities ranging from managers to marketers to mechanics to clerical and maintenance jobs.

Other Opportunities

A fairly comprehensive list of career opportunities has been presented. Others that do not fit the general categories listed are club management, entertainment management, corporate travel departments, hotel representative companies, in-flight and trade magazines, and trade and professional associations.

Career Paths in Tourism

In addition to considering one of the foregoing kinds of positions within a particular segment of the tourism sector, it is also useful to examine the various career paths that might be pursued. Because the tourism industry is so large and so diverse, it offers a broad range of challenging positions. While each of these positions offer its own unique opportunities and demands, people will find that the experience gained from working in a range of jobs in different sub-sectors of tourism can strengthen their understanding of the industry as a whole. Depending on one's career objectives, this broader understanding of tourism can be especially valuable when applying for certain types of positions. Examples include those in destination management organizations and national or provincial/state tourism offices.

To offer employees opportunities for growth and development, educators and personnel managers attempt continually to develop the concept of career paths in tourism. A schematic model illustrating the concept is shown in Fig. 7.1. The fundamental premise of this general model is that people can pursue a variety of reasonably well defined alternative routes, first through the educational system and subsequently through the industry itself. Based on the training and experience gained, combined with high-quality performance, a person can pursue a career path starting at different levels, with the ultimate goal of achieving the position of senior executive. While not everyone will have the ability or will necessarily want to pass through all levels of the model, it does provide defined career paths for those who are interested. It also indicates what combination of training and experience is normally required to achieve various positions.

Although clearly an oversimplification, the career path model demonstrates that people may take a variety of routes in pursuing their careers at different levels within and across the various sub-sectors of tourism. The specific positions that will appeal to different people will, of course, vary according to their particular educational background and their occupational skills. The chosen career path will also reflect a person's values and interests. Just how the chosen occupation might reflect individual values and interest is shown in Figure 7.2. As indicated, frontline staff (entry level and operations) must like dealing with people and possess a strong interest in providing them with high-quality service. Supervisors, managers, and entrepreneurs must possess additional values and interests that enable

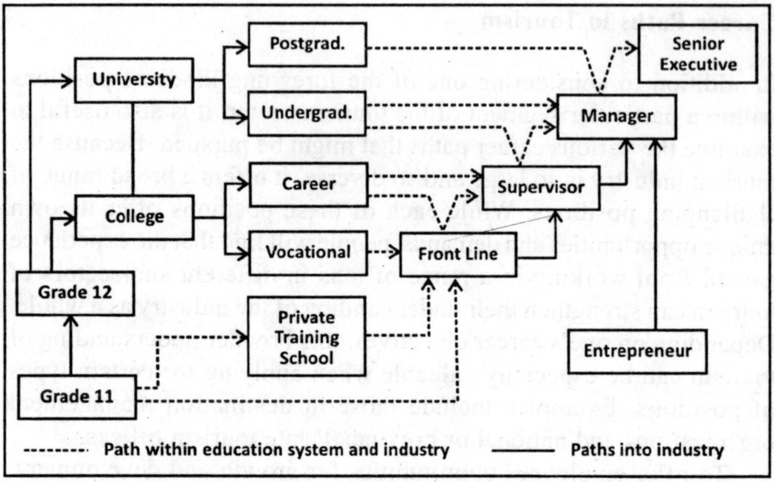

Fig. 7.2: Career Paths within the Tourism Industry.

them to face the challenges of change as they attempt to meet the needs of a demanding and ever-shifting marketplace.

Internships

One of the best ways to get the job you want is to have internship (cooperative education) experience. Internship opportunities abound in the tourism area. Most internship programmes are designed to provide students the opportunity to: (1) acquire valuable, hands-on experience to supplement their academic learning; (2) learn potential practical skills; (3) develop professionalism; (4) interact with segments of the local business community and develop an appreciation for the daily operation and long-term strategic direction of a corporate or small business environment; and (5) develop a further understanding of their chosen field. Some examples of internship programmes and sources of internships are Marriott, Hyatt, Disney, Universal Studios, the National Tourism Foundation, and the American Hospitality Academy. The Marriott Lodging Internship Programme is designed to stimulate student interest in hotel management and a career with Marriott International. Through the programme, students gain practical work experience necessary to pursue a management career in the hospitality industry. In addition, it provide Marriott with an

	Food and Beverage Restaurant Owner	*Accommodations Hotel Owner*	*Tour and Travel Tour Bus Line Owner*	*Attractions Amusement Park General Manager*	
Entrepreneur	• Independence • Flexible Work Hours • Financial and Personal Success • Control • Novelty/Change	• Independence • Irregular Work Hours • Control • Money • People • Novelty/Change • Success	• Quality • Commitment • Work Ethic • Optimism • People/Employees • Challenge • Growth • Humor • Flexibility • Organization • Working with Numbers	• Quality • Tourism and Tourists • Organization • Attention to Detail • Flexibility/ Diversity • People • Creativity • Business • Irregular Work Hours	PREDOMINANT VALUES AND INTERESTS
	Restaurant Manager	*Hotel Manager*	*Tour Bus Line Manager*	*Director of Special Attractions*	
Manager	• Quality • People • Leadership • Novelty/Change • Nutrition	• Influencing People • Novelty/Change • Curiosity • Competition • People • Problem Solving • Status	• Quality • Commitment • Work • People • Challenge • Flexibility • Growth • Humor • Organization • Innovation • Working with Numbers	• Young People • Professionalism • Work Ethic • Creativity • Irregular Work Hours • Variable Work Environment • Challenge • Economic Value • Leisure/Fun • Analysis	PEOPLE/QUALITY/CHALLENGE/FLEXIBILITY/NOVELTY/CHANGE
	Maitre D'	*Assistant Executive Housekeeper*	*Superintendent of Bus Maintenance*	*Amusement Park Supervisor*	
Supervisor	• People • Quality • Challenge • Food Industry	• Customers/ People • Quality • Cost Effectiveness • Team Efficiency • Problem Solving • Challenge	• People and their Safety • Quality • Variety/Novelty • Machinery • Problems • Organization	• People • Quality • Machinery • Challenge • Efficiency	
	Bartender	*Operations Chambermaid*	*Tour Bus Driver*	*Operations Ride Operator*	
Entry Level	• People • Quality • Creativity • Flexible Work Hours	• Customers/ People • Neatness • Fun • Variety • Cleaning	• People • Esteem • Power/Control • Being Busy • Routine	• People • Commitment • Initiative • Work • Teamwork • Being Busy	PEOPLE

(*Contd.*)

	Food and Beverage Server	Entry Chambermaid	Ticket Agent	Entry Ride Operator	
Pre-Employment	• People • Flexibility • Work Conditions	• People • Cleanliness • Cultural Variety	• People • Helpfulness • Challenge • Clerical Tasks • Math • Travel • Novelty/Variety	• People • Fun	PEOPLE
	Personal Woth Work				

* Created for the Industry Analysis and Training Information Branch, Department of Career Development and Employment Government, of Alberta by Career Development Institute.

Fig. 7.3: Career Paths in Tourism, Sample Occupations, Values, and Interests

opportunity to make sound evaluations of potential management candidates. Internship opportunities are available in their Marriott Hotels, Resorts, and Suites, Renaissance Hotels, Residence Inn, Courtyard, and Towne Place Suites brands and their time-share business, and Marriott Vacation Club International.

The Hyatt Hotels and Resorts Internship Programme was created to generate student interest in hotel management and spark a desire to join a hospitality leader after graduation. Internships also give Hyatt the opportunity to recognize potential managers and continue developing relationships throughout the academic year. Structured internship opportunities are available in over ten of their hotel and resort locations.

Universal Studios Florida has internships in advertising, convention sales, food services, human resources, information systems, marketing, merchandise, park operations, production, public relations, technical entertainment, and technical services. Active juniors, seniors, and graduate students are eligible for the programme.

Tourism Cares for Tomorrow, the non-profit foundation that was created from combining the National Tourism Foundation (NTF) and the Travellers Conservation Foundation (TCF) in January 2005, has announced the return of NTF's internship programme. Tourism Cares for Tomorrow assembles dozens of internship offerings to benefit both students and the industry. Go to their Web site at http://wvvw.Tourisrncaresfortoinorrow.org/tourismcares/students for information on internships and scholarships.

A career in tourism offers many exciting and challenging employment opportunities. As indicated in this chapter, tourism is the largest industry in the world today. In India and throughout the rest of the world the travel industry is expected to be a growth industry. The labour-intensive tourism industry has a need for motivated people of all ages and backgrounds. Those who prepare themselves, maintain high energy, have a talent for working with people, and have a dedication to high-quality service will find themselves climbing the career ladder to success.

The natural environment of Sikkim and its rich cultural diversity provide congenial conditions for the growth of tourism. The potential of tourism for the economy is well recognized in the state. Analyses of tourist influx suggest favourable trends and progressive state of growth for the development of tourism. The projections of trends for the next 10 years suggest a sizable increase in tourist numbers. Though, such an increase would create numerous job and income opportunities in the state, implications of the large turnout of tourists on the state's resources, infrastructure, cultural environment and eco-tourism would be significant. Accounting for the increase in population reveals that high-density, high-preference urban tourist areas such as Gangtok would receive the brunt of such impacts. The impacts of tourism in terms of monetization of rural pockets/economy are also showing in terms of changing agricultural traditions reflected in declining trends of livestock population, production of foodgrains, and apparent switch towards cash crops. Apart from the gradual drift from tradition, replenishing foodgrain supplies and livestock products from the outside would result in leakage and increase in the cost of living in the popular tourist pockets. Eco-tourism and its sustainability in the state would face a testing time and suitable management options are, therefore, needed.

References

Anderson, P., Crane, S., Stage, J. and Stage, J. (2005): "Potential Monopoly Rents from International Wildlife Tourism: An Example from Uganda's Gorilla Tourism", *Eastern Africa Social Science Research Review*, 21(1): 1-18.

Annual Report, 2006-07, Department of Tourism, Government of Sikkim.

Annual Report, 2008-09, Department of Tourism, Government of Sikkim.

Annual Report, 2009-10, Department of Tourism, Government of Sikkim.

Archer, B.H. (1973): *The Impact of Domestic Tourism: Bangor Occasional Papers in Economics* Number 2, Cardiff: University of Wales Press.

Aryal, B. (2008): Tourism Planning: Steps and Procedures, in Upadhyaya, R.P. (Ed.), *Readings in Rural Tourism*, Kathmandu: Sunlight Publication.

Atkins, W.S. (2001): *Eco-tourism Project Final Report* (3 Volumes), ADB TA 3332-NEP, Manila: Asian Development Bank.

Balaguer, J. and Cantavella-Jordà, M. (2002): Tourism as a Long-run Economic Growth Factor: The Spanish Case, *Applied Economics*, Vol. 34, pp. 877-884.

Bao, J. (1992): Application of the Gravity Model in Tourist Forecasting, *Journal of Zhongshan University* (Natural Science): 401: 133-135.

Banskota, K.; Sharma, B. and Kruk, E. (2006): "Economics of Sustainable Village Tourism: Experiences and Lessons from Sirubari, Nepal", *Journal of Tourism*, Srinagar Garhwal: HNB Garhwal University, Centre for Mountain Tourism.

Bhadauria, S.B.S. (1999): *Green State—Policies, Vision, Programme and Initiatives for Sustainable Development in Sikkim*, Gangtok: Author.

Bizcovering (2007): *Circular Flow of Income Model of an Economy*, (Online Document), Available: http://bizcovering.com/business-and-society/circular-flow-of-income-model-of-an-economy/. (Retrieved: 29 January, 2011).

Boo, F. (1990): *Ecotourism: The Potentials and Pitfalls*, Vols. 1 and 2, Washington, DC: Worldwide Fund for Nature.

Burkart, A.J. and Medlik, S. (1998): *Tourism— Past Present and Future*, London: Heinemann.

Census of Government Employee as on 1994, Government of Sikkim, Part-I, pp. 1-4.

Chakrabarti, Anjan (2008): "Sikkim Economy: The Present and Future and Interdependence with North Bengal", in Pankaj Kumar Debnath and Subhasis Bhattacharjee (Eds.), *Economy and Society of North Bengal*, Kolkata: Progressive Publishers.

Dwyer, L., Edwards, D., Mistilis, N., Scott, N. and Roman, C. (2009): Destination and Enterprise Management for a Tourism Future, *Tourism Management*, Vol. 30, pp. 63-74.

Godde, P.M., Price, M.F. and Zimmerman, F.M. (Eds.) (2000b): "Tourism and Development in Mountain Regions: Moving Forward into the New Millennium", in P.M. Godde, M.F. Price and F.M. Zimmerman, (Eds.) *Tourism and Development in Mountain Regions*, pp. 1-25, New York: CABI Publishing.

Government of Sikkim (1991): *Master Plan for Gangtok, 2020*, Urban Development and Housing Department, Government of Sikkim.

Hall, C.M. (1999): "Rethinking Collaboration and Partnership: A Public Policy Perspective", *Journal of Sustainable Tourism,* 7(3): 274-289.

Ogilvie, F.W. (1933): *The Tourist Movement: An Economic Study*, London: Staples Press.

Pradhan, K.M. (2008): *Macro- and Micro-Perspectives of Tourism in Nepal*, Kathmandu: Benchmark Education Support Pvt. Ltd.

Rasul, G. and Karki, M. (Eds.) (2008): *Policy Priorities for Sustainable Mountain Development*, Kathmandu: ICIMOD.

Sharma, P. (2002): "Tourism as an Instrument for Area Development and Poverty Alleviation with Focus on Nepal", in Jodha *et al.* (Eds.) *Poverty Alleviation in Mountain Areas of China*, pp. 221-244, Proceedings of the International Conference on Poverty in the Mountain Areas of China, Chengdu, China, 10–15 November, 2002, Kathmandu: In WEnt, IFAD, IMHE, ICIMOD.

Sinha, U.P. and Kumar, Swargesh (2011): *Bihar Tourism: Retrospect and Prospect*, New Delhi: Concept Publishing Company (P) Ltd.

State Socio-Economic Census (2006): Directorate of Economics, Statistics, Monitoring and Evaluation, Government of Sikkim, pp. 39-43.

UNWTO (2000): *Tourism 2020 Vision*, Madrid: United Nations World Tourism Organization.

8
Summary, Conclusion and Recommendations

This chapter deal with major summary of the study, conclusion and recommendation made by the researcher to improve tourism in the state is presented in brief. Summary, Conclusion and Recommendations have been presented respectively:

Summary

- In the view of natural, cultural resources or heritage, there is high potentiality of tourism development to generate multi-economic and social advantages in the study area. In the field of foreign exchange earnings, employment generation, regional development and advancement or modernization of rural life, tourism can significantly contribute to the nation in general and Sikkim in particular. Tourism industry in Sikkim has marked significantly multiplier effect.
- Eco-tourism is the second tourism activity in the State. From the view of diversification of tourism activities of tourism activities and lengthening the stay of tourist in Sikkim is a appropriate medium. From the study, average length of stay of tourist is five days. Especially, eco-tourism contributing to present varied taste or new products to the tourist. Likewise, by helping to increase tourist inflow and lengthen their stay in the State, these village and adventure tourism have remarkably been assisting to earn more exchanges to the state.
- The growth rate of tourist arrivals to Sikkim has been comparable to that of India as a whole. Since 1999, average

annual growth rates have been 11.20 per cent for domestic tourist arrivals and 14.20 per cent for international arrivals. Sharp increases in foreign arrivals are directly related to political problems in neighbouring Nepal, which suggests that Sikkim is currently perceived as an alternative to Nepal.

- Annual revenue receipt of Sikkim in the year 2012-13 was 300.00 lakhs (31.42%) against that is 70.69 lakhs (7.40%) in the year 2003-04. It shows that, there is tremendous increase in revenue receipt in the Sikkim. The neighbouring State of West Bengal is not surprisingly the main domestic market to visit Sikkim. The metro of Kolkata currently accounts for 45 per cent of all domestic visitors. However, it is reported by the Tourism Department that the share of domestic tourist traffic from other metros is increasing, with Delhi now accounting for 15 per cent of domestic visitors, Mumbai 10 per cent, Hyderabad 8 per cent, Bangalore 7 per cent, and Chennai and Ahmedabad 5 per cent, respectively. Foreign tourist come to Sikkim are as follows, the UK is the largest generating market, followed by the USA, Germany, and France. The largest market from the Asia Pacific region is Australia, followed by Thailand and Japan. Sikkim accounted for just 0.4 per cent of total international arrivals to India in 2013.
- It depicts that the highest 376 (94%) economic impact perceived by the tourists is on employment opportunities. other impacts as indicated by the tourism are, local business opportunity 300 (75%), development of infrastructure 125 (31.25%), improved standard of living 123 (30.75%), souvenirs 40 (16%), foreign exchange 23 (5.75%), tax in income 80 (20%) and other 50 (12.5%) respectively.
- The highest portion (100%) of respondents perceived the occurrences of economic impacts by way of employment opportunities. Similarly, the other major economic impacts pointed out by respondents are tax income (45%), foreign exchange (45%), souvenirs (67%), improved standard of living (50%), business opportunities (90%), better infrastructure (45%) and the gap between poor and rich increase (40%) respectively as mentioned by tourism entrepreneurs.

- The publicity materials relating to tourism published by the Government of Sikkim Tourism Department, TASS and other tourism related agencies is not satisfactory. Only 32.6 per cent tourist read the publicity materials relating to tourism by these agencies.
- Tourist visiting Sikkim are of the opinion that they are highly satisfied with some aspects of tourism like location, quality of food, behaviour of staff regarding hotels, hospitality, language communication, agencies, guide and tourism vendor and behaviour of local people and solid waste management. Similarly, they are moderately satisfied with some aspects of tourism like international airlines, domestic airlines, immigration, shopping facilities, currency exchange and naturally satisfied with tourism information centre, customs banking services.
- The highest number of (68.6%) tourist express the view that their friend/relatives are the main sources of information to come Sikkim. Followed by travel agent (13%), newspaper (15.2%), magazine (26.7%), television/radio (15.3%), internet (26.7%), guide book (32.6%), and business linkage (9.5%).
- The majority of tourists and entrepreneurs perceive economic, social and cultural effect of tourism in Sikkim.
- Unhealthy domestic competition (50%), and lack of skilled persons (68%), are the main problems of the tourism entrepreneurs, similarly, the security problem (13%) was also faced by tourism entrepreneurs.
- The majority of 95.55 respondents expressed their view that uniqueness is the major strength of Sikkim tourism product. Likewise, competitive (44.4%), location (42.2%), price (40%), repeat value (37.7%), emotional value (35.5%), access (31.1%), mass appeal (28,8%), source of achievement (34.1%), and others (31.1%) are the strength of tourism product of Sikkim respectively.
- 75 per cent tourism entrepreneurs are linked with international market through internet and words from mouth followed by direct contact 51.1 per cent and through travel link 33.3 per cent respectively.
- The entrepreneurs expressed their views that the government be initiated to promote destination by 95 per cent, followed

by development of infrastructure 87 per cent, special events (67%), marketing/publicity (45%) participation of festivals (34%), and facilitating tourism industry (23%), developed new products 12 per cent respectively.

- The tourism factors like Government policies, pollution control, safety measures, marketing and service are highly important factor to attract more tourists in Sikkim.
- Eco-tourism/nature tourism in the state is well supported by the institutional arrangements at village and community levels. Several capacity-building and awareness programmers are being continuously organized by NGOs and the State Tourism Department for the stakeholders to sensitize them on issues related to the environment and for better tourism culture and management in the state.
- Travellers to Sikkim need to follow some rules and regulations as the state has few entry restrictions that falls under the restricted area regime due to proximity with neighbouring country China. So, in order to promote smooth tourism in the state, constraints on the entry protocols have been relaxed by the government for foreign nationals. They can visit the famous tourism spots like Gangtok, Rumtek, Pemayangste, Phodong, and the Yuksom only after obtaining the restricted area permit from any of the concerned departmental offices in India. Inner Line Permit is issued from Sikkim Tourism Office at New Delhi and District Magistrate office of Darjeeling, Siliguri and Rangpo after you produce Indian Visa.
- About (31.25%) perceive impact of folk tradition followed by people begging for money or food (3%), overcrowding (6.5%), cultural loss of authenticity (70.5%), change in lifestyle/increase in western values (36.25%), modernization of facilities (41.75%), increase in urbanization (14%), increase in communication (75%), preservation of cultural monuments (11.25%), encourage education/knowledge (75%) and hygiene problem (6.5%) respectively. They are positive and negative socio-cultural impacts of tourism in Sikkim.
- Majority of the tourists that is (51.5%) are unsatisfied with the present royalty fee regarding tourism in Sikkim and (48.5%) tourists are satisfied with royalty fee.

- It can be said that the highest number of 95 per cent respondents perceive the social/cultural impact on mountain tourism on the inhabitants on mountain region at study area by the change in life/imitation of west preservation. Preservation of folk tradition (56%), people beginning for money or food (12%), overcrowding (45%), cultural loss/ loss of authenticity (85%), preservation of art or history (44%), urbanization (76%), increased communication (80%), encourage education/knowledge (87%) and hygiene problem (34%) respectively.
- The entrepreneurs are said that it is necessary for the human resource development for the tourism development. The highest portion (90%) of respondents emphasize on hospitality, education and knowledge (78%), tour/trekking guide (67%), language training (54%), similarly followed by mountaineering (34%) and others 23 per cent respectively.

Conclusion

The foregoing discussions reveal that the eco-tourism in Sikkim is the pioneer tourism activity and they introduced Sikkim and its unique natural product to tourists in the international markets. Due to the presence of immense snow-capped Himalayas of different awesome height and dimensions, Sikkim has immense potentials for the development of tourism and can accrue large economical benefit to the people of Sikkim.

Despite possessing high socio-economic advantages, Sikkim still could not have fully mobilized and exploited these immense natural gifts appropriately. Insufficient physical infrastructure and unskill/ unexperience tourism entrepreneurs along with deficiency of other supportive things tourism has not yet progressed in a desirable manner in the State. Until now, the contribution of tourism in the state of Sikkim economy is felt in the field of foreign exchange earning mainly in the area of employment opportunities and royalty. However, its contribution is nominal. Therefore, the government needs more attention and starts functioning as early as possible for overall development from where tourism may be able to generate significant socio-economic advantage in the State.

Recommendations

Based on the finding of the study the following recommendations are proposed for the development of mountain tourism especially with reference to Economic impact of tourism in Sikkim.

Recommendation on Tourism Development Policy

We know tourism is the important and popular economic activity in Sikkim. The level of importance of tourism in Sikkim is very high. There is still need of long-term perspective policy on tourism development in the country. So, in context of growing popularity day-by-day and socio-economic importance of it, a long-term comprehensive and appropriate policy in the field of tourism with explicit recognition, comprising all aspects of tourism development is most desirable. *Ad hoc* and frequent changing policies will never help mountain tourism to flourish smoothly. Considering this crucial fact, a long-term comprehensive policy with the integration of tourism development policy should be formulated and implemented as early as possible. This will not only help government to come out with a clear-cut vision and appropriate policy tools for sustainable and systematic tourism development, but it will also create confidence among the potential investors in different tourism destination.

While preparing a long-term perspective plan development due provisions for the diversification of tourism destination should be mentioned obviously. Until now tourism in Sikkim has been focused only in few specific places, but in the view on diversified and expending tourism destinations we have to expand it to various remote places which is far reaching from the eye of authorities. To encourage these places as a tourist destination, the government needs to develop various support infrastructure like transportation and communication, security, camping sites, accommodation, etc. PPP (Public Private Partnership) should be introduced. Providing various financial provisions, logistic facilities like hotels, restaurants, resort in remote places should be introduced.

The government should make solid commitment with clear provision for direct allotment of a certain amount of royalty out of the total receipt from particular region to the fund for the establishment of local infrastructure of the same particular region.

Different fees for different destination can lead to more revenue for the government. Say for example, if the mountaineers want to summit they can be asked to pay more, but if the person wants to climb to base camp-I he/she may pay less. This will introduce innovative approach to promote mountain tourism. Provision should be made in policy or regulation for providing certain percentage less/ concession during the time of fair and festivals so that more tourists are encouraged to visit Sikkim.

Recommendation of Infrastructure Development

Except some places, rest of all places of the state are lacking behind by the standard of basic infrastructure. All the mountain regions are beyond direct access of modern transport and communication. Being a mountainous state, road transportation is very tough and costly too, the government should give more emphasis to connect remote places to big cities with two lane road. To boost our tourism, railways and airways is equally important factor so, government should think for easy asses to consume these facilities, as the states do not have railways junction and airport. Nearest is 100 kilometre far from the capital in Siliguri, West Bengal. Ticketing facilities should be more systematize in order to check hackers from taking easy benefits.

Communication is another fundamental prerequisite for the development of tourism in the state. Due to the lack of communication facilities, neither tourist nor tourism entrepreneurs can communicate properly and can send their urgent news to others on time. Non-availability of direct communication has sometimes created serious accident in the mountain regions. So, the government should pay especial attention on these regards. Accommodation is another infrastructure facilities which is necessary for tourism boost in the region. Most of the regions do not have good facilities of accommodation as the number is comparatively less. If the percentage of tourist inflow increases by 20 per cent than there will no rooms for tourist to stay in Sikkim. Keeping under these considerations PPP is most needed to set-up various facilities like development of new hotel, lodging facilities, shopping, etc. in far reaching rural areas.

From the above survey, it is found that there is lack of trained manpower in tourism sector. The hotel management and tourism training centre vocational student in related field has been producing some basic skilled manpower in the field. But the centre has not given focus so far for providing training on different aspects of tourism in the study area. Occasionally, TAAS and ECOS conducts training about high altitude sickness and other tourism aspects. But due to the lack of physical and financial resources these NGOs has not been able to provide training at large scale. Consequently, tourism in Sikkim is still dominated by untrained guide, drivers, even some entrepreneurs. This has increased the possibilities of failures and accident in tracking and adventure activities. The government need to take-up this matter seriously and start some training through TAAS and Environmental Council of the States (ECOS) by upgrading its existing capacity in both physically and financially. And providing incentives to the NGOs related should be encouraged to establish at least one such kind of school.

Besides, the Ministry of Tourism, Sikkim has not been able to prepare any GIS profile covering information on different aspects of tourism. The ministry has neither developed any scientific map on caravan roots and published any adventure destination for the convenience of tourists. Till now almost all the tourists use the guidebook on rough map prepared by different tourism entrepreneurs for necessary information. Due to not fully scientific and based on rough estimation these maps and books are not helpful to the tourists. So, it is most urgent to prepare profile at least of some tourist destinations. Similarly, the map of caravan of tourist destination for major bus station or airport should be sketched and distributed to the tourists. Similarly, for mountaineers some new tourist information centres should be established in the major regions.

Till now, there is not any permanent institution with basic equipment and professional experts for rescue operation for tourist in emergency period. So, it is felt that high attention should be paid towards establishing a permanent rescue unit with necessary support to expand its existing programmees more efficiently in the new region also.

Recommendation on Promotion and Marketing

Sikkim's tourism marketing and promotional strategy have not remained so effective and stimulating. Still promotional marketing strategy has remained more or less static in terms of innovation, spread new technique, co-ordination, appropriate promotional materials and so on. Due to a lack of aggressive promotional campaign, tourism of Sikkim has not got appropriate publicity concern in the international market.

In order to promote Sikkim wide publicity and information about tourism, various construction works should be done. First of all, more attractive and clear promotional materials like books, booklets, magazines, brochures, pamphlets and audio and visual material should be produced and distributed to the major tourist generating regions. Sikkim houses in different states of India and information centre can be the best media to provide information of Sikkim. So more material should be publicly distributed from these place. Similarly, the exhibition of Film and documentaries about Sikkim and tourism should be made on the occasions of different social functions and gathering. Organizing different occasions, photo exhibitions, seminar, international tourism fairs and festivals, conferences focusing on Sikkim tourism should be made within and outside the country. Prevailing tourism information centres should be upgraded and extended both financially and physically to meet the requirement of tourist. Internet is providing to be a very effective media to market directly to the prospective customers. Sikkim needs to take advantage of this technology in marketing. Regular update of the website is also required.

Almost half of the trekkers and mountaineers visiting Sikkim are found to have their own travel agency, in this context the travel and tracking agencies should be encouraged by giving them various facilities and incentives to have more and more direct linkage with them and thereby bringing more trekkers and mountaineers in the Sikkim.

Recommendation on Foreign Exchange Policy

Liberal policy that has been adopted by the government in the field of foreign exchange at present should be continued and due precaution should be taken to adjust this policy with changing need of the state economy. Leakage of foreign exchange in the field of tourism and in the forms on import and illegal trafficking should be given to develop industries for import substitution by providing soft loans and incentives to the national entrepreneurs in the country immediately.

Till now exchange facilities services are available only in the major towns, but in course of journey they reach to far rural areas where exchange facilities are completely unavailable, so, there always remains high possibility of leakage of foreign exchanges. Therefore, the Government and State Banks like SDICO, SBS and SISCO should try to check such leakages by opening necessary exchange counters in major tourism traffic. Due to the existence of unauthorized tourism industries, their services are marketed with poor quality, limited capacity, poor sanitation and deficient management. It is, therefore, most urgent to find out such illegal industries and to penalize them strictly. The tourism industry should be brought within the border of the law, if they do not fulfil prescribed norms and conditions. Therefore, there is a growing need to monitor and supervise the data and information related with the income and expenditure of almost all the tourism industries regularly in the State.

Miscellaneous

- Co-ordination among various agencies such as TAAS, ECOS and local level tourism firms, etc. is essential for speedy and healthy development of tourism is Sikkim.
- Participation of local people in tourism destination should be encouraged.
- Tourism in Sikkim is seasonal so, efforts must be made to ensure of creating off season tourism. We should promote summer tourism in the time of off season by introducing rain tourism for gulf countries.
- Active and vigilant conservation acts and programmees should be identified and implemented.
- To prevent the deforestation, solar and hydro-power potential should be explored, afforestation programmes and supply of LPG and other supplementary things should be encouraged.
- Modernized rescue operation cells should be established.
- To sustain multiplier effect and to prevent the leakage of income, inputs of tourism activities should be made available locally.
- Cable car and ropeways services should be expended.
- Wildlife tourism should be developed in mountain areas in national parks.
- The entry formalities must be strict in parks and conservation areas for sustainable tourism.
- Organic tourism must be given more importance as Sikkim is only organic state in the country.
- Appropriate radio transmitting station should be established

to give information about weather forecasting, search and rescue operations.

- Flora and fauna and pastureland should be protected and properly preserved for adventure tourism.
- For the intersection of guest and host local fairs and festivals, *yoga*, meditation and other spiritual activities should be organized.
- Positive works of the people or political parties who are effective in preserving the tourism should be published.
- Awareness programme to local about the benefits and burdens of tourism and brochures of information about local customs and do's or do not for tourist should be published.
- Education and training for tourism are essential for local people to improve skills, develop understanding the tourism, increase motivation and to the effective use and management of resources.

To sum-up, tourism is Sikkim is marked by different weaknesses and shortcomings as mentioned in the study. Until and unless we show keen interest to avoid such weaknesses associated with tourism development, Sikkim's tourism cannot pay significant role in our economy. That is why, it is necessary for the government to consider seriously to get rid of such shortcomings as early as possible whereby, sustainable and more productive tourism activities will emerge in the state in the days to come.

ANNEXURE I(A)

Questionnaire for Tourists

1. Name: ....
2. Nationality: ....
3. Permanent Address: ....

Personal Details

1. Sex: Male ( ) Female ( )
2. What is your age?
   Below 30 years ( ) 30-40 years ( ) Above 40 years ( )
3. Marital status: Married ( ) Unmarried ( )
4. What is your education?
   School Education ( ) Under Graduate ( )
   Post Graduate ( ) Doctoral ( ) Any Other ( )
5. What is your occupation? ....

Tourism Related Informations

1. Have you ever been in Sikkim before? Yes ( ) No ( )
2. If yes, how many times did you visit Sikkim? Second time ( )
   Three–four times ( ) Five–six times ( ) Seven and more ( )
3. Did you visit other countries/state on this journey? Yes ( ) No ( )
   If answer is yes, name of the country/state. ....
4. What is the main purpose of Travel? (Multiple Responses Possible).
   - Professional ( )
   - Leisure ( )
   - Holiday ( )
   - Pleasure ( )
   - Business ( )
   - Official ( )
   - Diplomat ( )
   - Religious ( )
   - Research ( )
   - Others ( )
5. Before your trip to Sikkim how did you perceive Sikkim? (Multiple Responses Possible)
   - The State of Mountains ( )

- The State of Scenic Beauty ( )
- The State of Rich Flora and Fauna ( )
- The State of Strict Law ( )
- The State of Rich Culture and Tradition ( )
- The State of Beautiful Lakes ( )
- Others ( )

6. What kind of Destination you are going to visit? (Multiple Responses Possible)
   - Adventure ( )
   - Religious/pilgrims ( )
   - Peace loving ( )
   - Natural lover ( )
   - Others ( )
   - Sports Tourism ( )
   - Fairs and Festivals ( )
   - Official Tour ( )
   - Village Tourism ( )
7. How long are you staying in Sikkim? Days ( ) Months ( )
8. How do you rate on the scale of four for the following aspect of Tourism?

   ……………………………………………………………………………

Transportation and Communication

(i) International Airlines:

	Unsatisfactory	Fair	Good	Satisfactory	
	1	2	3	4	
Not Important	1	2	3	4	Very Important

(ii) Domestic Airlines:

	Unsatisfactory	Fair	Good	Satisfactory	
	1	2	3	4	
Not Important	1	2	3	4	Very Important

(iii) Railways:

	Unsatisfactory	Fair	Good	Satisfactory	
	1	2	3	4	
Not Important	1	2	3	4	Very Important

(iv) Roadways:

	Unsatisfactory	Fair	Good	Satisfactory	
	1	2	3	4	
Not Important	1	2	3	4	Very Important

(v) Communication Facilities:

	Unsatisfactory	Fair	Good	Satisfactory	
	1	2	3	4	
Not Important	1	2	3	4	Very important

Location, Facilities and Services Regarding Hotel

(i) Location:

	Unsatisfactory	Fair	Good	Satisfactory	
	1	2	3	4	
Not Important	1	2	3	4	Very Important

(ii) Sanitation:

	Unsatisfactory	Fair	Good	Satisfactory	
	1	2	3	4	
Not Important	1	2	3	4	Very Important

(iii) Quality of Food and Drink:

	Unsatisfactory	Fair	Good	Satisfactory	
	1	2	3	4	
Not Important	1	2	3	4	Very Important

(iv) Behaviour of Hotel Staff:

	Unsatisfactory	Fair	Good	Satisfactory	
	1	2	3	4	
Not Important	1	2	3	4	Very Important

Facilities and Services Regarding Tourism Activities

(i) Hospitality:

	Unsatisfactory	Fair	Good	Satisfactory	
	1	2	3	4	
Not Important	1	2	3	4	Very Important

(ii) Banking Facilities:

	Unsatisfactory	Fair	Good	Satisfactory	
	1	2	3	4	
Not Important	1	2	3	4	Very Important

(iii) Currency Exchange:

	Unsatisfactory	Fair	Good	Satisfactory	
	1	2	3	4	
Not Important	1	2	3	4	Very Important

(iv) Shopping Facilities:

	Unsatisfactory	Fair	Good	Satisfactory	
	1	2	3	4	
Not Important	1	2	3	4	Very Important

(v) Language Communication:

	Unsatisfactory	Fair	Good	Satisfactory	
	1	2	3	4	
Not Important	1	2	3	4	Very Important

(vi) Health Services:

	Unsatisfactory	Fair	Good	Satisfactory	
	1	2	3	4	
Not Important	1	2	3	4	Very Important

(vii) Tourist Informations Centres:

	Unsatisfactory	Fair	Good	Satisfactory	
	1	2	3	4	
Not Important	1	2	3	4	Very Important

(viii) Tourism Marketing:

	Unsatisfactory	Fair	Good	Satisfactory	
	1	2	3	4	
Not Important	1	2	3	4	Very Important

(ix) Services of Agencies:

	Unsatisfactory	Fair	Good	Satisfactory	
	1	2	3	4	
Not Important	1	2	3	4	Very Important

(x) Tourist Guide:

	Unsatisfactory	Fair	Good	Satisfactory	
	1	2	3	4	
Not Important	1	2	3	4	Very Important

(xi) Public Amenities:

	Unsatisfactory	Fair	Good	Satisfactory	
	1	2	3	4	
Not Important	1	2	3	4	Very Important

(xii) Behaviour of the Local People:

	Unsatisfactory	Fair	Good	Satisfactory	
	1	2	3	4	
Not Important	1	2	3	4	Very Important

(xiii) Solid Waste Collection and Disposal:

	Unsatisfactory	Fair	Good	Satisfactory	
	1	2	3	4	
Not Important	1	2	3	4	Very Important

(xiv) Security Arrangement:

	Unsatisfactory	Fair	Good	Satisfactory	
	1	2	3	4	
Not Important	1	2	3	4	Very Important

(xv) Facilities, Services and Other Goods:

	Unsatisfactory	Fair	Good	Satisfactory	
	1	2	3	4	
Not Important	1	2	3	4	Very Important

(xvi) Entry Fee:

	Unsatisfactory	Fair	Good	Satisfactory	
	1	2	3	4	
Not Important	1	2	3	4	Very Important

9. Did you see any publicity materials relating to tourism published by the Tourism Department of Sikkim/Travel Agencies or any other sources?
   Yes ( ) No ( )
10. What are the main sources of information that influenced your decision to come Sikkim? (Multiple Responses Possible)
    - Friends/Relatives ( )
    - Travel agent ( )
    - Newspaper ( )
    - Magazine ( )
    - Television ( )
    - Others ( )
    - Tourist Office ( )
    - Guide Book ( )
    - Business Linkage ( )
    - Trade Fairs/shows ( )
    - Airlines ( )
11. Do you think any environmental impact of Tourism in Sikkim?
    Yes ( ) No ( )
    If yes, what kinds of impact do you notice? (Multiple Responses Possible)
    - Degradation of Scenic appeal ( )
    - Measures of hold population ( )
    - Erosion of trekking trial/bridge ( )
    - Maintenance of scenic beauty/landscape ( )
    - Deforestation/destruction of flora and funna ( )
    - Lack of sanitation ( )
    - Narrow road ( )
    - Police protection ( )
    - Others ( )
12. Are you satisfied with the present royalty system of the Government regarding trekking, entry fee, passes etc. Yes ( ) No ( )
    If No, give comment. ....
13. Could you please, specify the quality of manpower involved in the Tourism Industry of Sikkim.
    Trained ( ) Untrained ( )
14. Is there any problem that you found here? Yes ( ) No ( )
    If Yes, why? (Multiple Responses Possible)
    - Terrorism/violence ( )
    - Pollution ( )
    - Inadequate infrastructure ( )
    - Service quality ( )
    - Transportation and communication ( )
    - Others ( )
15. Are you interested to visit Sikkim again? Yes ( ) No ( )
16. Would you like to extend some suggestions to improve Tourism in Sikkim?
    ....
    ....

ANNEXURE I(B)

Questionnaire for the Tourism Enterprises

1. Name of the Organization: ....
2. Name of the Managing Director: ....
3. Year of establishment: ....Reg. No.: ....
4. What kind of services have been provided to tourists by your agency? (Multiple Responses Possible)
   - Guiding ( )
   - Tour operating ( )
   - Ticketing ( )
   - Sightseeing ( )
   - Rafting ( )
   - Transportation ( )
   - Mountaineering ( )
   - Trekking ( )
   - Other ( )
5. What types of problems are you facing currently? (Multiple Responses Possible)
   - Domestic competition ( )
   - Lack of resources (Financial and equipments) ( )
   - Unfavorable Government policy ( )
   - Foreign competition ( )
   - Lack of skilled personnel ( )
   - Security problem ( )
   - Other ( )
6. How do you rate the performance of your agency in providing services to consumer in comparison to other agencies?
   - Highly satisfactory ( )
   - So, so ( )
   - Satisfactory ( )
   - Unsatisfactory ( )
7. How do you rate the performance of the travel agent and association of Sikkim (TASS) in context of Tourism Promotion?
   - Excellent ( )
   - Satisfactory ( )
   - Good ( )
   - Poor ( )
8. Which are the peak months for visiting Sikkim? ....
9. Which are the off seasons for visiting Sikkim? ....
10. Are you satisfied with the present tourism products? Yes ( ) No ( )
    If No, what kind of product should be developed? (Multiple Responses Possibie)
    - Preserve and promote our product as is it ( )

- Modify product to suit target market ( )
- Combine product features ( )
- Developed new product ( )
- Others ( )

11. What is the strength of our present product? (Multiple Responses Possible)
    - Uniqueness ( )
    - Repeat value ( )
    - Sense of achievement ( )
    - Price ( )
    - Location ( )
    - Mass appeal ( )
    - Emotional value ( )
    - Competitive ( )
    - Access ( )
    - Others ( )
12. What are the weaknesses of our present product? (Multiple Responses Possible)
    - Poor preservation ( )
    - No repeat value ( )
    - Lack of competitiveness ( )
    - Poor presentation ( )
    - Congestion ( )
    - Limited products ( )
    - Others ( )
13. What should we do to attract more tourists? (Multiple Responses Possible)
    - Government policies ( )
    - Marketing ( )
    - Hospitality ( )
    - Banking system ( )
    - Others ( )
    - Pollution control ( )
    - Transportation ( )
    - Communication ( )
    - Fairs and festivals ( )
14. In your opinion what should be done to increase the length of stay? (Multiple Responses Possible)
    - Enhancement of infrastructure ( )
    - Improve safety measures ( )
    - Shopping facilities ( )
    - Sustainable development (eco-tourism) ( )
    - Improve the quality of hotels ( )
    - Price limiting ( )
    - Emphasis on village tourism ( )
    - Explore new product ( )
    - Others ( )
15. In which area do you think more training is required for the development of human resources? (Multiple Responses Possible)
    - Language ( )
    - Mountaineering ( )
    - Education and knowledge about tourism ( )
    - Hospitality ( )
    - Tour and trekking guide ( )
    - Others ( )
16. Do you have direct linkage with international market? Yes ( ) No ( )
    If answer is Yes, how do you establish link with international market?
    ....

17. What do you think about the marketing effort done at present by the Government and the marketing agencies/advertising agencies?
    - Excellent ( ) • Good ( )
    - Satisfactory ( ) • Poor ( )
18. Are these effort sufficient to promote Sikkim as a Tourist Destination?

    Yes ( ) No ( )

    If answer is No, what effort should be made by the government to improve Sikkim as a Tourist Destination? (Multiple Responses Possible)
    - Destination promotion ( )
    - Development of infrastructure ( )
    - Develop new product ( )
    - Marketing/Publicity ( )
    - Special events ( )
    - Facilitating tourism industry ( )
    - Participation on fairs and exhibitions ( )
    - Others ( )
19. Do you think that there is any cultural/social impact of Tourism on the inhabitants of Sikkim? (Multiple Responses Possible)
    - Preservation of folk/tradition ( )
    - People begging for money or food ( )
    - Overcrowing ( )
    - Cultural loss/loss of authenticity ( )
    - Preservation of arts/history ( )
    - Urbanization ( )
    - Increased communications ( )
    - Encourage education/knowledge ( )
    - Hygiene ( )
20. Do you think that there is any environmental impact of Tourism in Sikkim? Yes ( ) No ( )

    If answer is yes, what kind of impact do you think?
    - Degradation of scenic beauty ( )
    - Measures of hold population ( )
    - Erosion of tracking trials ( )
    - Garbage/litter/pollution ( )
    - Maintenance of scenic landscape ( )
    - Deforestation/destruction of flora and fauna ( )
    - Disturbances of natural resources ( )
    - Better area protection ( )
    - Others ( )
21. How do you rate the pricing strategy of tourism service in Sikkim?
    - Excellent ( ) • Good ( )
    - Satisfactory ( ) • Poor ( )
22. How do you rate the different policies/plan regarding tourism till now?

    ....

Income Analysis

Annual Investment Expenditure

Sector of Investment	*Amount of Investment*
Destination promotion	
Development of Infrastructure	
Development of new product	
Marketing/publicity	
Facilitating Tourism Industry	
Fairs/exhibitions	
Preservation of culture/tradition/customs	
Preservation of scenic appeal	
Sanitations	
Orientation programme/training programme	
Others	

Annual Income

Sources of income	*Amount of income*
Funding by Tourism industry	
Package tour	
Tourism destination	
Transportation	
INGOs	
NGOs	
Any other sources	

Saving

- What is your average annual saving?
- Present status of saving during the last six month.
- Deposited in bank ₹ __________ amount used for promotion and development of tourism in Sikkim.

Debt Situation

Have you taken any loans? If Yes.

- Amount of loans ____________________
- Sources of loans ____________________
- Nature of loans ____________________
- Reasons for taking loans ____________________
- Amount of outstanding loan ____________________

23. Would you like to extend some suggestions to improve Tourism in Sikkim?

ANNEXURE I(C)

Questionnaire for Tourism Related Persons: (Diver/Potter/Tourist Guide and Agriculturist)

1. Name: ....
2. Nationality: ....
3. Permanent Address: ....
4. Present Address : ....

Personal Details:

5. Sex: Male ( ) Female ( )
6. What is your age?
   Below 30 years ( ) 30-40 years ( ) Above 40 years ( )
7. Marital status: Married ( ) Unmarried ( )
8. What is your education?
   School Education ( ) Under graduate ( )
   Post-Graduate ( ) Doctoral ( ) Any Other ( )
9. What type of work you are doing presently? ....
10. Details about the present Job:
    - Nature/types of work. Regular/*Ad hoc*/Contractual/Own
    - Name of the Employer: ....
    - Length of service : ....
    - Wage: Monthly ( ) Weekly ( ) Daily ( )
    - Any other ....
11. Nature of work.
    - Tourist seasons ( )
    - Daily ( )
    - Monthly ( )
    - Permanent ( )
12. Working hour Fixed ( ) Not Fixed ( )
    If fixed, duration of working hour. ....
13. Do you get holiday? Yes ( ) No ( )
    If Yes, number of holidays in a month ....
14. Nature of job prior to present job:
    - Wage labour ( )
    - Farmer ( )

- Contractor ( )
- Government Employee ( )
- Any other ( )

15. Reason for shifting the job:
    - Interest ( )
    - More earning ( )
    - Future scope ( )
    - Any other ( )
16. Economic Aspects:

Monthly Income of the Individual (Directly or Indirectly Depends Upon Tourism)

Sources of Income	*Amount Of Income*
Self	
Family member	
Other sources of earning (if any)	
Total	

Monthly Expenditure of the Individual

Fooding	
Clothing	
Education	
Accommodation	
Recreations	
Others	
Total	

Monthly Saving of the Individual

What is your monthly saving?

Present status of saving during the last six months.

Amount of deposited in bank ₹ _________ amount used for promotion and development of tourism in Sikkim.

Debt Situation

Have you taken any loans? If Yes

Amount of loans ____________________

Sources of loans ____________________

Nature of loans ____________________

17. Do you think that there is any economic impact of Tourism on the inhabitants of Sikkim? Yes ( ) No ( )
18. If Yes, what kind of impact do you think? (Multiple Responses Possible)
    - Employment opportunities ( )
    - Revenue ( )
    - Foreign exchange reserve ( )
    - Improvement of living standard ( )
    - Industrial opportunity ( )
    - Development of infrastructure ( )
    - Improvement of transport and communication ( )
    - Modernization of facilities ( )
    - Increase in urbanization ( )
    - Others ( )

19. Do you think that there is any Social/Cultural impact of Tourism on the inhabitants of Sikkkm? Yes ( ) No ( )

    If yes, what kind of impact do you think? (Multiple Responses Possible)

    - Education ( )
    - Souvenir ( )
    - People begging for money or food ( )
    - Cultural Loss/loss of authenticity ( )
    - Preservation of cultural monuments ( )
    - Hygienic ( )
    - Preservation of Folk tradition ( )
    - Overcrowding ( )
    - Change in lifestyle/increase in western values ( )
    - Others ( )

20. Is government effort sufficient to promote Sikkim as a Tourism Destination? Yes ( ) No ( )

    If No, what should be done to promote Sikkim as a Tourism Destination? (Multiple Responses possible)

    - Destination promotion ( )
    - Developed new product( )
    - Special events ( )
    - Participation on fairs and exhibitions ( )
    - Development of infrastructure( )
    - Marketing/Publicity ( )
    - Facilitating tourism industry ( )
    - Orientation programme ( )
    - Others ( )

21. What should be done to attract more tourists? (Multiple Responses Possible)

    - Improvement of government policies ( )
    - More safety and security should be given to tourists ( )
    - Pollution control ( )
    - Marketing ( )
    - Service ( )
    - Orientation programme to Drivers/potter/tourist guide ( )
    - Others ( )

22. How do you rate the different policies, plan regarding tourism till now?

	Unsatisfactory	Fair	Good	Satisfactory	
	1	2	3	4	
Not Important	1	2	3	4	Very Important

    Give comments.

23. Would you like to extend some suggestions to improve Tourism in Sikkim?

ANNEXURE II

Place of Interest in Sikkim

Mountain View

Lachung Valley, North Sikkim

Himalayas of Sikkim

Pilling West Sikkim

Evening at M.G. Marg

North Sikkim

View of Kanchenjunga from Pilling

Evening at Singtam Valley

North Sikkim

Yak at Valley

Organic Temi Tea Garden

Natural Beauty of Sikkim Himalayas

Baba Dham Tsomgoo Lake Nathula

Night Out for Tourists

On the Way to Zuluk, Old Silk Route

Flowers of Sikkim

Flowers of Sikkim

Flowers of Sikkim

Sikkim Valley in May

Sikkim Valley in May

Gurudongmar Lake in Winter

Gangtok Town

Sidayshora Dham Rhenock East Sikkim

Valley at Top Hill

Unique Bridge, South Sikkim

Hanging Bridge

Way to Solaphok, Char Dham

Gangtok Town

Rabongla South Sikkim

Bibliography

A Guidebooklet for Shingba Rhododendron Sanctuary.

A Guidebooklet for Kyongnosla Alpine Sanctuary—Brochures of the Wildlife Circle, Sikkim Forest Department, Websites:www.sikkiminfo.com

ADB (2000): Memorandum of Understanding between the Government of Lao PDR and the Asian Development Bank for the Mekong Tourism Development Project, Manila: Asian Development Bank.

ADB (2004): Asian Development Bank and South Asia Sub-Regional Economic Cooperation Tourism Working Group's Final Report, Report prepared by Tourism Resource Consultants Ltd., New Zealand, in Association with Metcon Consultants PTE Ltd., Nepal, Manila: Asian Development Bank.

ADB (2006): SASEC Human Resource Development Strategy and Capacity Building in the Tourism Sector, Final Report, Manila: Asian Development Bank.

ADB (2008): SASEC *Tourism Development Project*, TA 6362-REG, July 2008, Manila: Asian Development Bank.

ADB (2010): Updated Situation Analysis for the Tourism Sector in the South Asia Sub-Region, Appendix-1 of Discussion Paper for Tourism Planning Workshop in Kathmandu, 4-6 August 2010, Barcelona and Madrid: Europraxis Consulting.

Abhishek, Varun, Palash, Saurabh and Dipayan (2011): *Tourism Demand Forecasting, Sikkim.*

Acharya, B.K. (2008): Bird Communities and their Distribution Pattern Along the Elevation Gradient of Teesta Valley, Sikkim, Ph.D. Thesis (Unpublished), Coimbatore: Salim Ali Centre for Ornithology and Natural History and Bharathiar University.

Aima, Ashok, Bhasin, Jaya and Gupta, Rachna (2011): "Heritage Tourism in Rajasthan: Study of Leadership Styles", Presented

Paper in Colombo Conference of India Tourism Congress, June 2011.

Ali, S. (1962): *The Birds of Sikkim*, New Delhi: Oxford University Press.

Andriotis Konstantinos (2000): "Local Community Perceptions of Tourism as a Development Tool: the Island of Crete", Ph.D. Thesis, Greece: Bournemouth University.

Annual Report, 2003-04. Department of Tourism, Government of Sikkim.

Annual Report, 2004-05. Department of Tourism, Government of Sikkim.

Annual Report, 2005-06, Department of Tourism, Government of Sikkim.

Annual Report, 2006-07. Department of Tourism, Government of Sikkim.

Annual Report, 2008-09. Department of Tourism, Government of Sikkim.

Annual Report, 2009-10, Department of Tourism, Government of Sikkim.

Annual Report, 2010-11. Department of Tourism, Government of Sikkim.

Annual Report, 2011-12. Department of Tourism, Government of Sikkim.

Annual Report, 2012-13. Department of Tourism, Government of Sikkim.

Archer, B.H. (1973): *The Impact of Domestic Tourism:* Bangor Occasional Papers in Economics Number 2. Cardiff: University of Wales Press.

Archer, B.H. (1977a): *Tourism in the Bahamas and Bermuda: Two Case Studies*: Bangor Occasional Papers in Economics Number 10, Cardiff: University of Wales Press.

Archer, B.H. (1977b): *Tourism Multipliers: The State of the Art*: Bangor Occasional Papers in Economics Number 11, Cardiff: University of Wales Press.

Archer, B.H., Shea, S. and Vane, R. (1974): *Tourism in Gwynedd: An Economic Study*, Bangor: Institute of Economic Research, University College of North Wales.

Archer, B.H. (1982): "The Value of Multipliers and Their Policy Implications", *Tourism Management*, December.

Archer, B.H. (1984): "Economic Impact: Misleading Multiplier", *Annals of Tourism Research*.

Aryal, B. (2008): "Tourism Planning: Steps and Procedures," in Upadhyaya, R.P. (ed.), *Readings in Rural Tourism*, Kathmandu: Sunlight Publication.

Ashley, C. (2006): How Can Governments Boost the Local Economic Impacts of Tourism? Options and Tools, the Hague: SNV, London : Overseas Development Institute, http://www.propoor tourism.org.uk/toolbox091106.pdf (accessed 23, July 2010).

Ashley, C., Roe, D. and Goodwin, H. (2001): *Pro-poor Tourism Strategies : Making Tourism Work for the Poor,* a Review of Experiences, London: Overseas Development Institute.

Ashley, C., Meyer, D., Roe, D. and Goodwin, H. (2004): *Tourism and Poverty Reduction—Making the Links*, Pro-Poor Tourism Information Sheets, Sheet No. 3. London: Pro-Poor Tourism Partnership. http://www.propoortourism.org.uk/info_sheets/ 3%20info%20sheet.pdf (accessed 25 July, 2010)

Ashraful, Mohammad, Chowdhury, Ferdous and Shahriar, Faisal Mohammad (2012): "The Impact of Tourism in a Deficit Economy: A Conceptual Model in Bangladesh Perspective," *Business Intelligence Journal*.

Asian Development Bank (2013): *Cost-benefit Analysis for Development: A Practical Guide*, Mandaluyong City, Philippines: Asian Development Bank, ISBN: 978-92-9092-957-4 (Print), 978-92-9092-958-1 (PDF).

Australian Bureau of Statistics (2009): Australian National Accounts: Tourism Satellite Account, 2007-08. Australian Bureau of Statistics, Canberra, ACT, Retrieved from:http://www.abs.gov. au/ AUSSTATS/abs@.nsf/DetailsPage/5249.02007-08?Open Document

Avasthe, R. (2005): Biodiversity Conservation Issues in Sikkim: I. High Priority Biologically Rich Areas of North Sikkim, *ENVIS Bulletin: Himalayan Ecology*.

Avasthe, R.K. and Jha, A. (1999): *Mammals of Sikkim*, Gangtok: WWF— India, Sikkim Field Office, Deorali.

Babu, S.S., *et al.* (Eds.) (2008): *Tourism Development Revisited*, London, New Delhi: Response.

Bader, E. and Lababedi, A. (2007): "Hotel Management Contracts in Europe," London: Palgrave MacMillan, First Published in the *Journal of Leisure Management*.

Baaijens, S.R., Nijkamp, P. and Montfort, K. Van (1998): *Explanatory Meta-analysis for the Comparison and Transfer of Regional Tourist Income Multipliers*, Regional Studies.

Bajracharya, S.B. (1998): "Tourism Development and Management in the Annapurna Area", In East, P., Luger, K., Inmann, K. (Eds.) *Sustainability in Mountain Tourism: Perspective for the Himalayan Countries*, Delhi: Book Faith India, Innsbruck: STUDIEN Verlag.

Balaguer, J. and Cantavella-Jordà, M. (2002): "Tourism as a long-run Economic Growth Factor: The Spanish case, *Applied Economics.*

Bao, J. (1992): "Application of the Gravity Model in Tourist Forecasting." *Journal of Zhongshan University (Natural Science).*

Beaumont, N. (2001): *Ecotourism and Conservation Ethic*, J. Sustain, Tourism.

Becken, S. and Hay, John, E. (2007): *Tourism and Climate Change—Risks and Opportunities*, Toronto and Bufallow: Channel View Publication.

Bertalanffy, L. Von. (1972): "General System Theory: A Critical Review," In J. Beilshan and G. peters (eds.), *System Behaviour*, London: Open University Press.

Bhadauria, S.B.S. (1999): *Green State—Policies, Vision, Programme and Initiatives for Sustainable Development in Sikkim*, Gangtok: Author.

Bhatia, A.K. (1994): *International Tourism*, New Delhi: Sterling Publishers Private Limited.

Bhatia, A.K. (2010): *Tourism Development: Principles and Practice*, New Delhi: Sterling Publishers Private Limited.

Bhuyan, Anjan (2008): "A study on the Development of Tourism Entrepreneurship in Assam, with Special Reference to Accommodation Industry", Ph.D. Thesis, Assam, India: Tezpur University.

Bisht, H. (2007): "Prospects and Problems of Ecotourism in Uttarakhand." In: H. Bisht and G. Rajwar, (Eds.) *Tourism & Himalayan Biodiversity*, Srinagar: Transmedia Publication.

Bizcovering (2007): Circular Flow of Income Model of an Economy. (Online Document). Available: http://bizcovering.com/business-and-society/circular-flow-of-income-model-of-an-economy/. (Retrieved: 29 Jan., 2011).

Boniface, B.G. and Cooper, C.P. (1987): *The Geography of Travel and Tourism*, London: Heinemann.

Boo, F. (1990), *Ecotourism: The Potentials and Pitfalls*, Vols. 1 and 2. Washington, DC: Worldwide Fund for Nature.

Buckley, R.A. (1994): "A Framework for Eco-tourism", *Annals of Tourism Research*.

Burkart, A.J. and Medlik, S. (1998): *Tourism: Past Present and Future*, London: Heinemann.

Butler, R. (1992): "Alternative Tourism: The Thin Edge of the Wedge." In: V.L. Smith and W.R. Eadington (eds.), *Tourism Alternative*, New York: John Wiley & Sons.

Butler, R.W. (1980): "The Concept of Tourist Area Cycle of Evolution, Implications for Management of Resources", *Can. Geogr.*, 24, 5-12, as displayed in p. 203. In: *Tourism, Environment and Sustainable Development*: *Environmental Conservation* (ed. Butler, R.W.), 1991.

Campbell, J.G. and Kruk, E. (2005): *Sustainable Mountain Tourism in the Greater Himalayan Region, Proceedings Mountaineering and Tourism Meet*, Mussoorie, India, May 2005.

Cater, E.A. (1987): "Tourism in the Least Developed Countries", *Annals of Tourism Research,* 14(2): 202-226.

Census of India (2011): District Census Handbook, Part (xii) A293, Series 22, Directorate of Census Operations, Gangtok, Sikkim. Paul, S., *European Journal of Geography,* 4. 2: 46-54 (2013).

Centre for Interdisciplinary Studies of Mountain Hill Environment (2006): Carrying Capacity Study of Teesta Basin in Sikkim (2005) Volume VI, *Biological Environment—Terrestrial and Aquatic Research*, Delhi: University of Delhi.

Chakrabarti, Anjan (2001): "No More Theories", *The North-Eastern Week End Review*, Vol. 1, No. 5 (5-11th April, Gangtok), (2007): "Sikkim Economy: The Present and Future", In Fr. P.J. Victor, Prabhat Pradhan, Devika Lama, Aniruddha Das (eds.), *Discursive Hills—Studies in History, Polity and Economy*. Darjeeling: St. Joseph's College (2008): "Sikkim Economy: The Present and Future and Interdependence with North Bengal". In Pankaj Kumar Debnath and Subhasis Bhattacharjee (Eds.), *Economy and Society of North Begal*, Kolkata: Progressive Publishers.

Chakrabarti, Anjan (2009): "Tourism in Sikkim: Quest for a Self-Reliant Economy", *The NEHU Journal.*

Chakrabarti, Anjan (2009): *Economic Development and Employment in Sikkim*, New Delhi: Authorspress, Laxmi.

Chakrabarti, Anjan (2010): "A Critical Review of Agrarian Reforms in Sikkim", *Economic and Political Weekly*.

Chakrabarti, Anjan and Chakraborty, Anup Sekhar (2010): "Emergent Development Approach: A Critique of "Money-bags' Centre directed Dole Development in North-East India", *Indian Journal of Political Science*.

Chakrabarti, Anjan (2014): "Economic Development and Tourism in Sikkim: A Critical Review", *International Journal of Research in Commerce, Economics and Management*, A Monthly Double-Blind Peer Reviewed (Refereed/Juried) Open Access International e-Journal—Included in the International Serial Directories, http://ijrcm.org.in

Chandra, Prakash (2010): *Rajasthan Tourism in India—Explore Its Attractions*, July, 2010.

Chandra, Satish and Menezes, Dennis (2001): "Applications of Multivariate Analysis in International Tourism Research: The Marketing Strategy Perspective of NTOs", *Journal of Economic and Social Research*.

Chaudhary, P. (2009), *Tourism: Concepts and Principles*, New Delhi: Adeline Books.

Chumni, Maeta (2001): "Tourism Demand Model: Determinants of Thailand's International Tourist Receipts", Ph.D. thesis, Thailand: Chulalongkom University.

Cohen, E. (1979): "Rethinking the Sociology of Tourism", *Annals of Tourism Research*. Jan/March 18-35.

Craigwell, Roland (2007): "Tourism Competitiveness in Small Island Developing States", *World Institute for Development Economics Research* (*WIDER*), Finland: United Nations University, April.

Cook, R.A., Yale, L.J. and Marqua (2006): *Tourism: The Business of Travel*, New Delhi: Dorling Kindersley.

Cooper, C., Fletcher, J., Gilbert, D., Shepherd, R. and Wanhill, S. (eds.) (1998): *Tourism: Principles and Practice*, Essex, UK: Longman.

Corneliu, I. and Mihai, B. (2011): "New Approach in Evaluating Tourism Attractiveness in the Region of Moldavia (Romania)", *International Journal of Energy and Environment*: 2 (5): 165-174.

Crompton, J.L. (1993): *Economic Impact Analysis: Myths and Misapplication, Trends*.

Crompton, L., Lee, S. and Shuster, T. (2001): "A Guide for Undertaking Economic Impacts Studies: The Springfest example", *Journal of Travel Research.*

Das, Sunita, Das, T.H. and Goswami, A. (1993): "Soil Type and Land Use Planning of Sikkim", *Indian J. of Landscape System and Ecological Studies.*

De, U.K. and Devi, Amrita (2011): "Valuing Recreational and Conservational Benefits of a Natural Tourist Site: Case of Cherrapunjee", *Journal of Quantitative Economics*, Vol. 9, No. (2), July.

Department of Economics, Statistics, Monitoring and Evaluation, Government of Sikkim (DESME) (2006): *State Socio-Economic Census 2006*, Gangtok: Author.

Department of Economics, Statistics, Monitoring and Evaluation, Government of Sikkim (DESME) (2007): *Sikkim—A Statistical Profile 2006-07*, Gangtok: Author.

Department of Information Technology (2009): *The Official Portal of the Government of Sikkim*, Gangtok: Author, Retrieved June 24, from http://sikkim.gov.in/

Department of Rural Management and Development (RMDD), Government of Sikkim (n.d.), *Panchayati Raj in Sikkim*, Gangtok: DRMD.

Development Planning, Economic Reforms and North-Eastern Council (DP, ER and NEC) Affairs Department, Government of Sikkim (2007): *Draft Eleventh Five Year Plan* (*2007-2012*) *and Annual Plan* (*2007-08*): Gangtok: Author.

Department of Tourism (1996): *Report of the Working Group on Tourism for the Ninth Five Year Plan.*

Department of Tourism (2012): *Kerala Tourism Policy 2012*, Thiruvanthapuram, Kerala: Government of Kerala.

Department of Tourism, Government of Sikkim (2002): *Sikkim's Tourism Master Plan*, Gangtok: Department of Tourism, Government of Sikkim.

Dhaka, Suresh (1991): "Personnel Policies & Practices in RTDC", Ph.D. Thesis, Jaipur: University of Rajasthan.

Directorate of Economics, Statistics, Monitoring and Evaluation, Government of Sikkim, 2004-05, *Sikkim: A Statistical Profile*, Gangtok: Government of Sikkim.

Divisekera, Sarath (2003): "A Model of Demand for International Tourism", *Annals of Tourism Research Journal*, Vol. 30, No. 1, Great Britain.

Domestic Tourism Survey 2002-03 by NCAER, Ministry of Tourism and Culture, Government of India.

Dixit, S.K. (2005): *Management in Tourism*, New Delhi: Mohit Publications.

Dixit, Saurabh and Barua, C.S. (2011): "Tourism Linkages between India and Sri Lanka", Presented paper at India Tourism Congress—Colombo Conference, 14th June.

Dowling, Ross Kingston (1993): "An Environmentally Based Approach to Tourism Planning", Ph.D. Thesis, Western Australia: Murdoch University.

Duc Pham, T., Dwyer, L., Spurr, R., Ruhanen, L. and Scott, N. (2008): Queensland Regional Tourism Satellite Account Scoping Study, *Sustainable Tourism Cooperative Research Centre*, Gold Coast, Queensland.

Dwyer, L., Edwards, D., Mistilis, N., Scott, N., Roman, C. and Cooper, C. (2008): "Trends Underpinning Tourism to 2020: An Analysis of Key Drivers for Change", *Sustainable Tourism Cooperative Research Centre*, Gold Coast, Queensland.

Dwyer, L., Forsyth, P. and Spurr, R. (2007b): "Productivity and Yield Measurement in Australian Inbound Tourism Using Tourism Satellite Accounts and Computable General Equilibrium Models". In J. Tribe and D. Airey (Eds.) *Advances in Tourism Research*, UK: University of Surrey.

Dwyer, L., Forsyth, P., Spurr, R. and van Ho, T. (2005): *Economic Impacts and Benefits of Tourism in Australia: A General Equilibrium Approach*, Sustainable Tourism Cooperative Research Centre, Gold Coast, Queensland.

ENVIS (2009): *ENVIS Sikkim Newsletter 2008-2009*, Ministry of Environment and Forest, Government of India.

ENVIS TEAM : Eco-destinations of India "Sikkim Chapter", *Envis Centre Sikkim on Ecotourism*, (online).

Eijgelaar, Eke, Peeters Paul and Pieter Piket (2008): "Domestic and International Tourism in a Globalized World", paper presented paper in International Conference "Ever the twain shall Meet-relating International and Domestic Tourism" of *Research Committee RC50 International Tourism*, Jaipur, Rajasthan, India: International Sociological Association.

Fletcher, John (1994): "Economics and Forecasting, Economic Impact", In *Tourism Marketing and Management Handbook*, 2nd ed. S.F. Witt and L. Moutinho, New York: Prentice Hall.

Fletcher, John (1994): "Input-output Analysis", In: *Tourism Marketing and Management Handbook*, 2nd ed., S.F. Witt and L. Moutinho, New York: Prentice Hall.

Fondeux, Adele, Benisti, Antonin, Wanduragala, Gehan, Assedo, Maxime and Sharma, Shiv Kumar (2011): "Jaipur International Tourist Survey", Survey Report, Kanvic Management Consulting Firm, April, 2011.

Forest, Environment, and Wildlife Management Department (FEWMD), Government of Sikkim (2009): *Wildlife Management Plan for the Maenam Wildlife Sanctuary South Sikkim*, 2008-2018, Gangtok: Author.

Franklin, Adrian (2003): *Tourism: An Introduction*, London: Sage Publications.

Frechtling, Douglas, C. (1994): "Assessing the Economic Impacts of Travel and Tourism—Introduction to Travel Economic Impact Estimation", In: *Travel, Tourism and Hospitality Research*, Second edition, J.R. Brent Ritchie and Charles R. Goeldner (Eds.), New York: John Wiley & Sons Inc.

Ganguli-Lachungpa, U. (2002): "Avifauna of Trans-Himalayan and Alpine Grasslands in Sikkim, India", In Rahmani, A.R. and Ugra, G. (Eds.), *Birds of Wetlands and Grasslands: Proceedings of the Salim Ali Centenary Seminar 1996*, Mumbai: Bombay Natural History Society.

Gawande, Rohan and Dethe, Sudhir (2008): "Branding Indian Tourism: Entering Second Phase" in *Conference on Tourism in India—Challenges Ahead*, Kanpur: Indian Institute of Management.

George, P.O. (2003): "Management of Tourism Industry in Kerala", Ph.D. Thesis, Kottayam, Kerala: Post-Graduate Department of Commerce.

Ghimire, A. (2010): *Travel and Tourism*, Kathmandu: Ekta Books Distributers Pvt. Ltd.

Ghosh, R.N., Siddiqui, M.A.B. and Gabby. R. (2003): "Tourism, Ecotourism and Economic Development: An Overview", In: R. Canrady and M. Buck (eds.), *Trends and Issues in Global Tourism*, New York: Springer.

Goeldner, C.R., Brent, J.R. and Robert, M. (2000): *Tourism Principles, Practices, Philosophies*, New York: John Wiley & Sons Inc.

Goswami, B.K. and Ravindran, G. (2001): *A Textbook of Tourism*, New Delhi: Har Anand DSB Management Service.

Government of India, Ministry of Tourism, *Annual Report 2012-13*, pp. 61-62.

Government of India, Press Information Bureau release, dated 8.5.2000, www.incredibleindia.org/travel/eco-tourism.

Government of Sikkim, *Memorandum to the Thirteenth Finance Commission*, Volume I, Finance, Revenue and Expenditure Department, 2010.

Government of Sikkim (1991): *Master Plan for Gangtok, 2020*, Urban Development and Housing Department, Government of Sikkim.

Government of Sikkim, Sikkim: A Statistical Profile 2002, Directorate of Economics, Statistics, Monitoring and Evaluation: Government of Sikkim, Gangtok.

Government of Sikkim, "An Adventure Odyssey", *Sikkim Tourism*, Gangtok, Government of Sikkim.

Government of Sikkim. *The Land of Mystic Splendor*, *Sikkim Tourism*, Gangtok, Government of Sikkim.

Government of Sikkim, *Annual Administrative Report, 2001-2002*, Forests, Environment and Wildlife Department, Government of Sikkim, Gangtok.

Gupta, A. (2002): "Status of Primates in Tripura", *ENVIS Bulletin*.

Gupta, Deepika (2008): "A Study of Evaluating Economic Impact Assessment and Physical Carrying Capacity at Tourist Destination Areas of Rajasthan", Ph.D. Thesis, Ajmer: MDS University.

Gupta, S. and Bansal, S.P. (2001): *Tourism Towards 21st Century*, New Delhi: Deep & Deep Publications Pvt. Ltd.

Haldar, Piali (2007): "Rural Tourism—Challenges and Opportunities", Presented paper in International Marketing Conference on Marketing and Society at Indian Institute of Management, Kanpur, April 2007.

Hans, V. Basil (2008): "India's Tourism Industry—Progress and Emerging Issues", Presented paper in State Level seminar on *World Tourism Day*, Srinivas College of Hotel Management, Pandeshwar, Mangalore and Karnataka, 27th September.

Haribal, M. (1992): *The Butterflies of Sikkim Himalaya and their Natural History*, Gangtok: Sikkim Nature Conservation Foundation.

Harris, P. (1997): "Limitations on the use of Regional Economic Impact Multipliers by Practitioners: An Application to the Tourism Industry", *Journal of Tourism Studies*.

Home Department (HD), Government of Sikkim (2007): *Annual Report 2006-2007*, Gangtok: Author.

Hudson, I. (2001). "The Use and Misuse of Economic Impact Analysis: The Case of Professional Sports", *Journal of Sport and Social Issues*, 25, 20-39.

Husain, Tarannum (2007): "Promotional Strategies of Tourism Industry in Uttranchal State of India", Ph.D. Thesis, New Delhi: Jamia Millia Islamia University.

IMF (2009): *World Economic Outlook Database*, Washington, DC: International Monetary Fund.

Indian National Trust for Arts and Cultural Heritage (2002): *Master Plan for Trekking—Sikkim*, New Delhi.

Information and Public Relations Department, Government of Sikkim (2003): Our Natural Resources Our Responsibilities, Green Initiatives for Sustainable Development by Hon'ble Chief Minister Shri Pawan Chamling, Gangtok: Information and Public Relations Department, Government of Sikkim & New Delhi: Indus Publishing Company.

Information and Public Relations Department, Government of Sikkim (2003): Sikkim Perspectives and Vision, Speeches of Chief Minister Pawan Chamling, Gangtok: Information and Public Relations Department, Government of Sikkim & New Delhi: Indus Publishing Company.

Information and Public Relations Department, Government of Sikkim (2007): Sikkim Perspectives and Vision, Speeches of Chief Minister Pawan Chamling, Gangtok: Information and Public Relations Department, Government of Sikkim & New Delhi: Indus Publishing Company.

Information and Public Relations Department (IPRD), Government of Sikkim (2008): *Our Natural Resources Our Responsibilities*, Gangtok: Author.

International Consultants and Technocrats Pvt. Ltd. (2005): "Documentation of Best Practices Adopted by the State Governments for the Development of Tourism", *Survey Report*, New Delhi, India.

International Labour Organization (2010): "Development and Challenges in the Hospitality and Tourism Sector", Geneva, Switzerland: International Labour Office.

JICA (2009): Study Team for Japan International Cooperation Agency (JICA) IC Net Limited (GOJ) Report, November 2009.

Jafari, Jafar (1983): "Anatomy of the Travel Industry", *Dirndl Hotel and Restaurant Administration Quarterly*.

Jafari, J., *et al.* (2000): *Encyclopedia of Tourism*, London: Routledge Publications.

Joshi, R. and Dhyani, P.P. (2009): "Environmental Sustainability and Tourism—Implications of Trend Synergies of Tourism in Sikkim Himalaya", *Current Science*, Vol. 97, No. 1, 10 July.

Kala, Neha (2008): "Host Perception of Heritage Tourism Impact with Special Reference to the City of Jaipur", *South Asian Journal of Tourism and Heritage*, Vol. 1, No. 1.

Kamalakhi, M.V. (1996): "Hotel Industry in Kerala with Special Reference to Tourism", Ph.D. Thesis, Cochin, Kerala: Cochin University of Science & Technology.

Khan, Nafees A. (2008): "Human Resource Development in Tourism Industry in India: A Case Study of Air India Ltd., New Delhi", in Elperiplo Sustentable No. 14, *Faculty of Tourism and Gastronomy*, Mexico State.

Khatri, Nitasha M. (2012): "Profitability Analysis of Rajasthan Tourism Development Corporation" in *Journal of Commerce and Management Thought*, Volume 3, Issue 2.

Kruk, Ester (2009): "Tourism in the Himalaya—Mountain of Opportunities in a Changing Climate", Nepal: International Center for Integrated Mountain Development.

Kruk, E. (2010): "Marketing the Uniqueness of the Himalayas", In Hoermann, B., Choudhary, D., Choudhary, D., Kollmair, M. (2010): Integrated Value Chain Development as a Tool for Poverty Alleviation in Rural Mountain Areas, *An Analytical Framework*, Kathmandu: ICIMOD.

Kumari, Anita (2004): "Problems and Prospectus of Tourism Administration in Rajasthan", Ph.D. Thesis, Jaipur: University of Rajasthan.

Kunwar, R.R. (1997): *Tourism and Development, Science and Industry Interface*, Kathmandu: Laxhmi Kunwar.

Kurukshetra, May 2012.

Lahiri, A.K., S. Chattopadhyaya and Bhasin, A. (2001): *Sikkim*: *The People's Vision*, New Delhi & Government of Sikkim, Gangtok, Sikkim: Indus Publishing Company.

Lalnunmawia, H. (2010): *Development and Impact of Tourism Industry in India*.

Lama, Mahendra P. (2001): *Sikkim Human Development Report 2001*, New Delhi: Social Science Press & Government of Sikkim.

Lama, Mahendra P. (2007): *The Economic Survey 2006-2007*. Gangtok: Sikkim State Planning Commission, Government of Sikkim.

Lane, M. (2006): "Critical Issues in Regional Natural Resource Management", Paper prepared for the 2006 Australian State of the Environment Committee, Department of the Environment and Heritage, Canberra: Australian State of the Environment Committee.

Leiper, Neil (1979): "The Framework of Tourism: Towards a Definition of Tourism, Tourist, and the Tourism Industry", *Annals of Tourism Research*, October-December.

Lindberg, K. (2001): "Economic impacts", In Weaver, D.B. (ed.) *The Encyclopaedia of Ecotourism,* Oxon: CABI Publishing.

Maharana, Iyata (2000): "Economic Benefits and Conservation Linkages from Tourism Development in the Sikkim-Himalaya".

Maru, M.K. (2001): "Progress, Problems and Prospects of Tourism Industry in Saurashtra and Kuttchh", Ph.D. Thesis, Rajkot: Saurashtra University.

Mathieson, A. and Wall, G. (1982): *Tourism: Economic, Physical, and Social Impacts*, New York: Longman.

McIntosh, R.W. and Goeldner, R. (1990): *Tourism: Principles, Practices and Philosophies*, USA: John Wiley & Sons Inc.

Menon, A.G. Krishna (1993): "Case Study on the Effects of Tourism on Culture and The Environment: INDIA—Jaisalmer, Khajuraho and Goa," Bangkok: published in UNESCO Principal Regional Officer for Asia and the Pacific.

Ming, Sze (2009): "Forces Shaping the Trends and Patterns of China's Outbound International Tourist Flows", Ph.D. Thesis, Lismore, NSW: Southern Cross University,

Ministry of Tourism (1997): *India Tourist Statistics*.

Ministry of Tourism (1998): *Draft National Tourism Policy*.

Ministry of Tourism (1998): *Eco-Tourism Policies and Guidelines*.

Ministry of Tourism, *Annual Report 2012-13*.

Muhammed, Ajims P. and Jagathyraj, V.P. (2008): "Challenges Faced by Kerala Tourism Industry" in conference on *Tourism in India—Challenges Ahead* at Indian Institute of Management, Kanpur.

Murphy, P. (ed.), Tourism in Canada: Selected Issues and Options, Western Geographical Series, 1983, Vol. 21, p. 136, as displayed in p. 10, In *Policies for Maximizing Nature Tourism's Ecological and Economic Benefits* (ed., Lindberg, K.), World Resource Institute, 1991.

National Atlas and Thematic Mapping Organisation (NATMO) (2009): *Natural Resources Atlas of Sikkim*, Kolkata: Department of Science and Technology, Government of India.

National Bureau of Soil Survey (NBSS) (1997): *Soils of Sikkim for Optimizing Land use* (NBSS Publ.60).

National Skills Development Corporation. Human Resource and Skill Requirement in Tourism, Travel, Hospitality and Trade Sector (2022)—A Report, http://www.nsdcindia.org/pdf/tourism.pdf.

National Tourism Policy (2002): Ministry of Tourism, Government of India.

Negi, J. (1990): *Tourism and Travel: Concepts and Principle*, New Delhi: Gitanjali Publishing House.

Negi, M. (1994): River Alaknanda, In Nautiyal, P. (Ed.), *Mahseer the Game Fish*, Dehradun: Jagdamba Publication.

Nepal, S.K. (2002): *Mountain Ecotourism and Sustainable Development Ecology, Economics, and Ethics*, Mountain Research and Development.

Nepal, S.K. (2003): *Tourism and the Environment: Perspectives from the Nepal Himalaya*, Lalitpur and Innsbruck: Himal Books and STUDIEN Verlag.

Ogilvie, F.W. (1933): *The Tourist Movement: An Economic Study*, London: Staples Press.

Pandey, Hari D. (2008): "Concept of Tourism", In R.P. Upadhyaya (Ed.), *Readings in Rural Tourism*, Kathmandu: Sunlight Publications.

Pasricha, A. (2009): *International Tourism*, New Delhi: Regal Publications.

Patil, Ashok T. and Choubey, Kailash (2010): "Geographical Analysis of Tourism and Concerning Problems in Goa (India)", SSMRAE, *International Referred Research Journal*, Jaipur: Rajasthan, Issue 19.

Poonia, Anamika (2011): "Spatial Availability of Tourism Services in Rajasthan with its Sustainability Concept", *South Asian Journal of Tourism and Heritage, An International Referred Research Journal*, Vol. 4, No. 1.

Pourafkari, Bahareh (2007): "A Comparative Study on Cultural Tourism Development in Iran and Turkey", Ph.D. Thesis, Iran: Lulea University of Technology.

Praveen Rizal and R. Asokan (2013): "An Overview of Tourism Industry and Its Impact on the Health Status in Sikkim State", *Language in India*, www.languageinindia.com

RTDC (2010): "RTDC—A Model for Tourism Sector in India", *The Team of RTDC*, 20th February, 2010.

Raina, A.K. and Jain, Neelu (2004): *Dynamics of Tourism—Concept, Philosophy and Strategies.*

Ranjit, Sanuraja (1978): *Tourism Industry with Special Reference to Foreign Exchange Earnings and Resort Development*, Unpublished Masters Dissertation, T.U. Kathmandu.

Rasul, G., Manandhar, P. (2009): "Prospects and Problems in Promoting Tourism in South Asia: A Regional Perspective", *South Asia Economic Journal.*

Rathore, Ashok Singh and Jodhana, Lokeshver Singh (2012): "An Empirical Analysis of the Service Operations of Rajasthan Tourism Development Corporation Hotels", *South Asian Journal of Tourism & Heritage, International Referred Research Journal*, January.

Rathore, Ashok Singh, Prasad, Hanuman and Jodhana, Lokeshver Singh (2010): "Financial Performance of Rajasthan Tourism Development Corporation (RTDC)—An Analysis", *South Asian Journal of Tourism and Heritage, International Referred Research Journal*, Volume 3, No. 1, January 2010.

Ratti, Hanish (2007): *History and Geography of Tourism*. New Delhi: Rajat Publication.

Raveendran, G. (1993): *Tourism Planning and Measurement Methods.*

Rhodes, A.R. (2005): "Institutional Arrangements Study of the Recreation and Tourism Management on Protected Natural Areas of New Zealand and Mexico", Ph.D. Thesis, New Zealand: Lincoln University.

Rizal, Praveen and Asokan, R. (2013): "An Overview of Tourism Industry and Its Impact on the Health Status in Sikkim State", Language in India, www.languageinindia.com

Ritchie, J.R. Brent and Goeldner, R. (1995): *Travel, Tourism and Hospitality Research*, Second edition, New York: John Wiley & Sons Inc.

Roy, B.N. and Thapa, M. P. (1998): "Lakes of Sikkim: A limnological study". In Rai, S.C., Sundriyal, R.C. and Sharma, E. (Eds.), *Sikkim: Perspectives for Planning and Development*, Gangtok: Sikkim Science Society.

Saeed, Simad (1997): "Environment Impact Management in the Tourism Industry of Maldives", in EDI/SAARC Regional

Seminar on "*Economic Globalization and Environmental Sustainability*" in Goa.

Saha, Subhasish (1994): "Tourism Development—Accommodation Sector: A Study of Pondicherry Accommodation Sector", Ph.D. Thesis, Pondicherry: Pondicherry University.

Sarah, Li Fung Mei (2005): "Chinese Common Knowledge, Tourism and Natural Landscapes", Ph.D. Thesis, Western Australia: Murdoch University.

Satyal, Y.R. (1988): *Tourism in Nepal—A Profile*, Varanasi: Nath Publishing House.

Sawkar, Kalidas, Noronha, Ligia, Mascarenhas, Antonio and Chauahan, O.S. (1997): "Tourism and the Environment Issues of Concern in the Coastal Zone of Goa", presented in EDI/ SAARC Regional Seminar on *Economic Globalization and Environmental Sustainability*, Goa.

Sharma, A.S. (2009): *Tourism Management*, New Delhi: Essential Books.

Sharma, G., Liang, L. and Tanaka, K. (2006): On-farm Agro-biodiversity Management in Mountain Marginal Farms in the Sikkim Himalaya, Proceedings of the International Workshop on Shifting Agriculture, Environment Conservation and Sustainable Livelihood of Marginal Mountain Societies (Unpublished), Guwahati.

Sharma, P. (2002): "Tourism as an Instrument for Area Development and Poverty Alleviation with Focus on Nepal", In Jodha, *et al.* (Eds.) *Poverty Alleviation in Mountain Areas of China*, pp. 221-244, Proceedings of the International Conference on Poverty in the Mountain Areas of China, Chengdu, China, 10-15 November, Kathmandu: In WEnt, IFAD, IMHE, ICIMOD.

Sheldon, Pauline J. (1990): "A Review of Tourism Expenditure Research", In *Progress in Tourism, Recreation and Hospitality Management*, C.P. Cooper (Ed.), New York: Belhaven Press.

Shreshtha, H.P. (2000): *Tourism in Nepal: Marketing and Challenges*, New Delhi: Nirala Publication.

Shreshtha, P. (1999): *Tourism in Nepal: Problems and Prospects*, Ph.D. Dissertation, Banaras: Banaras Hindu University.

Shreshtha, S.H. (1995): *Simple Geography of Nepal*, Kathmandu: Educational Enterprises.

Shreshtha, V.P. (2007): *A Concise Geography of Nepal*, Kathmandu: Mandala Publication.

Sikkim: The Hidden Paradise, Glimpses of Sikkim—Brochures of Sikkim Tourism.

Sikkim (2010): India Brand Equity Foundation (IBEF), November.

Sikkim: A Statistical Profile 2002, Directorate of Economics, Statistics, Monitoring and Evaluation, Government of Sikkim, pp. 75-95.

Sikkim: A Statistical Profile 2004-05, Directorate of Economics, Statistics, Monitoring and Evaluation, Government of Sikkim, p. 9.

Sikkim: A Statistical Profile 2006-07, Directorate of Economics, Statistics, Monitoring and Evaluation, Government of Sikkim, pp. 5-81.

Sikkim Tourism Development Corporation (STDC), (2003): "Master Plan for Trekking Sikkim", Gangtok: STDC.

Sikkim Tourism Policy (2010): Tourism Department, Gangtok, Government of Sikkim, Planting Seeds of Hope for a Greener Tomorrow.

Sinclair, M.T. and Sutcliffe, C. (1988): "The Estimating of Keynesian Income Multipliers at the Sub-National Level", *Applied Economics*.

Singh, A.K. and Rana, P.S. (2006): *Tism Geography*, Lucknow: New Royal Book Co.

Singh, J.P., Mohanty, M.K., Jena, S.N. and Mishra, Akhilesh (2006): "Tourism Industry in Jaipur: Size and Status", *Vision R.I.*, New Delhi: Connexion Services Private Ltd.

Singh, Kishor (2006): "A Study of Tourism Management and Organization in State of Rajasthan", Ph.D. Thesis, Ajmer: MDS University.

Singh, Ratandeep (1994): *Tourism Today*, Volumes 1-3, New Delhi: Kanishka Publishers & Distributors.

Singh, Tejvir (1975): *Tourism and Tourist Industry,* Delhi: New Heights.

Sirgy, M.J. and Su Chanting (2004): Destination Image, Self-congruity, and Travel Behaviour: Towards an Integrative Model, *Journal of Travel Research*.

Smith, V. (1977): *Hosts and Guests: The Anthropology of Tourism*, Philadelphia: University of Pennsylvania Press.

Sood, V.K. (1999): Impact of Tourism on Socio-cultural Setup of Laddakh, *Geogr. Rev. India*, 61, 173-182.

Spurr, R., Van Ho, T., Forsyth, P., Dwyer, L., Pambudi, D. and Hoque, S. (2007): Tourism Satellite Account 2003/04: Summary

Spreadsheets, Sustainable Tourism Cooperative Research Centre, Gold Coast, Queensland.

Sr. M.V. and Croes, R.R. (2003): "Growth, Development and Tourism in small economy: Evidence from Aruba", *International Journal of Tourism Research.*

Srivastava, A.K. (2006): *Sikkim: Small and Beautiful—A Traveller's Companion*, Tourism Department, Government of Sikkim.

State Policy of Environment, Forest and Land Use (2000): Department of Forest, Environment and Wildlife Management, Government of Sikkim.

State Socio-Economic Census (2006): Directorate of Economics, Statistics, Monitoring and Evaluation, Government of Sikkim.

Stynes, Daniel J. (1999): *Economic Impact of Tourism*, (Online Document), https://www.msu.edu/course/prr/840/econimpact/pdf/ecimpvol1.pdf (Retrieved on 03 Jan., 2011).

Subhajit, D. and Priyom, R.K. (2012): "Village Tourism in Sikkim, India: A Precolonial Approach for Sustainability", *International Journal of Social Science Tomorrow.*

Sustainable Tourism Cooperative Research Centre (2009): The Impacts of Climate Change on Australian Tourism Destinations: Developing Adaptation and Response Strategies—Summary. Sustainable Tourism Cooperative Research Centre, Gold Coast, Queensland.

Sutheeslina, B.S., *et al.* (2008): *Tourism Development Revisited*, New Delhi: Response.

TECS (1998): Tourism Master Plan of Sikkim 1997-2011, Tata Economic Consultancy Service, I-V, submitted to the Department of Tourism, Sikkim, Tata Economic Consultancy Services (TECS), New Delhi.

TRPAP (2007): Nepal's Experience Implementing Sustainable Tourism Development Models, UNDP/Tourism for Rural Poverty Alleviation Programme, NEP/99/013. Nepal: MoCTCA-UNDP/TRPAP and NTB/STDU.

Tata Economic Consultancy Services (TECS) (1998): *Main Report: Tourism Master Plan of Sikkim 1997-2011*, New Delhi www.incredibleindia.org

Tiwari, Ajay (1992): "Organization and Working of RTDC", for his Ph.D. Degree from Jaipur: University of Rajasthan.

Tewari, S.P. (1994): *Tourism Dimensions*, New Delhi: Atma Ram & Sons.

Thaker, Manisha D. (2004): "Problems and Prospects of Tourism Industry in Gujarat", Ph.D. Thesis, Rajkot: Saurashtra University.

The Steering Committee on Tourism of Planning Commission, Government of India : Committee Reports, Role of Tourism during the Eleventh Five Year Plan (2007-12).

Theobold, W.F. (Ed.) (1997): *Global Tourism: The Next Decade*, London: Butterworth.

Trikha, Pradeep (2008): "Cultural Heritage of Rajasthan *vis-à-vis* Politics of Travel Information", *South Asian Journal of Tourism and Heritage*, Vol. 1, No. 1.

Tourism Policy Uttarakhand Tourism, Government of Uttarakhand.

Tourism Policy (1998): Department of Tourism, Government of Uttar Pradesh.

Tourism Policy (2005): Department of Tourism, Himachal Pradesh.

Tourism Policy (2006): Department of Tourism, Government of Andhra Pradesh.

Tourism Policy (2008): Department of Tourism, Government of West Bengal.

Timothy, D. (1999): "Cross-border Partnership in Tourism Resource Management: International Parks along the US-Canada Border", *Journal of Sustainable Tourism*.

Travel Agent Association of Sikkim (TAAS), (2000): *Achievement and Activities*, Gangtok, Sikkim.

Turton, S., Hadwen, W. and Wilson, R. (Eds.) (2009): The Impacts of Climate Change on Australian Tourism Destinations: Developing Adaptation and Response Strategies—A Scoping Study, *Sustainable Tourism Cooperative Research Centre*, Gold Coast, Qld.

UNDESA (1992) Agenda 21. UN Department of Social and Economic Affairs, Division for Sustainable Development. www.un.org/esa/sustdev/documents/agenda21/index, html (accessed July 2009)

United Nations Conference on Trade and Development (1998): Developing Countries Could Target Tourism to Boost Economic Growth, 9 June. <http://www.unctad.org/en/press/pr2755en.htm

UNESCAP (2003): Poverty Alleviation through Sustainable Tourism Development, Bangkok: United Nations Economic and Social Commission for Asia and the Pacific.

UNESCAP (2005): "Major Issues in Tourism Development in the Asian and Pacific Region: Enhancing the Role of Tourism in Socio-economic Development and Poverty Reduction", United Nations Economic and Social Council, General Information, E/ESCAP/STD/3, 21 November.

UNWTO (1998): *Guide for Local Authorities on Developing Sustainable Tourism*, Madrid: United Nations World Tourism Organization.

UNWTO (2001): *Tourism Vision 2020*, Madrid: United Nations World Tourism Organization.

UNWTO (2002): *Tourism and Poverty Alleviation*, Madrid: United Nations World Tourism Organization.

UNWTO (2003): *Sustainable Development of Ecotourism—A Compilation of Good Practices in SMEs*, Madrid: United Nations World Tourism Organization.

UNWTO (2004): *Tourism and Poverty Alleviation: Recommendations for Action*, Madrid: United Nations World Tourism Organization.

UNWTO (2009): *UNWTO World Tourism Barometer*, January, Madrid: United Nations World Tourism Organization.

UNWTO (2009): *World Tourism Barometer*, Madrid: United Nations World Tourism Organization.

UNWTO (2010): *UNWTO World Tourism Barometer*. Vol. 8, No. 1, January, Madrid: United Nations World Tourism Organization.

UNWTO (2010): United Nations World Tourism Organization, www.unwto.org/index.php

Upadhyaya, R. (2008): "A Case Study: Rural Tourism in Sirubari, Bandipur, and Ghalegaon", In : R. Upadhyaya (Ed.) *Readings in Rural Tourism*, Kathmandu: Sunlight Publications

Vogt, J.W. (1978): "Wandering Youth and Travel Behaviour", In: Lamore, M.D. (Ed.), *Tourism and Behaviour*, Williamburge, U.S.A.: College of William and Many Press.

WTO (1994): *Recommendation on Tourism Statistics*, Madrid: World Tourism Organization.

WTTC (2010a): About WTTC. London: World Travel and Tourism Council, www.wttc.org/eng/About_WTTC/ (accessed 22 July, 2010).

WTTC (2010b): *Travel and Tourism Economic Impact Nepal*, London: World Travel and Tourism Council. www.wttc.org/bin/pdf/original_pdf_file/ nepal.pdf (accessed 17 July, 2010).

WWF (2008): International Living Himalayas Development Initiative: Eastern Himalayas Eco-region Tourism Scoping Study Report, November 2008. Kathmandu: WWF.

Wagner, J.E. (1997): "Estimating the Economic Impacts of Tourism", *Annals of Tourism Research.*

Wells, M.P. (1994): "Parks Tourism in Nepal: Reconciling the Social and Economic Opportunities with the Ecological and Cultural Threats", In Munasinghe, M., McNeely, J.A. (Eds.) *Protected Area Economics and Policy: Linking Conservation and Sustainable Development*, pp. 319-331. Washington, DC: The World Bank.

Wen, J. and Tisdell, C.A. (1996): "Spatial Distribution of Tourism in China", *Tourism Economics*, Vol. 2.

World Bank (2008): *World Development Indicators: Poverty Data. A Supplement to World Development Indicators*, Washington, DC: World Bank.

World Travel and Tourism Council (2010): *Tourism Economic Research 2010*, World Travel and Tourism Council, London, Retrieved from: http://www.wttc.org/eng/Tourism_Research/Economic_Research/

World Travel and Tourism Council (2013): *Travel and Tourism Economic Impact 2013, Various Tables and Countries*, http://www.wttc.org/research/economic-impact-research/, London, United Kingdom.

World Tourism Organisation (UNWTO) (2013): *UNWTO Tourism Highlights*, http://mkt.unwto.org/en/publication/unwto-tourism-highlights-2013-edition.

Yadav, P.K., Singh, P.B. and Saxena, R.K. (2011): "Tourism Perspectives in South-Asian Region", Presented paper in India Tourism Congress—Colombo Conference, 14th June.

Zortuk, Mahmut (2009): "Economic Impact of Tourism on Turkey's Economy: Evidence from Cointegration Tests", *International Research Journal of Finance and Economics*, Issue 25, http://www.patientsbeyondborders.com/medical-tourism-statistics-facts.

Index